"This exploration of justice begins where every discussion should start, but, unfortunately, few do: with the Word of God. The result is a richer and deeper understanding of justice than any secular social theory is able to provide."

—**Timothy Paul Jones**, PhD, C. Edwin Gheens chair of Christian Family Ministry, professor of Apologetics, Ethics, and Philosophy, The Southern Baptist Theological Seminary

"The meaning of justice has been discussed and debated intensely, but too often the whole matter is sundered from the biblical text. In this work the meaning of justice in the various biblical corpora is carefully investigated. At the same time, the biblical conception of justice is applied to today's world. An important contribution that deserves to be read widely."

—**Thomas R. Schreiner**, PhD, James Buchanan Harrison professor of New Testament interpretation and associate dean, The Southern Baptist Theological Seminary

"Most books about social justice begin with cultural or political or ideological concerns. *Let Justice Flow Like Water* begins where all Christians should begin: with the Bible. What is justice? What does God think about justice? How is justice revealed in the character of God? What is the role of justice within God's covenant community? The authors provide detailed, insightful answers to these questions rooted in a careful reading of the Bible, rather than in sociological theories or partisan commentary. The result is an invaluable resource for pastors and lay Christians alike."

—**Neil Shenvi**, PhD, teacher, speaker, and author

Let Justice Flow Like Water

edited by

Joshua M. Greever | D. A. Horton | Justin McLendon

Let Justice Flow Like Water: Toward a Theology of Biblical Justice

Published by B&H Academic®
Brentwood, Tennessee

ISBN: 978-1-0877-6549-5

Dewey Decimal Classification: 261.1
Subject Heading: SOCIAL JUSTICE \ JUSTICE \ CHRISTIAN SOCIOLOGY

Cover design by Emily Keafer Lambright.
Cover image by Susan Wilkinson / Unsplash.
Back cover image by Olga Aniven / Shutterstock.

Printed in the United States of America
30 29 28 27 26 25 VP 1 2 3 4 5 6 7 8 9 10

CONTENTS

INTRODUCTION

The Biblical Ground, Call, and Hope for Justice

Therefore the Lord is waiting to show you mercy, and is rising up to show you compassion, for the Lord is a just God. All who wait patiently for him are happy.
—Isa 30:18 (CSB)

For Christ also suffered for sins once for all time, the just for the unjust, so that he might bring us to God.
—1 Pet 3:18a (NASB)

Pure and undefiled religion before God the Father is this: to look after orphans and widows in their distress and to keep oneself unstained from the world.
—Jas 1:27 (CSB)

There is no evil in justice.
—Andrew Peterson, *North! Or Be Eaten*

The aim of this book is to articulate the biblical ground, call, and hope for justice in the world. Since justice is an essential attribute of God (Isa 30:18), our praxis in imitating him as our Father is "to look after orphans and widows in their distress" (Jas 1:27). However, we face a significant obstacle in our pursuit of justice: we ourselves are not inherently just, and we consistently fail to love one another in right ways. To use the language of James, we do not have "pure and undefiled religion," nor do we keep ourselves "unstained from the world" (1:27). Yet in the mire and misery of our sin, we hear God's merciful declaration towards us: "Christ also suffered for sins once for all time, the just for the unjust" (1 Pet 3:18). Christ the just has died for us, the unjust, to bring us to God. In the death of Christ we are therefore freed both from the penalty and the power of our sin, so that now we are free to imitate our Father in loving and pursuing justice.

Accordingly, as Romans 8 puts it, in this book we want to look *back* at what God has done for us through the death of Christ (Rom 8:1–4); *around* at what God is doing among us through the Spirit who enables us to live with justice (8:5–17); and *forward* to what God will one day do when he completely restores all things and eradicates injustice (8:18–25). Through this panorama of redemptive history, we aim to show that justice, rightly understood, is an essential part of our sanctification, for it is propelled and fueled by the past redemptive work of Christ, the present life-giving work of the Spirit who dwells within us, and the future hope of our consummate redemption.

Assistance for Pastors and Ministry Leaders

While we wish to serve readers of all types, we specifically want to assist pastors and ministry leaders to speak with biblical fidelity and pastoral sensitivity in their respective ministry contexts. The first part of the twenty-first century has seen an influx of scholarly and popular-level treatments on the question of justice and the Bible. To give but a few examples, Ronald Nash critiques evangelical social action in his now dated 2002 volume, *Social Justice and the Christian Church*.[1] His concerns focus upon the compatibility of biblical

[1] Ronald Nash, *Social Justice and the Christian Church* (Lima, OH: Academic Renewal, 2002).

fidelity and social causes. Ron Sider's *Rich Christians in an Age of Hunger: Moving from Affluence to Generosity*, now in its sixth edition, addresses both liberals and conservatives in their collective missteps in posturing the church toward biblical social engagement.[2] Adam Taylor's *Mobilizing Hope: Faith-Inspired Activism for a Post-Civil Rights Generation* considers the applicability of Martin Luther King Jr.'s work to contemporary settings. His work explores the meaning of activism, critiquing the "American Dream," and how justice advocacy is an aspect of Christian discipleship.[3] Jim Wallis, the highly regarded leader of Sojourners, has written several volumes addressing various themes within the conversation about justice. One of his recent volumes, *Christ in Crisis? Why We Need to Reclaim Jesus*, calls for healing among America's religious and political divide. In his view, Christians are called upon to heal national wounds by rediscovering Jesus's own method of engaging others.[4] One of the more recent popular evangelical treatments on justice is Timothy Keller's *Generous Justice: How God's Grace Makes Us Just.* Working through Scripture and church tradition, Keller argues Christians are empowered to enter into a wide array of social causes for the purposes of human flourishing.[5] In addition to these broader treatments, numerous attempts have been made to apply biblical justice to various cultural issues, such as criminal justice, economics, and ethnicity.[6]

---

[2] Ronald J. Sider, *Rich Christians in an Age of Hunger: Moving from Affluence to Generosity*, 6th ed. (Nashville: Thomas Nelson, 2015).

[3] Adam Taylor, *Mobilizing Hope: Faith-Inspired Activism for a Post-Civil Rights Generation* (Downers Grove, IL: IVP, 2010). Similarly, see Michael J. Rhodes, *Just Discipleship: Biblical Justice in an Unjust World* (Downers Grove, IL: IVP, 2023).

[4] Jim Wallis, *Christ in Crisis? Why We Need to Reclaim Jesus* (San Francisco: HarperOne, 2019).

[5] Timothy Keller, *Generous Justice: How God's Grace Makes Us Just* (New York: Dutton, 2010).

[6] For example, see Matthew T. Martens, *Reforming Criminal Justice: A Christian Proposal* (Wheaton, IL: Crossway, 2023); Brent Waters, *Just Capitalism: A Christian Ethic of Economic Globalization* (Louisville: Westminster John Knox, 2016); George Yancey, *Beyond Racial Division: A Unifying Alternative to Colorblindness and*

But this subject is also not without controversy or critique. For example, in 2018 some evangelical leaders collaborated to publish "The Statement on Social Justice & the Gospel."[7] This group believes current conversations about justice can too easily obscure the Bible's presentation of the gospel and its implications for social action. Similarly, other evangelicals have wondered if the category of "social justice" can be redeemed from secularism, suffused as it is with unbiblical assumptions.[8]

In short, pastors and ministry leaders are inundated with a barrage of voices speaking into the subject of justice and the Bible. Further complicating the task is that pastoral ministry transpires in different locales and communities. The questions about justice that a pastor may face in an urban context may sound vastly different from questions about justice that arise in suburban or rural contexts. Lay Christians seek guidance from their pastors as they pursue justice in their respective workplace environments or as they face the challenge and threat of injustice around them. Such ministerial diversity requires that pastors speak with nuance and sensitivity when they

---

Antiracism (Downers Grove, IL: IVP, 2022). For broader treatments of justice in the public square, see Alasdair MacIntyre, *Whose Justice? Which Rationality?* (Notre Dame, IN: University of Notre Dame Press, 1988); Michael Sandel, *Justice: What's the Right Thing to Do?* (New York: Farrar, Straus and Giroux, 2009).

[7] "The Statement on Social Justice and the Gospel," located at https://statementonsocialjustice.com/.

[8] For example, see Scott David Allen, *Why Social Justice is Not Biblical Justice: An Urgent Appeal to Fellow Christians in a Time of Social Crisis* (Grand Rapids: Credo House, 2020); Voddie T. Baucham Jr., *Fault Lines: The Social Justice Movement and Evangelicalism's Looming Catastrophe* (Washington, DC: Salem, 2021). For the view that "social justice," rightly understood, remains a useful concept, see Michael Novak and Paul Adams, *Social Justice Isn't What You Think It Is* (New York: Encounter, 2015). For the various uses of "social justice" in our current culture, see Thaddeus J. Williams, *Confronting Injustice Without Compromising Truth: 12 Questions Christians Should Ask About Social Justice* (Grand Rapids: Zondervan Academic, 2020), 1–11, 162–66. See also Neil Shenvi and Pat Sawyer, *Critical Dilemma: The Rise of Critical Theories and Social Justice Ideology—Implications for the Church and Society* (Eugene, OR: Harvest House, 2023), 127–28.

synthesize and apply the Bible's teaching on justice. In recognition of the challenges pastors face, this book aims to assist pastors and ministry leaders by analyzing various biblical texts on justice, synthesizing those texts into theological formulation, and probing practical ways for Christians and pastors to apply those principles in their communities.

Outline of the Book

Such analysis, synthesis, and application corresponds to the three parts of this book—exegetical, theological, and practical. As an introduction to this approach, chapter 1 frames the discussion by exploring the variegated use of justice across the American Protestant landscape of the twentieth century. Cory Higdon explains the use of the concept within the so-called social gospel movement of the early twentieth century, as well as the response to that movement from the neo-evangelicals of the mid-twentieth century. Higdon shows how the evangelicals both rejected the social gospel movement—they foregrounded the church's mission to preach the gospel for the sake of individual redemption—and emphasized vocational Christian engagement in the public square. Higdon warns that one cannot simply accept or reject the term *social justice* without first considering the meaning and use of the term within its historical context. As such, chapter 1 is foundational for the book inasmuch as it provides historical parameters in order to frame the current discussion.

Part 1 analyzes some key biblical texts often cited in support of various notions of justice. These chapters do not exhaust the biblical data but illustrate a proper hermeneutical approach to the biblical text. In chapter 2, Peter Gentry probes the nature of justice in Isaiah and how that justice is achieved through God's plan of redemption. Gentry contends that Isaiah's word pair "justice and righteousness" is a hendiadys and summarizes Israel's covenant stipulations. Thus, a right grasp of justice in Isaiah must take its covenantal context into account. Additionally, Gentry shows that the transformation of Zion from a faithless city to a city of justice and righteousness is based on the accomplished work of Isaiah's suffering servant. Hence, Isaiah does not support a project of social justice using government policies; rather, biblical justice arrives only in the new covenant community created through the work of the Messiah.

In chapter 3, Paul Raabe summarizes the presentation of justice in the prophecy of Amos. Raabe cautions against reading our assumptions of justice back into the Old Testament. Indeed, justice in the Old Testament often refers to what Raabe calls "rightly-distinguishing-judgment." With regard to Amos, Raabe interprets the oft-quoted Amos 5:24 as God's call for such right judgment. In light of the literary context of Amos 5 and Amos's concluding vision of the return of the Davidic dynasty, Raabe shows that Amos's expectation was that right judgment would only come to pass through the Messiah.

In chapter 4, Brian Tabb assesses the presentation of justice in the books of Luke and Acts. Tabb highlights the interplay between justice and mercy both in Jesus's ministry and teaching and in the early church. Since Jesus and the early church emphasized justice and mercy, Tabb suggests that doing good works, giving generously, and acting justly are a necessary implication of a right preaching of the gospel. At the same time, Tabb recognizes the reality of current injustice and points the reader to hope in the eschatological justice Jesus will bring when he returns.

In chapter 5, Chris Morgan assesses the presentation of justice in the letter of James. Morgan shows that James's "genuine religion" includes justice, for faith in Christ necessarily is manifested in social good. Morgan also draws out the eschatological nature of James's hope, in which justice will finally come to fruition when Jesus returns. In the meantime, the church should display that future hope as it seeks to imitate the character of God in the world.

In chapter 6, Joshua Greever investigates the relationship of the new covenant to justice. Greever suggests that a vision for justice was part of the eschatological hope of the Old Testament prophets, in which they foresaw a day when the people of God would treat one another with justice and righteousness. However, they also saw that such an Edenic hope would only be accomplished in the arrival of the new covenant through the work of the Messiah. Greever shows that the through the inauguration of the new covenant, Jesus reigns with justice and righteousness on behalf of his people and transforms them through the Spirit to live in just ways towards one another.

Part 2 builds on the exegetical analysis of Part 1, drawing those themes together in theological reflection. In chapter 7, Justin McLendon explores the Bible's theological framework as the foundation for justice. Particularly, God's attributes of goodness, holiness, and justice define for humanity the good, the true, and the beautiful. The just character of God gives shape to and grounds the Christian life as we seek to reflect God's justice to the world. Additionally, the redemptive power of the cross, Christ's lordship over all, and the Christian hope for the future renewal of the cosmos undergird the Christian effort to address sin in society.

In chapter 8, Kenneth Reid explores the theme of redemption in Scripture and examines how that relates to the notion of biblical justice. Reid suggests that redemption is holistic in the sense that our freedom from sin through the gospel necessarily bears fruit in just actions towards others. Reid emphasizes that since God is just, those he redeems are to imitate him in acts of justice. Reid also grounds the Christian mandate for justice in the death of Christ, the empowerment of the Spirit that every believer possesses, and the hope for cosmic justice at the eschaton.

In chapter 9, John Wind roots the notion of justice and the mission of the church in the covenantal framework of the biblical metanarrative. Wind contends that a proper understanding of two covenants—the Noahic fallen creation covenant and the inaugurated new covenant—clarifies the mission of humanity and individual Christians, respectively, to do good deeds. Wind carefully distinguishes between God's own perfect justice in the age to come and humanity's limited and imperfect justice in this age. Critiquing both the use of critical theory to constitute social justice and the notion that social justice is obtained through equality of outcome, Wind locates the mission of the local church in the preaching of the gospel, because only through the new covenant and Christ's redemptive work can ultimate and cosmic justice be obtained.

Part 3 shifts from exegesis and theology to practical application for pastors, local churches, and individual Christians. In chapter 10, D. A. Horton explores the intersection between the mission of the church, mercy ministries, and the role pastors play in shaping and mobilizing the church. With Eph 4:1–16 as a model for pastoral leadership and the church, Horton highlights pastors as those who should exemplify the work of the ministry and mobilize the church to join in that ministry. Under such pastoral guidance, the church bears responsibility to do the work of the ministry, a holistic work that includes mercy ministries. To accomplish this, Horton provides a practical framework for pastoral mobilization of qualified and interested congregants in the various internal and external mercy ministries of a local church.

Finally, in the book's conclusion the editors address some lingering questions that readers may pose in response to specific issues addressed or raised throughout the book. Neither the questions nor their respective answers are meant to be exhaustive. Instead, they represent the kinds of questions the book may raise and the kinds of answers Christians may provide. The questions also are meant to probe some of the ramifications of this book for the local church, pastoral ministry, and how Christians conceive of justice.

A Final Word

A final word is in order: We do not envision this book as the final and definitive statement on this important discussion, nor are we seeking to be belligerent and divisive. We are aware that conversations about justice can be hurtful and produce more heat than light. Rather, we hope that this volume will be an irenic reminder to pastors, students, and interested Christians to engage the biblical text as the source of our faith and practice. We eagerly desire to "keep the unity of the Spirit through the bond of peace" (Eph 4:3) among Christians and local churches by unpacking the

Bible's ground, call, and hope for justice. The premise of this book is that our Christian unity is best served by looking together at the biblical text and by speaking the truth of God's word to one another in love. Similarly, we long for this book to serve pastors in a variety of contexts—whether urban, suburban, or rural—and to support them in their effort to shepherd God's people with biblical fidelity and pastoral sensitivity. Our prayer is that God would use these efforts for the sake of the gospel, the mission of the church, and the glory of God as we await the return of our King who will one day finish making all things new.

The Editors

1

Justice

Toward a Definition and Historical Framework

— Cory D. Higdon —

> Evangelicals no less than liberals recognize social justice as authentic Christian concern, despite serious differences over definition and content.
>
> —Carl F. H. Henry, "Evangelicals in the Social Struggle"

Introduction

The phrase "social justice," like many labels that describe movements or ideologies, redounds with complexity. It evokes a wide range of emotions and responses, including everything from celebration to visceral hostility. The realities of our politically charged and hyperpartisan age explain the dilemma Christians face when dealing with labels. Indeed, the plurality of responses Christians have towards social justice compares with recent debates over terms like "Christian nationalism." Some proudly wear the label while others find it utterly abhorrent. The term, furthermore, could mean everything from basic Christian activity in the public square to fully investing the civil magistrate with authority over the first table of the law.[1] While no label enjoys unvarnished homogeneity, "Christian nationalism" has become egregiously elastic to the point that some wonder if we can even have a meaningful conversation about its merits and vices.[2]

In the same way, social justice can leave Christians confused to the point where it is common to question the usefulness of the term to describe Christian public ethics. After all, is social justice a God-honoring pursuit or a trojan horse for a left-wing progressivist social agenda fundamentally at odds with biblical Christianity?[3] What is justice? Can justice not be social? Can it be achieved? What means or mechanisms secure this "justice"? To be clear, uncertainty about "social justice" does not mean Christians should have objections to building, as best we can, righteous societies moored in good laws and God's creation order. On the contrary, numerous passages of Scripture provide imperatives for Christians to pursue justice.[4]

---

[1] For examples that Christians face in the "Christian nationalism" dilemma, see Stephen Wolfe, *The Case for Christian Nationalism* (Moscow, ID: Canon, 2022); Kevin DeYoung, "The Rise of Right-Wing Wokeism: A Review of Stephen Wolfe's *The Case for Christian Nationalism*," *The Gospel Coalition*, November 28, 2022, https://media.thegospelcoalition.org/wp-content/uploads/2022/12/02195248/The-Rise-of-Right-Wing-Wokeism.pdf; Cory D. Higdon, "Our Christian Nationalist History? America's Founding in Stephen Wolfe's *The Case for Christian Nationalism*," *American Reformer* (blog), December 9, 2022, https://americanreformer.org/2022/12/our-christian-nationalist-history/.

[2] See Miles Smith, "The Uselessness of 'Christian Nationalism'," *Mere Orthodoxy* (blog), July 18, 2022, https://mereorthodoxy.com/the-uselessness-of-christian-nationalism.

[3] See, for example, R. Albert Mohler Jr., "Black Lives Matter: Affirm the Sentence, Not the Movement," *Public Discourse*, June 18, 2020, https://www.thepublicdiscourse.com/2020/06/65132/; R. Albert Mohler Jr., "Systemic Racism, God's Grace, and the Human Heart: What the Bible Teaches about Structural Sin," *Public Discourse*, June 25, 2020, https://www.thepublicdiscourse.com/2020/06/65536/. See also, Thaddeus J. Williams, *Confronting Injustice without Compromising Truth: 12 Questions Christians Should Ask about Social Justice* (Grand Rapids: Zondervan Academic, 2020), 4–5.

[4] See Ps 82:3; Isa 1:17; Mic 6:8; Luke 11:42.

The quagmire, rather, pertains to the usage of a phrase that could mean everything from the biblical pursuit of civil justice in the corporeal sphere to a radicalized social agenda imbibing a worldview animated by critical theory, which aspires to overthrow "oppressive" societal structures and customs via revolution.[5]

Thus, part of what makes the discussion over social justice difficult is attempting to define it. The meaning of the term will necessarily determine whether Christians can and should pursue "social justice." Furthermore, even if Christians craft a biblical and sensible definition of "social justice," reasonable believers may end up rejecting the term because of its ambiguity, elasticity, or the fear of associating the cause of Christ with a phrase which, in the hands of progressivists, embodies an unbiblical worldview.[6] As Michael Novak noted, the literature about social justice floats around "in the air as if everyone will recognize an instance of it when it appears. . . . The minute one begins to define social justice, one runs into embarrassing intellectual difficulties."[7]

---

[5] Williams, *Confronting Injustice*, 7.

[6] For examples of "social justice" that have, at best, questionable credentials as a faithful representation of biblical justice, see Anthea Butler, *White Evangelical Racism: The Politics of Morality in America* (Chapel Hill: The University of North Carolina Press, 2021); Ibram X. Kendi, *How to Be an Antiracist* (New York: One World, 2019). Owen Strachan, an evangelical Christian, wrote a book in response to these kinds of "social justice" arguments, further demonstrating how complex the situation is when it comes to the usefulness of social justice as a Christian moral imperative. See Owen Strachan, *Christianity and Wokeness: How the Social Justice Movement Is Hijacking the Gospel—and the Way to Stop It* (Washington, DC: Salem, 2021). See also, Bob Smietana, "Woke War: How Social Justice and CRT became Heresy for Evangelicals," *Religion News Service*, February 7, 2022, https://religionnews.com/2022/02/07/woke-war-why-social-justice-became-heresy-for-evangelicals-owen-strachan-crt-southern-baptists-trump/. For an example of evangelical hesitancy to use the phrase "social justice," see "The Statement on Social Justice and the Gospel," found at https://statementonsocialjustice.com/.

[7] Michael Novak, "Defining Social Justice," *First Things*, December 2000, https://www.firstthings.com/article/2000/12/defining-social-justice. See also Kevin

Despite these difficulties, and as this volume makes clear, Christians have a mandate and obligation to pursue social justice (Deut 16:19–20; Ps 37:27–29; Prov 21:3; Mic 6:8).[8] The Bible leaves no question about the responsibility of Christians to contend for the good, beautiful, and true as acts of love for their neighbors—neighbors who are made in the image of God. Social justice, moreover, has historically surfaced among conservative evangelicals throughout the twentieth century as a positive good, rooted in the Scriptures, and viewed as an extension of God's character and common grace towards all of creation. Thus, if social justice is indeed a matter of obedience to God, Christians need to properly define it, especially amid current political turmoil. This will require not only serious contemplation but an audit of the history of political theology and social ethics within American Protestantism during the twentieth century.

This chapter argues that social justice cannot be understood—nor can a definition be attempted—apart from its connectivity to historical conditions and how the term changed over time as a meaningful category for Protestant engagement in the public square. Thus, the dilemma facing Christians over how to define "social justice" and whether to publicly adopt the label comes from a complex history of Protestant ethical thought. This chapter analyzes the historical contours of social justice throughout twentieth-century American Protestantism and suggests that theological presuppositions as well as historically constrained political circumstances determined the parameters and ends called for by social justice advocates. In other words, as a constituent of the social gospel movement in the earliest decades of the twentieth century, social justice meant something quite different than what conservative evangelicals understood during the postwar period. Alterations in the political landscape certainly explained some of the shifts in emphasis and terms between liberal and conservative Protestants. This chapter also

---

DeYoung and Greg Gilbert, *What Is the Mission of the Church? Making Sense of Social Justice, Shalom, and the Great Commission* (Wheaton, IL: Crossway, 2011), 180.

[8] Williams, *Confronting Injustice*, 1.

reveals, however, that theological distinctives between liberals and conservatives clarified the way social justice was understood during the twentieth century. These theological currents adumbrate our own predicament when assessing the usability and verity of a term like "social justice." Indeed, while reasonable Christians can disagree over whether "social justice" as a term has merit in our present context, this chapter will show that notwithstanding the clear theological divide between liberal and conservative Protestants, all of them shared a conviction to pursue social justice as an indispensable mark of Christian faithfulness.

Social Justice and the Social Gospel

Social justice emerged as a concept sometime in the 1840s, before the first stirrings of the social gospel movement took off in the latter part of the nineteenth century.[9] The social gospel movement, however, adopted social justice as an important category for its public theology and public ethics, catapulting the term into more mainstream usage among Protestant ethicists, theologians, and pastors. The kind of social justice pursued by social gospel advocates was defined by political circumstances in America during the late nineteenth and early twentieth centuries. Political progressives sought significant reform during this time, especially on issues related to labor conditions, unions, economic inequality, and women's rights. These historical conditions fused with theological commitments of Protestant liberalism and provided the foundation for what became the social gospel movement. As this chapter argues, the theological disposition and historical contingencies of American Protestants framed their various conceptions of social justice.

---

[9] On the historical roots of the term, see the following: Gary Dorrien, *Social Ethics in the Making: Interpreting an American Tradition* (Southern Gate, UK: Wiley Blackwell, 2009); Gary Dorrien, *The Making of American Liberal Theology: Idealism, Realism, and Modernity, 1900–1950* (Louisville: Westminster John Knox, 2003); Novak, "Defining Social Justice"; DeYoung and Gilbert, *What Is the Mission of the Church?*, 179–81.

Thus, to understand social justice under the umbrella of the social gospel movement requires a consideration of its theological distinctives.

The Formation and Distinctives of the Social Gospel Movement

The social gospel materialized as a subsidiary of Protestant liberalism during the latter decades of the nineteenth century. Figures like Washington Gladden, Lyman Abbott, and Charles Monroe Sheldon provided the intellectual and theological foundations for the movement, which ascended into prominence in large part because of Walter Rauschenbusch.[10] The social gospel movement synthesized prominent aspects of liberal Protestantism with political and cultural issues facing the United States in the early 1900s. It relied upon a postmillennialism that "applied Christian ethics to social problems," seeking to inaugurate the kingdom of God through social transformation.[11] As a movement, it sought a "progressive theological vision to engage American social, political, and economic structures" that advocated for "systemic, structural changes in American institutions."[12]

---

[10] For the importance of earlier social gospel figures, especially Washington Gladden, see Dorrien, *Social Ethics in the Making*, 60–69. For a history of the African American social gospel movement, which focused much more on issues of racial equality than economic equality, see Gary Dorrien, *The New Abolition: W. E. B. Du Bois and the Black Social Gospel* (New Haven, CT: Yale University Press, 2015). For a history of conservative, fundamentalist African American Christianity during this same time, which would have rejected much of the theological categories of the Black social gospel movement, see Daniel R. Bare, *Black Fundamentalists: Conservative Christianity and Racial Identity in the Segregation Era* (New York: New York University Press, 2021).

[11] Daniel G. Hummel, *The Rise and Fall of Dispensationalism: How the Evangelical Battle over the End Times Shaped a Nation* (Grand Rapids: Eerdmans, 2023), 53.

[12] Christopher H. Evans, *The Social Gospel in American Religion: A History* (New York: New York University Press, 2017), 3.

The theological affinity between Protestant liberalism and the social gospel came down to shared views on the rejection of human depravity, an emphasis on the immanence of God, and a repudiation of historic Christian orthodoxy on matters of Christology and the doctrine of Scripture.[13] Christopher Evans, however, noted that figures like Walter Rauschenbusch self-consciously distinguished the social gospel movement from mainstream Protestant liberalism in at least two important ways. First, it deemphasized individual conversion, reorienting redemption around societal structures—entire systems of government—or viewing the mores of cultural structures as the proper objects of atonement.[14] As Rauschenbusch argued, "The chief purpose of the Christian Church in the past has been the salvation of individuals. But the most pressing task of the present is not individualistic. . . . our present task deals with society."[15] The focus on societal ills led to the second distinctive of the social gospel movement, namely, deploying particular theological and expositional categories as doctrinal grounds for "creating a

---

[13] Evans, 7–9; Russell D. Moore, "The Kingdom of God in the Social Ethics of Carl F. H. Henry," in *Essential Evangelicalism: The Enduring Influence of Carl F. H. Henry*, ed. Matthew J. Hall and Owen Strachan (Wheaton, IL: Crossway, 2015), 188; Henry, "Evangelicals in the Social Struggle," 40.

[14] Evans, *The Social Gospel in American Religion*, 5. Aaron Weaver and Gary Dorrien, however, made important points of clarification about the social gospel movement as it related to individual conversion. It would be a mistake to read social gospel advocates as rejecting the need for individual conversion. Indeed, Shailer Mathews (1863–1941), who was another important figure in the social gospel movement, made it clear that the gospel extended both to "individuals and social groups." Shailer Mathews, "Social Gospel," in *A Dictionary of Religion and Ethics*, ed. Shailer Mathews and Gerald Birney Smith (New York: Macmillan, 1923), 416. Historians, furthermore, have noted that the emphasis on societal regeneration among social gospel advocates was, in fact, not mutually exclusive of individual conversion. See Aaron Douglas Weaver, "Progressive Baptists: The Activist Faith of Walter Rauschenbusch, Henlee Barnette, and James Dunn," in *Baptist Political Theology*, ed. Thomas S. Kidd, Paul D. Miller, and Andrew T. Walker (Nashville: B&H Academic, 2023), 293.

[15] Walter Rauschenbusch, *Christianizing the Social Order* (repr. Baylor, TX: Baylor University Press, 2010), 41–42.

mandate to structurally change society."[16] Specifically, social gospel proponents leaned upon prophetic, Hebraic literature found in the Old Testament, as well as select teachings of Jesus found in the Gospel narratives.[17] Indeed, biblical prophetic literature and the prophetic role of Jesus in the Gospels served as vital pillars of the social gospel movement. As Dorrien noted, the advocates of the social gospel viewed prophetic religion—which drew upon prophets condemning established authorities for their lack of care to social and economic ills—as the "'beating heart' of Scripture."[18]

For figures like Rauschenbusch, Hebraic motifs served as the guiding hermeneutic of the social gospel movement. The Old Testament prophetic literature provided for Rauschenbusch a wellspring of narrative and biblical exhortation around which to frame his conception of the social gospel. The prophets, by his estimation, "were trying to beat back the hand of tyranny from the throat of the people."[19] The Old Testament prophet's primary target was, in essence, political: "Their concern," he wrote, "was for the largest and noblest social group with which they were in contact,—their nation."[20] As such, their prophetic ministry had little to do with souls but much to do with society.[21] Rauschenbusch, furthermore, funneled this Hebraic emphasis of the Old Testament prophetic office into the person and work of Jesus Christ. Rauschenbusch argued that Jesus emerged as the antitype of the Old Testament prophetic office, contending that his mission prepared "men for the righteous social order. The goodness which he sought to create in men was always the goodness that would enable them to live rightly with their fellow-men and to constitute true social life."[22]

---

[16] Evans, *The Social Gospel in American Religion*, 8.

[17] Evans, 84–85; Dorrien, *The Making of American Liberal Theology*, 98–100, 110.

[18] Dorrien, 98.

[19] Rauschenbusch, *Christianizing the Social Order*, 51.

[20] Rauschenbusch, 52.

[21] Rauschenbusch, 52.

[22] Walter Rauschenbusch, *Christianity and the Social Crisis in the 21st Century: The Classic That Woke Up the Church*, ed. Paul B. Rauschenbusch (New York: HarperCollins, 2007), 55.

For social gospel advocates, these prophetic and Hebraic underpinnings led to a conscious rejection of the hellenization of Christianity. Hellenistic Christianity tended toward an unbiblical fixation on the spirit at the expense of the body. It overemphasized eternal life and the salvation of the individual from his or her corporeal state, which in turn perverted the ministry of the church. In other words, Hellenistic Christianity made Christians and the church too heavenly minded for any earthly good.[23] Rauschenbusch, for example, ridiculed several facets of the Protestant Reformation. The Reformers, according to Rauschenbusch, bequeathed to Protestantism an unhealthy, Pauline-centric theology, which wrongly accentuated individual justification before a holy and just God. The social gospel, on the other hand, sought to remedy this by reorienting the Christian faith around the Hebraic, prophetic ministry of the prophets and of Jesus's ethical teachings. Rauschenbusch, furthermore, implicitly argued that Paul, to a certain degree, opposed the true teachings of Jesus. As Rauschenbusch put it, "The theology of the Reformation was not modeled on the teachings of Jesus, in which the Kingdom is central, but on the doctrinal system of Paul."[24] Thus, while the social gospel emphasized the redemption of society from systemic evil, it did not preach penal-substitutionary atonement. For Rauschenbusch, God's wrath against sin and the justification offered to men and women through Jesus's death on the cross was too Pauline; the fundamental pursuit of the social gospel movement was the eschatological realization of God's kingdom on earth through the eradication of systemic or political wickedness.

The reason figures like Rauschenbusch deemphasized doctrinal categories associated with Paul's letters—matters related to individual justification and the pursuit of heaven—came down to one of the most important theological distinctives of the social gospel movement, namely, immanentizing the kingdom of God.[25] The prophetic and Hebraic contours of the social

---

[23] Dorrien, *The Making of American Liberal Theology*, 101.

[24] Rauschenbusch, *Christianizing the Social Order*, 85.

[25] Moore, "The Kingdom of God in the Social Ethics of Carl F. H. Henry," 182.

gospel movement fed a broader mission to establish God's kingdom on earth—a kingdom, in theory, that mirrored the ethical teachings of Jesus Christ.[26] Shailer Mathews, for example, contended that the teachings of Jesus necessitated the outworking of love as both the foundation of God's kingdom as well as membership in it. This was in contradistinction with the standard pursuit of the church throughout its history, which accentuated ecclesiology and "pictures of heaven."[27] Indeed, as Mathews argued, the failure of the early church to appropriate the message of the gospel to systems and physical realities multiplied in the wake of both the Enlightenment as well as the revivals of the eighteenth and nineteenth centuries. Natural rights, spiritualism, and an emphasis on the substitutionary atonement of Christ, according to Mathews, culminated in the "indifference to the social needs of the masses."[28] The kingdom of God, on the other hand, was supremely concerned with remedying social needs and prophetically condemning social sins.

For Rauschenbusch, the social gospel prized the kingdom of God and its realization in this present dispensation. "The Kingdom of God," he argued, "is the first and the most essential dogma of the Christian faith. It is also the lost social ideal of Christendom." Indeed, he stated that while Protestantism busied itself with Pauline theology, the social gospel arose as "a revival of the spirit and aims of Jesus himself."[29] Under the "refracting and distorting" influences of Pauline-centric Protestantism, the kingdom of God morphed into a distant, abstruse doctrine rather than the perspicuity of the "social significance of Jesus and the gospel of the Kingdom of God."[30]

Thus, as Rauschenbusch defined it, the social gospel's notion of the kingdom of God encompassed the totality of man's earthly life in relation to the collective community of image-bearers. It provided the

---

[26] Evans, *The Social Gospel in American Religion*, 5.

[27] Mathews, "Social Gospel," 416.

[28] Mathews, 416.

[29] Rauschenbusch, *Christianizing the Social Order*, 49.

[30] Rauschenbusch, 50.

theological ligaments to connect religion with the political and social ills of early twentieth-century America; it enabled the preachers of the social gospel to connect Jesus's teachings to business practices, child labor laws, governmental programs, and the engines of cultural production.[31] The kingdom of God, he argued, "is not a matter of saving human atoms, but of saving the social organism. It is not a matter of getting individuals to heaven, but of transforming the life on earth into the harmony of heaven."[32] Indeed, when Protestants tethered the kingdom of God to a heavenly, other-worldly concept, it made the purpose of the gospel inherently concerned with the eternal life of the individual rather than viewing God's kingdom as the "task of saving the social order."[33]

These theological distinctives, by-and-large, marked much of the social gospel movement. An offshoot of Protestant liberalism, the social gospel emphasized the need for the redemption of social structures, viewing the totality of communal life in the body politic as objects of redemption. Rooted in a postmillennialist eschatology, social gospel proponents stressed the immanence of God's kingdom and undergirded their claims about the earthly realization of the kingdom of God in the prophetic, Hebraic contours of Old Testament literature. Jesus Christ, the ultimate fulfillment of prophetic witness, provided for society a kingdom ethic that was not other-worldly but something tangible and achievable in this life.

Social Justice and the Social Gospel

The theological commitments of the social gospel movement along with its historical circumstances at the start of the American twentieth century

---

[31] Evans, *The Social Gospel in American Religion*, 6; Weaver, "Progressive Baptists," 289.

[32] Rauschenbusch, *Christianity and the Social Crisis*, 54.

[33] Walter Rauschenbusch, *A Theology for the Social Gospel* (New York: MacMillan, 1917), 137.

defined its conception of social justice. In other words, the sociopolitical context of the early 1900s melded together with the theological convictions of social gospel advocates, which explained the framework they developed for social justice. Under this scheme, social justice emerged as a fundamental agenda for the church of Jesus Christ, and it pursued sociopolitical reformation for the purposes of inaugurating the kingdom of Christ on earth. Social justice sought to reorient the public realm—which included political policy as well as cultural mores—around theologically defined goals. Achieving social justice, moreover, was tantamount to applying the atoning work of the gospel to systems of oppression and social corruption. As Rauschenbusch contended, Jesus's ministry summoned subsequent generations to the building of a "righteous society on earth."[34] The "gospel" of the social gospel included repentance and faith, but it was a collective repentance over systemic sins, not individual sins; it was faith not in the Savior but in "the possibility of a new social order."[35] These progressivist theological beliefs defined the mission of social justice for the social gospel movement.

Indeed, in 1915, the Federal Council of the Churches of Christ—an ecumenical association of theologically liberal denominations and churches—adopted what became known as *The Social Creed of the Churches*. This document outlined the telos of social justice under the umbrella of the social gospel movement. The statement adumbrated the social and economic issues that were the focus of social justice reforms. These goals included ending poverty, stemming rising trends in divorce, ending child labor, and aiding in the formation of labor unions to improve work conditions and worker representation.[36] These social justice ambitions became standard among social gospel advocates, and were, by and large, connected

[34] Rauschenbusch, *Christianity and the Social Crisis*, 55.

[35] Rauschenbusch, 285.

[36] Harry Frederick Ward, *The Social Creed of the Churches* (New York: Abingdon, 1915).

to progressivist political aspirations of Americans during the early twentieth century.[37]

In fact, the liberal, or progressive, contours of the social gospel's conception of social justice necessarily rejected the principles of conservatism, both politically and theologically. Conservative theology, according to Rauschenbusch, promoted a stale, bleak spirituality, which imprisoned Christianity in grey cells of tradition and creeds. The American political system mirrored the vices of conservative theology. Indeed, as Rauschenbusch argued, "Law has the same conservative bent as theology. Its customs and precedents and traditions are as faithful and clinging as an hereditary disease."[38] He went on to suggest that *both* theology and the American political order needed a reformation—one defined by progressivist political and doctrinal commitments. Religion's power over a people and a nation, according to Rauschenbusch, "must satisfy the highest moral and religious desires of that age. If it lags behind, and presents outgrown conceptions of life and duty, it is no longer in the full sense of the Gospel."[39] Thus, religion and doctrine must evolve over time with the demands of the age if Christianity will have anything meaningful for society, especially on issues related to social justice. This was a Hegelian worldview, wherein all world history—including the Christian tradition—progressed towards a "self-realization of the Absolute."[40] Humanity, as well as Christian political theology, naturally evolved and advanced from one degree of enlightenment to another, which meant that "all life and history are somehow borne along by the progressive

---

[37] Rauschenbusch, *Christianizing the Social Order*, 14–15. To be clear, "progressive" in this context had much more to do with economic justice and worker conditions than it did with sexual ethics typically associated with progressive politics in our modern times.

[38] Rauschenbusch, *Christianizing the Social Order*, 33.

[39] Rauschenbusch, *Christianizing the Social Order*, 47.

[40] Carl F. H. Henry, *Remaking the Modern Mind* (Grand Rapids: Eerdmans, 1948), 40; Moore, "The Kingdom of God in the Social Ethics of Carl F. H. Henry," 188.

manifestation of divinity."[41] As such, eradicating social injustice under the social gospel worldview necessitated a reimagined Christianity that possessed relevance for the contemporary issues facing society. Tradition and orthodoxy inhibited the ability of the church to heal the nation's moral vector and to realize God's kingdom in America.[42]

Determining, therefore, what was "social justice" was, to a certain degree, subjective under the Hegelian hermeneutic of social gospel advocates. Scholars of the social gospel movement identified extrabiblical threads of political philosophy—ideas that included socialism, Marxism, and communism—which intertwined with the theological liberalism of figures like Rauschenbusch.[43] As Dorrien notes, social gospel advocates allied themselves with American socialism and democratic socialism, believing that "making socialism Christian" paved the way for the realization of social justice.[44] This made sense given that social gospel proponents sought to decouple theological dogmatism and creedalism from their version of "Christianity." The minimization of doctrinal orthodoxy along with a reduction of the penal-substitutionary work of Jesus allowed social justice a certain elasticity.[45] "Christianizing" the social order, then, was not a nod towards the exclusivity or superiority of Christianity to other religions or social philosophies, including Marxism, communism, and socialism. On the contrary, Rauschenbusch, for example, believed that social demands of Christianity were universally achievable, regardless of one's religious or

---

[41] Henry, 40.

[42] Evans, *The Social Gospel in American Religion*, 3; Moore, "The Kingdom of God in the Social Ethics of Carl F. H. Henry," 182.

[43] Evans, for example, chronicled the influence of Karl Marx on Walter Rauschenbusch during his education in the late 1880s. He also highlighted the influence of socialism and progressivism in his thought, which became paradigmatic for the broader social gospel movement. See Evans, *The Social Gospel in American Religion*, 79–84.

[44] Dorrien, *The Making of American Liberal Theology*, 103.

[45] Rauschenbusch, *Christianizing the Social Order*, 67; Moore, "The Kingdom of God in the Social Ethics of Carl F. H. Henry," 188.

cultural background. Jesus, moreover, was less the Savior who had come to redeem mankind from sin and instead an "ultimate exemplar" of the social ideal and of social justice.[46]

This was not to suggest that some of the justice goals of the social gospel movement lacked virtue. On the contrary, conservative evangelicals living at that time could have celebrated efforts to end child labor atrocities or to stymie burgeoning divorce rates. As the twentieth century progressed, the concern of conservative evangelicals, as we shall see, took issue with the *theology* of the social gospel movement and how that affected its view of social justice, especially since social justice became the means with which the social gospel inaugurated the kingdom of God. Thus, as conservative evangelicals during the postwar period considered social justice, they did not reject the term nor its significance for Christian faithfulness and stewardship. They did, however, reframe the structure of theology in order to present social justice within a biblically defined framework.

Social Justice and the Evangelical Response

While present-day evangelicalism wrestles with the usefulness of the term *social justice*, conservative evangelicals in the postwar period embraced the label. One of the most important evangelical theologians at the midpoint of the twentieth century was Carl F. H. Henry, and Henry called social justice an "authentic Christian concern."[47] Indeed, crafting a biblically rooted conception of social justice and political theology surfaced as a primary concern for postwar evangelicals like Henry. Contextually, conservative Christianity throughout the twentieth century receded into obscurity and marginalization. By the early 1940s, figures like Carl F. H. Henry, Harold Ockenga, Charles Fuller, and Billy Graham cast a new vision for conservative evangelicals—what became known as neo-evangelicalism—hoping to

[46] Dorrien, *The Making of American Liberal Theology*, 110; Rauschenbusch, 85.

[47] Henry, "Evangelicals and the Social Struggle," 44.

correct the failures of orthodox Christianity to properly engage the world for Jesus Christ. They founded institutions like Fuller Theological Seminary, the National Association of Evangelicals, the Evangelical Theological Society, and the publication *Christianity Today*.[48] These endeavors sought to course correct from the perceived failures of fundamentalism in the early 1900s as well as to respond to the social gospel movement and liberal Protestantism by providing a robust evangelical theology.

Indeed, in his salvo against fundamentalism and modernism, Henry framed the neo-evangelical resurgence as the biblically faithful model for Protestant engagement in the American twentieth century, arguing that while orthodox Christians in the early 1900s rightly revolted against the social gospel, they did so to an extreme.[49] Conservative Christianity had abandoned the "Christian social imperative."[50] Thus, Henry and his neo-evangelical compatriots spent much of their careers attempting to reorient conservative Christianity in two ways: First, they wanted to see the development of an evangelical mind that was intellectually capable of refuting

---

[48] See the following for historical overviews of what became known as "neo-evangelicalism": George M. Marsden, *Fundamentalism and American Culture: The Shaping of Twentieth-Century Evangelicalism, 1870–1925* (Oxford: Oxford University Press, 1980); George M. Marsden, *Understanding Fundamentalism and Evangelicalism* (Grand Rapids: Eerdmans, 1991); George M. Marsden, *The Twilight of the American Enlightenment: The 1950s and the Crisis of Liberal Belief* (New York: Basic, 2014); George M. Marsden, *Reforming Fundamentalism: Fuller Theological Seminary and the New Evangelicalism* (Grand Rapids: Eerdmans, 1987); Owen Strachan, *Awakening the Evangelical Mind: An Intellectual History of the Neo-Evangelical Movement* (Grand Rapids: Zondervan, 2015); Neil J. Young, *We Gather Together: The Religious Right and the Problem of Interfaith Politics* (New York: Oxford University Press, 2016). For one of the most important primary resources that highlighted the distinctives of neo-evangelicalism with fundamentalism and Protestant liberalism, see Carl F. H. Henry, *The Uneasy Conscience of Modern Fundamentalism* (Grand Rapids: Eerdmans, 1947).

[49] Moore, "The Kingdom of God in the Social Ethics of Carl F. H. Henry," 181.

[50] Henry, *The Uneasy Conscience of Modern Fundamentalism*, 22.

modernism, secularism, and especially Protestant liberalism. Second, they wanted to create a thoroughly evangelical vision for social justice—one that avoided fundamentalist isolationism, on the one hand, while also refuting the parameters of social justice under the scheme of the social gospel movement. As Moore states, "The new evangelical theologians maintained that their agenda was far from a capitulation to the Social Gospel but was instead the conservative antidote to it."[51] Henry and other neo-evangelicals therefore resisted the urge to jettison phrases or categories for Christian engagement merely on the grounds that such words or phrases had a checkered history. They sought to provide clear definitions that were, by their estimation, derived from the Bible as the starting point of Christian theological reflection.

Evangelicals, according to Henry, possessed a God-given mandate to preach the gospel of Jesus Christ *and* to promote social justice. "The Lordship of Christ over all life," Henry argued, "involved socio-cultural obligations."[52] The social gospel, however, inhibited a viable pursuit of social justice because of its belief that the kingdom of God could be realized "through political and economic changes."[53] Henry believed that a proper vision of social justice required the disentangling of the term from the erroneous political-theological worldview of the social gospel—a movement that, by Henry's estimation, subverted biblical theology, reduced the wrath of God against individual sin, minimized the demands of righteousness that only Jesus achieved, and robbed the love of God of its truly glorious power and beauty.[54] Additionally, the social gospel crafted social justice goals that were contrary to the full counsel of God's word. Indeed, Henry believed the social gospel allowed the tentacles of socialism and communism to constrict

---

[51] Moore, "The Kingdom of God in the Social Ethics of Carl F. H. Henry," 177.

[52] Henry, "Evangelicals in the Social Struggle," 37.

[53] Henry, 40.

[54] Henry, 40–42.

a biblical conception of justice. A comprehensive framework for social justice cannot violate, as Henry argued, precepts of the Bible and implications drawn out of the *imago Dei*. By allying itself with socialistic impulses, the social gospel inadvertently repudiated fundamental goods and natural rights that were either explicitly revealed in the Scriptures or reasonably deduced from its instruction. In this way, the social gospel could not achieve true social justice because it adopted an erroneous epistemological method—a method which did not root the knowledge of true justice in the full counsel of what God had revealed in his Word.[55]

In fact, one of the most important distinctions between the social gospel's summons for social justice with that of conservative evangelicalism in the latter decades of the twentieth century came down to the place of biblical authority. As Dorrien notes, neo-evangelicals believed that the social gospel movement—and Protestant liberalism generally—amounted to nothing less than "misguided betrayals of Christian orthodoxy."[56] Henry contended that "the present civilizational crisis calls for recovering the transcendent basis of law and justice as well as the truth of revelation."[57] God spoke in his Word and revealed the principles of justice, love, and morality. This moral transcendence formed the basis of true social justice and societal stability. The will of God, disclosed in the Bible, provided a stable, cohesive foundation around which to frame society's laws and policies in a way that nourished justice.[58] "Either we return to the God of the Bible, or we perish in the pit of lawlessness," Henry warned.[59]

Henry, however, did not equate the transcendence of biblical authority as the basis of social justice to mean that the Bible provided specific answers to modern-day political concerns. On the contrary, the neo-evangelical

---

[55] Henry, 43.

[56] Dorrien, *Social Ethics in the Making*, 447.

[57] Carl F. H. Henry, *God, Revelation, and Authority: God Who Stands and Stays, Part Two* (Wheaton, IL: Crossway, 1999), 436.

[58] Henry, 454.

[59] Henry, 454.

conception of social justice, in distinction with the social gospel movement, stressed sphere sovereignty between the church and civil realms—each had its own authority and mandate. "The Church as a corporate body," Henry contended, "has no spiritual mandate to sponsor economic, social, and political programs."[60] For Henry, competency served as a principle that defined the boundary between church and state. The church, as an institution, lacked expertise and biblical warrant to offer governments sound economic or trade policies in the same way that government and the civil mechanisms of power lacked competency to instruct the church on the content of orthodoxy and doctrine. Individual Christians, on the other hand, may possess—and should acquire—expertise and competency via their respective vocations and education.[61]

A second divergence from the social gospel worldview that neo-evangelicals insisted upon was redemption. While the social gospel amplified the need for societal redemption from systemic sin, conservative evangelicals reasserted the fundamental need for *individual* salvation. Henry believed that while evangelicals had a responsibility to contend for justice in the public square, their primary goal must remain "the preaching of the Gospel, in the interest of individual regeneration by the supernatural grace of God."[62] Where the social gospel diminished the spiritual obstacles that inhibited social justice, neo-evangelicals like Henry magnified them. As Henry articulated: "The great contemporary problems are moral and spiritual. They demand more than a formula. The evangelicals have a conviction of absoluteness concerning their message, and not to proclaim it, in the assault on social evils, is sheer inconsistency."[63] For Henry and the new evangelicals, a prioritization of social justice must not confuse or confound

---

[60] Carl F. H. Henry, "The Church and Political Pronouncements," *Christianity Today*, August 28, 1964, 29.

[61] Henry, 30.

[62] Henry, *The Uneasy Conscience of Modern Fundamentalism*, 88–89.

[63] Henry, *The Uneasy Conscience of Modern Fundamentalism*, 89.

the mission of the church and the summons of the gospel to reconcile sinners to God.

This focus on individual salvation, regeneration, and the gospel's message about the penal-substitutionary atonement of Jesus Christ explained a third distinctive between the social gospel movement of the early twentieth century and the social justice advocacy of the new evangelicals. The majority of neo-evangelicals rejected the postmillennialism of Rauschenbusch, especially any notion of immanentizing the kingdom of God on earth through political mechanisms. Henry rejected attempts to create an idyllic kingdom this side of Christ's return; in fact, no amount of social justice or human activity could realize the perfect kingdom of Christ.[64] Indeed, Henry indicted the social gospel for surrendering the "redemptive-regenerative view of man" to a seemingly utopic society secured through political revolution.[65] "The social gospel," he continued, "became readily identified with a Socialist and sometimes Communist critique of society, with espousal of a welfare state based on the political redistribution of wealth."[66] The embrace of worldly, unbiblical ideologies—especially those that promised reprieve from social ills—made sense in a theological system committed to immanentization of an idealized state. This was not the way of biblical Christianity, and any approach to social justice that believed a righteous society could be achieved through political power was prone to abandon the mission of the church and the message of the gospel. Henry, rather presciently, believed that this propensity not only existed among liberal Protestants, but arose as a temptation among "right-wing, culture-ideology," which could easily forget "personal religion and God's searching judgment of all human history."[67]

---

[64] Henry, *Remaking the Modern Mind*, 41–42; Henry, "Evangelicals in the Social Struggle," 40, 44.

[65] Carl F. H. Henry, *A Plea for Evangelical Demonstration* (Grand Rapids: Baker, 1971), 117.

[66] Henry, 117.

[67] Henry, 109.

Thus, the social gospel reduced the kingdom of God to something worldly and corporeal and hitched it to extrabiblical ideologies. For neo-evangelicals, the church had a God-given mission to proclaim the excellencies of Jesus Christ to a lost and dying world. As Dorrien notes, Henry and the new evangelicals believed that the church must "pray for and give witness to the regenerative power of God in human souls. God's very Spirit was the answer to the world's troubles, not government, education, or an unregenerate conscience."[68] By God's grace, when the church proclaimed the gospel, it wrought salvation—and through the salvation of individuals, "society was a beneficiary."[69] Pursuing social justice from an evangelical perspective, then, required a resilient reliance upon the Word of God as the basis of ethical and theological reflection. It also necessitated a proper prioritization of evangelical activity—one that summoned evangelicals into the public square as ambassadors for a biblically defined ethic that, at the same time, resisted temptations to forget Paul's reminder in Phil 3:20: "But our citizenship is in heaven, and from it we await a Savior, the Lord Jesus Christ." Social justice was a Christian imperative but one that was always tempered by the realities of a Genesis 3 world.

These distinctives led Henry to articulate four controlling convictions for an evangelical vision of social justice. First, social transformation comes via the work of the Holy Spirit through the church of Jesus Christ proclaiming the gospel to unbelievers. This marked the church's primary and "dynamic" task for social renewal. Second, Henry charged pastors to preach and proclaim the full counsel of God from the pulpit. Individual Christians needed biblical, expositional instruction if they hoped to pursue social justice in a way that accorded with the revealed will of God. The proclamation of God's Word from the pulpit, in other words, bequeathed to Christians engaged in the public square guardrails and principles that enabled a more faithful representation and advocacy of justice from God's people. Third, Henry

[68] Dorrien, *Social Ethics in the Making*, 453.

[69] Dorrien, 454.

magnified vocation and daily work as the "most natural transition from private to social action." Everyday labor, done to the glory of God, nourished conditions conducive to a just society. Unlike the social gospel, which leaned upon governmental mechanisms to secure justice, Henry asserted a bottom-up approach. Individual Christians, deployed throughout the economy, carried with them the obligations of faithfulness and justice to their respective vocations. The presence of Christian businessmen, Christian laborers, Christian lawyers, Christian doctors, Christian teachers, and Christians in every other sector of the economy would foster justice, peace, and prosperity. This meant that Christians needed to take their vocations seriously, and that the church needed to take an active part in encouraging and training young Christian men and women for this kind of service. Finally, individual Christians needed a constant reminder that they lived as "citizens of two worlds." The Christian, therefore, took on a dual prerogative and divinely ordained mandate. As Henry put it, this dual mandate constituted the extension of "God's purpose of redemption through the church, and also to extend God's purpose of justice and order through civil government."[70]

Taken together, the evangelical corrective to the social gospel did not abandon social justice as a category for Christian ethical engagement. Henry and the neo-evangelicals summoned conservative Christianity to a pursuit of justice that was inherently connected to the Bible as the norming principle for ethical reflection and theological conviction. They also redirected the focus of social justice away from systemic sins and towards individuals who remained unregenerate. It was a pursuit of justice tempered by the realities of a fallen world as well. No amount of political power or governmental might could, in the end, cure what truly plagued mankind. The only remedy—and the only hope for lasting justice—was the proclamation of the gospel.

---

[70] The preceding quotes and these four principles can be found in Henry, "Evangelicals in the Social Struggle," 57.

Conclusion

Evangelical consternation over the term "social justice" comes from a long, complex history of an idea that stretched back into the earliest days of the twentieth century. Social justice as a category for Christian political engagement, then, is complex. The phrase did not emerge out of a vacuum, which means that it should not be flippantly defined without due attention to the history of this contested idea. Evangelicals should not be surprised that social justice can be coopted for ungodly, unbiblical causes and purposes. The social gospel movement co-opted social justice as a significant feature of its entire theological paradigm. Though many of the goals were commendable, figures like Rauschenbusch tethered social justice to a worldview and philosophical system at odds with a biblical worldview. Conservative evangelicalism in the twentieth century, however, sought to correct these issues by linking social justice to the Bible and reminding the church of its primary mission.

Knowing this history will help pastors and Christian leaders avoid the pitfall of thinking that social justice is an easy, uncomplicated matter. On the contrary, as this chapter has shown, Protestants—liberal and conservative alike—wrestled with the term. What is justice? How can Christians achieve it? What role does the Bible play in matters of public policy? How political should the church be? How political should the individual Christian be? All these questions are inherently tethered to the idea of social justice and none of them are easy to answer.

Finally, this brief historical survey should remind Christians of the need for patience and grace with one another. As the old adage goes, families should never discuss religion and politics if they hope to coexist. Social justice from a Christian perspective requires consideration of both religion and politics. It is a recipe for contention. Christians, however, must meet this challenge, consider the demands of social justice, and think deeply and biblically *together* about an incredibly complex topic.

Questions for Further Discussion

1. How can one's eschatology affect one's view of social justice?
2. Should Christians partner with nonbelievers on issues of social justice?
3. How does historical analysis help us with our present challenges as we think through social justice?
4. How can Christians avoid falling into the extremes of either cultural isolationism or an idolization of the public square?
5. What theological weaknesses did the social gospel adopt that made its pursuit of social justice improbable and unhelpful?
6. How did neo-evangelicals attempt to correct course during the midpoint of the twentieth century? What theological categories did they emphasize in order to craft a more biblical approach to social justice?

Suggested Reading

Ballor, Jordan J., and Robert Joustra, eds. *The Church's Social Responsibility: Reflections on Evangelicalism and Social Justice* (Grand Rapids: Christian's Library, 2015).

DeYoung, Kevin, and Greg Gilbert. *What is the Mission of the Church? Making Sense of Social Justice, Shalom, and the Great Commission* (Wheaton, IL: Crossway, 2011).

Henry, Carl F. H. *The Uneasy Conscience of Modern Fundamentalism* (Grand Rapids: Eerdmans, 1947; repr. Wheaton, IL: Crossway, 2022).

Kidd, Thomas S., Paul D. Miller, and Andrew T. Walker, eds. *Baptist Political Theology* (Nashville: B&H Academic, 2023).

Williams, Thaddeus J. *Confronting Injustice without Compromising Truth: 12 Questions Christians Should Ask about Social Justice* (Grand Rapids: Zondervan Academic, 2020).

2

Justice in Isaiah

— Peter J. Gentry —

Introduction

Prophets of the Old Testament are well-known for addressing issues of social justice. It is not surprising, then, that those concerned in some way for social justice in their own context have appealed to prophets like Amos or Isaiah.

An important question arises in appealing to the prophets. When the prophets describe scenarios where the powerful and rich oppress the poor and powerless, is it appropriate for us to appeal to the prophets and apply their message directly and simply to our situation? For example, in his historic "I Have a Dream" speech during the 1963 March on Washington, Martin Luther King Jr. quoted Amos 5:24, applying it to the concerns of social justice that he raised. If appealing directly to the prophets is perhaps inappropriate, what interpretive method would allow us to transfer the authority of the prophetic word in Scripture to concerns of social justice in our own culture and society?

Here we will consider questions of social justice raised in the book of Isaiah in the Old Testament, seek to discover the context in which those questions were raised, and ask how they might be legitimately transferred to similar questions of social justice current in our society.

Biblical Texts and Exegesis

Social Justice in Isaiah: An Example from Isaiah 5

One obvious way to discuss social justice in Isaiah is to collect examples pointed out in particular by the prophet himself. The "Song of the Vineyard" in Isaiah 5 and the application of the "bad grapes" to Judah is just such an example that I considered in an earlier publication.[1] I propose now to review briefly this example in order to reevaluate the way in which examples such as these must be contextualized before applying them to our society today.

Explanation of Isaiah 5

Outline or Structure of Isa 5:1–30

I. Song of the Vineyard	5:1–7
A. A Song of a Vineyard and Its Fruit	1–2
B. The Listeners Asked for a Verdict	3–4
C. The Decision of the Owner	5–6
D. The Application to Judah	7
II. Bad Grapes: Indictment of God's People	5:8–24
A. Round 1	8–17
1. Woe: Land Grabbing	8–10
2. Woe: Partying and Revelry	11–12
a. Therefore 1	13
b. Therefore 2	14–17
B. Round 2	18–24
3. Woe: Mocking Divine Justice	18–19

[1] Unless otherwise noted, all translations are by the author. This essay reuses exposition of Isa 5:1–30 and 16:5. Nonetheless, a radically new analysis and synthesis is proffered here. See Peter J. Gentry, "Sizemore Lectures I: Isaiah and Social Justice," *Midwestern Journal of Theology* 12, no. 1 (2013): 1–16 and Peter J. Gentry, *How to Read and Understand the Biblical Prophets* (Wheaton, IL: Crossway, 2017).

4. Woe: Inverting God's Standards	20
5. Woe: Self-Approved Wisdom	21
6. Woe: Partying and Inverting Social Justice	22–23
a. Therefore 3	24
III. The Vineyard Ravaged: Announcement of Punishment	5:25–30
A. The Final Therefore	5:25

The text is divided into three sections. The first is a parable or song about a vineyard, in vv. 1–7. The second section goes from vv. 8–24 and applies the parable to the people of Judah and Jerusalem in Isaiah's time. The last section describes the coming judgment: God will bring a distant nation to conquer them and destroy their civilization.

The "Song of the Vineyard" in the opening section can be briefly summarized. The parable is divided into four stanzas. The first stanza relates in song a story of a farmer preparing a vineyard and expecting good vintage. Instead, he is met by rotten, stunted grapes. In the second stanza the listeners are asked for a verdict. The third part confirms the rhetorical question posed in the second stanza by relating the decision of the owner of the vineyard. He will do exactly as the listeners expect him to do—he will destroy this useless vineyard. Then comes the punch line of the parable, and what a great shock it is. The parable is applied to Judah and Jerusalem in the last stanza; they are the bad grapes!

Verses 8–24, which I have entitled "Bad Grapes," constitute a damning indictment of the people of God. A series of six woes details and specifies the bad grapes indicated in vv. 2 and 4 of the parable. The literary structure is the clue to the meaning of the text. The key words are "woe" and "therefore." "Woe" is a key word used to describe and identify the sins for which the people will be punished. "Therefore" is a key word used to detail the divine punishment for these specific sins. The punishment is based squarely upon retributive justice, since this is the main principle of the Torah (Genesis through Deuteronomy).

Notice, however, how these woes are presented. First there are two "woes" in vv. 8 and 11, which are followed by two "therefores" in vv. 13–14.

Then there are a series of four more "woes," in vv. 18, 20–21, and 22, given in rapid staccato fashion. This is followed by another "therefore" in v. 24. The word "therefore" divides the woes into two groups; here Isaiah, in typical Hebrew literary style, is going around the topic twice from two different angles or points of view.

The section indicting the people of God is then followed by an announcement of imminent punishment. This last paragraph is introduced by a conjunction that also means "therefore," but the word in Hebrew is different because this is the big "therefore" that takes up the three little "therefores" in the previous verses (Isa 5:13–14, 24).

Consequently, the six woes are divided into two groups, two in the first group and four in the second. At the heart of all of them is the violation of social justice as indicated by the last line of v. 7—the punch line of the parable—where we have the word pair "justice-righteousness" split over parallel lines of Hebrew poetry.

Isaiah 5 in Light of Ancient Hebrew Literature

Before we can explain the parable of the vineyard and interpret its application to Judah, we must grasp how ancient Hebrew authors communicated. For those of us whose culture is based upon a civilization that is modern and Western rather than ancient and Eastern, the biblical texts communicate in a completely different manner.

The normal pattern in Hebrew literature is to consider topics in a recursive manner, which means that a topic is progressively repeated. Such an approach seems monotonous to those who do not know and understand how these texts communicate. Using the recursive approach, a Hebrew author begins a discourse on a particular topic, develops it from a particular perspective, and then concludes his conversation. Then he begins another conversation, taking up the same topic again from a different angle, perspective, or point of view. When these two conversations or discourses on the same topic are heard in literary sequence, they function like the left and right speakers of a stereo system. In one way, the music from the left speaker is identical to that of the right, yet in another way it is slightly different so that the effect is stereo instead of just one-dimensional. In Hebrew literature, then, the ideas presented can be experienced like 3D IMAX movies with Dolby surround sound.

This approach to communication can occur across genres: Exodus 14 and 15 give first a prose and then a poetic account of crossing the Sea of Reeds while Judges 4 and 5 give first a prose and then a poetic account of the destruction of Sisera and his military unit of iron chariots. Genesis 1:1–2:3 and 2:4–3:24 show the phenomenon within the same genre of narrative. These narratives of the creation story were not composed from different sources, as scholars have mistakenly proposed from the eighteenth century onward; what we find in those accounts is the chief characteristic and method of how a single author communicates.

This approach in Hebrew literature—aimed at developing ideas in a three-dimensional manner, so to speak—is followed not only in every genre and across genres, whether prose or poetry, but also recursively at both the micro and macro levels. Let me illustrate from Exod 19:5–6, where Yahweh announces his purpose for making the covenant at Sinai. He says to Israel:

> "You shall be my treasured possession among all peoples . . . and you shall be to me a kingdom of priests and a holy nation."

Two clauses or sentences joined by the conjunction "and" constitute the declaration by Yahweh. The first is "You shall be my treasured possession among all peoples" (v. 5). The second is "and you shall be to me a kingdom of priests and a holy nation" (v. 6).

If we begin with the second sentence (v. 6), we notice that there are two phrases, "kingdom of priests" and "holy nation," also joined by "and." These two phrases are like the left and right speakers of a stereo system. A holy nation is a nation completely devoted to loving God and serving him.

A kingdom of priests is a group of priests exhibiting the rule of God and in their ministry bringing others to experience God's rule in their lives—bringing others to devote themselves to the worship of God. Both phrases then, each in a slightly different way, speak of a group of people completely devoted to serving and worshiping God. The phrase "treasured possession" is used in ancient Near Eastern literature and in the Old Testament of a king who is completely devoted to serving and worshiping his god or of an obedient son who is devoted to the service of his father.[2]

In this way the two phrases in v. 6 are like the left and right speakers of a stereo system, saying the same thing. Verse 6, in turn, is also the right speaker in relation to v. 5, because both verses speak of Israel's relation to Yahweh as a devoted and obedient son, serving and worshiping him. We can see, then, that the approach is both repetitive and recursive. First, the two verses serve as a left and right speaker. Second, within the second verse there is another left and right speaker.

Such an approach is completely opposite to scientific writing in our culture, which is based on our Greco-Roman heritage going back especially to Aristotle. In our culture, a writer, perhaps a philosopher or scientist, begins at a certain point A and moves slowly in a straight line to point B using arguments, evidence, and logic.

Repetition in Isaiah 5

The recursive nature of the discourse in Isaiah 5 is clear. Two "woes" in vv. 8 and 11 bring the charges of social injustice: (1) adding fields and houses together to amass a huge farm and (2) partying from dawn to dusk. The partying represents how the newly gained and ill-gotten riches are being

[2] For a detailed exegesis of Exod 19:5–6, see Peter J. Gentry and Stephen J. Wellum, *Kingdom through Covenant: A Biblical-Theological Understanding of the Covenants*, 2nd ed. (Wheaton, IL: Crossway, 2018), 346–65.

spent. These "woes" are followed by two "therefores" in vv. 13–17 to delineate punishment from God based on retributive justice to fall on those who have mistreated the poor and powerless.

Then the discourse in vv. 18–24 goes over the same topic again from a different angle or perspective. In the second round, the last four woes actually repeat the first two in a recursive development of the topic. The third woe talks about the upper classes carrying a burden of sin bound by big ropes of deceit and mocking God by calling upon him to hurry up with the judgment that he has promised. The fourth woe shows that the system of virtue and vice, of right and wrong, is completely inverted in this society. The fifth woe accuses the people of depending on self-approved knowledge and skill. They are confident in and reliant on their technology and mastery of the powers of nature.

The woes, then, are all ways of elaborating the original charge of perverting social justice. The last woe is the climax and summarizes by combining the two original charges of gaining wealth by social injustice and living a life of pleasure to spend that wealth. In this way, the last four woes elaborate the original two indictments. These indictments and the punishments are based entirely upon the retributive justice (*lex talionis*) of the Torah as prescribed in the covenant made at Sinai (Exod 21:23–25). The penalty always exactly matches the crime. The wrongdoer must repay as much as but no more than the wrong done.

Social Justice in Isaiah: Analysis from Poetry and Word Pairs in Ancient Hebrew Literature

The recursive nature of Hebrew writing is further revealed in the couplet of Hebrew poetry and in word pairs.

If we keep in mind the analogy of a stereo system, Hebrew poetry is based on juxtaposing short lines as couplets: the first line functions as the left speaker and the second line as the right speaker. Ideas are presented in brief, but they are full-orbed and multi-dimensional.

There is a unit in Hebrew literature, smaller than the couplet in poetry, that functions in the same way—like the left and right speakers of a stereo system—called a word pair. Just two words, joined together with the conjunction *and*, mean something different and also greater than either of the words by themselves or the sum of the parts.

An example is the word pair loyalty-faithfulness found in Josh 2:14. There the Israelite spies make a deal with Rahab to preserve her and her family if she maintains secrecy about their activities:

> The men answered her, "We will give our lives for yours. If you don't report our mission, we will show kindness and faithfulness to you when the Lord gives us the land" (CSB).

In the English translation of the CSB, the words "kindness" and "faithfulness" are rendering the Hebrew word pair *ḥesed̲* and *ʾĕmet̲*.

This word pair is frequently used to summarize the attitudes and obligations in a covenant relationship. In Gen 47:29–30 we have the same word pair used to describe the obligations of the relationship between Jacob and Joseph. In the ancient Near East, family relationships were the basis of covenantal relationships and were comprehended in terms of *ḥesed̲* and *ʾĕmet̲*.

Now, according to the Hebrew poetry of Isa 5:7—which is based upon placing lines in parallel pairs—"justice" is matched in the first line by "righteousness" in the second. Normally, when the words "justice" and "righteousness" are joined together in prose, they form a single concept or idea—best expressed in English by the term *social justice*. This is a figure of speech known as a "hendiadys," one concept expressed through two words. The word pair becomes an idiom expressing a single thought that is both different and greater than the words considered independently. Just as one cannot analyze the expression "by and large" in English by studying "by" and "large" separately, so one cannot determine the meaning of this expression by analyzing "justice" and "righteousness" separately. Hebrew poetry, however, allows such a word pair to be split so that half is in one line of the couplet and the other half is in the matching parallel line. The word pair "justice-righteousness" is central to the discourse of Isaiah and occurs some eighteen times, always at critical or key points in the discourse.[3]

It is important to grasp and understand that the prophets used certain word pairs as a way of summarizing the covenant commands, requirements, and stipulations. Bible scholars and religious leaders came to Jesus and asked him, "Which is the greatest commandment in the Law?" Similarly in the Old Testament, many years earlier, as Isaiah and other prophets sought to apply the covenant with Moses and Israel to their situation and times, they found new ways to condense and summarize in a single sentence or even a phrase the apparently unwieldy mass of commands and instructions in the Torah.[4] Even the Ten Commandments, upon which some 600 or so instructions are based, could be further condensed and summarized. An example is the famous passage in Mic 6:8, "What does the Lord require of you but to do justice, and to love kindness, and to walk humbly with your God?" Micah is summarizing in brief what the covenant relationship entails.

The heart of Isaiah's message is that the covenant between God and Israel given by Moses at Sinai is broken. He summarizes this covenant, consisting of the Ten Commandments and the Judgments in Exodus 20–23, using expressions or idioms for social justice and faithful, loyal love or being truthful in love. Isaiah's prophecy in Isa 16:5 is an excellent example to illustrate this:

> In *love* a throne will be established;
> in *faithfulness* a man will sit on it—
> one from the house of David—
> one who in judging seeks *justice*
> and speeds the cause of *righteousness* (NIV, italics added).

---

[3] The word pair "justice-righteousness," frequently split over poetic parallelism, is discussed below in detail.

[4] See Matt 22:36–40.

In contrast to the regime of the kings of Isaiah's time, a future king is promised who will rule in justice and righteousness. Again, like in Isa 5:7, the word pair is split so that half is in one line of the couplet and half in the parallel line. Similarly, in the first half of the verse we have "love" in the first half of the couplet and "faithfulness" in the second. This is another word pair that focuses on fulfilling one's obligations and doing what is right in a covenant relationship (such as marriage).

Now, Isaiah's promise of a future king in Isa 16:5 is based upon Deuteronomy 17. Deuteronomy 17:16–20 describes the manner in which the future king of Israel is to fulfill his responsibilities. Three negative commands in vv. 16–17 are followed by three positive commands in vv. 18–20, all relating to the Torah: (1) the king shall copy the Torah; (2) the king shall have the Torah with him; and (3) the king shall read the Torah.[5] In other words, the only positive requirement is that the king embodies *torah*, i.e., the instruction of the covenant as a model citizen. This is exactly what Isaiah is saying in 16:5, only he uses the concept of social justice, expressed by the broken word pair "justice-righteousness" as a *summary* for the covenant or Torah. Deuteronomy calls for a king who implements the Torah in his regime and Isaiah predicts a king who will deliver social justice in his rule. They are saying the same thing.

Although scholars have published lexical studies of *mišpāṭ* (justice) and *tsĕdāqāh* (righteousness), in general they have not paid attention to the function of these two words as a word pair, nor have they noted that the word pair functions, especially in the prophets, as a summary of the covenant commands. As an example, one may mention the contribution of Charles Lee Irons, *The Righteousness of God: A Lexical Examination of the Covenant-Faithfulness Interpretation*.[6] In general the method of semantic

---

[5] Cf. Daniel I. Block, "The Burden of Leadership: The Mosaic Paradigm of Kingship (Deut. 17:14–20)," *BibSac* 162 (2005): 259–78.

[6] Charles Lee Irons, *The Righteousness of God: A Lexical Examination of the Covenant-Faithfulness Interpretation* (WUNT 2/386; Tübingen: Mohr Siebeck, 2015), 120–26, 344–82.

study he follows as well as his results are sound. Nonetheless, there is no consideration of the function of justice-righteousness as a word pair and especially as a way of summarizing the character of the covenant requirements. The evidence in the Old Testament for this word pair can be briefly laid out as follows:

Analysis of Word Pairs Entailing "Justice" and "Righteousness"
Hebrew *ṣeḏeq* = "righteousness" = 119x
Hebrew *ṣəḏāqāh* = "righteousness" = 157x
Hebrew *mišpāṭ* = "judgment"/"justice" = 424x

Word Pair *mišpāṭ wāṣeḏeq*
Ps 119:121; Eccl 5:7 [MT; Eng. 5:8]

Broken Word Pair *mišpāṭ . . . ṣeḏeq*
Job 8:3; 35:2; Isa 1:21; 16:5; Eccl 3:16

Word Pair *ṣeḏeq ūmišpāṭ*
Pss 89:15 [MT; Eng. 89:14]; 97:2; Prov 1:3; 2:9
(צֶדֶק וּמִשְׁפָּט וּמֵישָׁרִים)

Broken Word Pair *ṣeḏeq . . . mišpāṭ*
Job 29:14; Pss 37:6; 72:2; Isa 32:1; Jer 22:13; Hos 2:19

This accounts for 17 of 119 occurrences of צֶדֶק (14.3%).

Word Pair *ṣəḏāqāh ūmišpāṭ*
Gen 18:19; Prov 21:3

Broken Word Pair *ṣəḏāqāh . . . ūmišpāṭ*
Deut 33:21 (*ūmišpāṭāw*); Pss 36:7 [MT; Eng. 36:6]; 103:6; Prov 8:20; 16:8; Isa 58:2 (*ṣəḏāqāh . . . ūmišpāṭ*)

Word Pair *mišpāṭ ūṣəḏāqāh*
2 Sam 8:15; 1 Kgs 10:9; 1 Chr 18:14; 2 Chr 9:8; Pss 33:5; 99:4; Prov 21:3; Isa 33:5; 59:14; Jer 9:24; 22:3, 15; 23:5; 33:15; Ezek 18:5, 19, 21, 27; 33:14, 16, 19; 45:9; Amos 5:7, 24

Broken Word Pair *mišpāṭ . . . ṣəḏāqāh*
Deut 16:18 (*mišpāṭ ṣeḏeq*); 33:21; Job 37:23; Pss 72:1 (*mišpāṭîm*); 106:3; Isa 1:27; 5:7, 16; 9:6 [MT; Eng. 9:7]; 28:17; 32:16; 56:1; 59:9; Jer 4:2; Amos 6:12

This accounts for 46 of 157 occurrences of *ṣəḏāqāh* (29.3%).

In my Sizemore Lectures at Midwestern Baptist Theological Seminary, I listed nineteen instances of justice and righteousness for the book of Isaiah alone.[7] Only fourteen of these instances are really cases of the nouns as word pairs split over parallel lines as indicated in the following table:

A Line	B Line
1:21a	1:21b
1:27a	1:27b
5:7a	5:7b
5:16a	5:16b
9:6a	9:6b
16:5a	16:5b
28:17a	28:17b
32:1a	32:1b
32:16a	32:16b
33:5a	33:5b
56:1a	56:1b
58:2a	58:2b

[7] Gentry, "Isaiah and Social Justice," 6 n3. The nineteen instances are: 1:21, 27; 5:7, 16; 9:6 [MT; Eng. 9:7]; 11:4; 16:5; 26:9; 28:17; 32:1, 16; 33:5; 51:5; 56:1; 58:2 [2x]; 59:4, 9, 14. In 11:4; 51:5; 59:4, verbal forms of the root *špṭ* are employed instead of the noun *mišpāṭ*. The instance in 51:5 is not listed in the rather exhaustive and excellent study of Thomas Leclerc, although it appears as valid as the instance in 11:4. See Thomas L. Leclerc, *Yahweh Is Exalted in Justice: Solidarity and Conflict in Isaiah* (Minneapolis: Fortress, 2001), esp. 10–13, 88, 157; Gentry and Wellum, *Kingdom through Covenant*, 501–2.

59:9a	59:9b
59:14a	59:14b

In addition to this evidence from Isaiah, Ezekiel seems to employ the word pair "statutes and judgments" as an alternative summary for the covenant requirements. The evidence is as follows:

Hebrew *ḥōq* = "statute" = 129x

Word Pair "Statutes and Judgments"
Word Pair *ḥuqqîm . . . mišpāṭîm*
Ezek 11:12; 20:18, 21, 25; 36:27

Word Pair *ḥuqqōwṯ . . . mišpāṭîm*
Ezek 5:7; 11:20; 18:9; 20:11, 13, 19, 21

Word Pair *mišpāṭîm . . . ḥuqqōwṯ*
Ezek 5:6 (2x); 18:17; 20:16, 24; 37:24

Using Three Terms to Summarize
Ezek 18:19, 21; 44:24

This accounts for 21 of 129 occurrences of *ḥuqqîm* or *ḥuqqōwṯ* (16.3%). In total, this accounts for 84 of 424 occurrences of *mišpāṭ* (19.8%).

Thus, terms like "justice" and "righteousness" are employed in a variety of ways. This analysis seeks to identify places where word pairs are used to summarize in a single sound bite, so to speak, all the requirements and stipulations in the covenant that have to do with "loving our neighbor as ourselves," i.e., justice and righteousness in the context of everyday human interactions and relations. The analysis here could be extended by including all occurrences of the word pair *ḥesed* and *'ĕmet* which would no doubt describe not only treating each other in genuinely human ways but also signal faithfulness and loyalty in the divine-human relationship.

Isaiah 1–37 and Isaiah 56–66: The Restoration of Social Justice in Zion

As Isaiah develops his main theme, going around the topic in Isa 1:2–2:4; 2:5–4:6; and 5:1–12:6, it is abundantly clear that Jerusalem is completely corrupt and lacking in social justice. A central question, therefore, is: How does Isaiah envision the restoration of social justice in Zion? How will the current Jerusalem be remade and renewed as the future Zion where the reign of the king will be characterized by social justice as Isa 16:5 predicts and, in fact, where all in the community will reflect the fear of the Lord and the knowledge of God as Isaiah 11 portrays the new creation Davidic kingdom.

The introduction or prologue to Isaiah contains a remarkable and striking statement: "Zion will be ransomed by justice and those in her who repent by righteousness" (Isa 1:27). We see here the key word pair "justice and righteousness" split over parallel lines. This same word pair occurs in Isa 5:7, the punch line of the parable of the vineyard, and also in Isa 5:16, which is the key statement and charge against Israel in the application of the parable that follows. In fact, the word pair is only found at critical junctures in the literary structure. What does it mean to be ransomed by social justice in Isa 1:27?

This verse has created difficulties for interpreters because on the surface it seems to endorse some kind of salvation by works. With considerable exegetical skill, Hugh Williamson devotes several pages to determine the function of the *beth* preposition in the phrase *bəmišpaṭ*.[8] Is it a *beth-pretii* showing the cost of the ransom or a *beth-instrumenti* showing the means of the ransom?

It is important to realize that in the introduction or prologue to the work as a whole, certain ideas are only hinted at or given in germ form. It requires a careful reading of the book as a whole to see how this program of

[8] Hugh G. M. Williamson, *Isaiah 1–5*, ICC (London: T&T Clark, 2006), 156–58.

salvation unfolds. It is not until we come to Isa 56:1–8, the last section of the book, that this becomes clear.

The first half of Isa 56:1 is a call and command to "keep justice and do righteousness." Right away we can see the word pair "justice and righteousness" distributed over the lines of poetry in parallelism that form an idiomatic phrase for social justice. The second half of v. 1 gives a motive or reason for the command: "because my salvation is about to happen, and my righteousness is about to be revealed." So the first half of v. 1 is a call to practice social justice and the second half of v. 1 bases the command on the sovereign work of God who provides his righteousness as an act of deliverance and salvation.

Before we go further, it is important to see that the first verse of this final section of Isaiah is interlocked and interwoven with the earlier sections. The word pair "justice and righteousness," frequently split over poetic parallelism, is found so far only in chapters 1–37, but never in the section marked by chapters 38–55 that is sometimes referred to as deutero-Isaiah.[9] The word pair "righteousness-salvation" or "salvation-righteousness" in the second half of v. 1 speaks of righteousness as an attribute or characteristic of God; it is the way he works in all his relationships, and since humans do not possess this characteristic in their relationships, it must come from God as an act of deliverance and salvation, as a gift. And this word pair (salvation-righteousness) is found only in the second part of Isaiah, constituted by chapters 38–55 (Isa 45:8, 21; 46:13; 51:5–6, 8). This first verse, then, of the last section of Isaiah combines phrases that are found only in the first and last sections, respectively, with a phrase found only in the middle section. This is a testimony to the unity of the book and also to the fact that this third section will now build on these two ideas. I have difficulty believing

---

[9] In chapters 1–37: 1:21, 27; 5:7, 16; 9:6 [MT; Eng. 9:7]; 11:4; 16:5; 26:9; 28:17; 32:1, 16; 33:5. It is found six times in the last section (sometimes called trito-Isaiah): 56:1; 58:2 (2x); 59:4, 9, 14. See Leclerc, *Yahweh is Exalted in Justice*, esp. pp. 10–13, 88, 157.

that the occurrences of these word pairs split over parallel lines are either accidental or due to the disciples of Isaiah and their redactional work. It is a coherence that comes from a single mind.

Thus in the first and last third of the book, we see that social justice is necessary to live in God's presence because it is fundamental to faithful covenant partners. We see that the people do not have this social justice. In the middle third of the book, we see that social justice comes as a divine gift through the work of a mysterious servant of Yahweh. This is the only way to understand correctly the statement in Isa 1:27 that Zion will be ransomed by social justice. It is a germ idea which requires the entire book to be unfolded. The magisterial exegetical treatment by Williamson of the function of *beth* cannot by itself resolve the difficulty in Isa 1:27.[10]

Isaiah 38–55: Deliverance and Formation of the New Covenant Community

According to the plot structure of the book of Isaiah, Zion will be ransomed and rescued by social justice and this will entail an act of deliverance given as a free and gracious gift. It remains to show in summary fashion how this deliverance is directly tied to the new covenant community, whether in connection with Israel or the nations. As we shall see, this has implications for appropriating the message of the prophets for today.

Isaiah foretells deliverance from exile through a coming king, and this rescue from sin results in a new covenant community. The following outline, adapted from commentaries by J. Alec Motyer, is effective

---

[10] After arriving at my position on righteousness in Isaiah, John Oswalt kindly pointed out that his own position, already published, is similar. See John Oswalt, "Righteousness in Isaiah: A Study of the Function of Chapters 56–66 in the Present Structure of the Book," in *Writing and Reading the Scroll of Isaiah*, ed. Craig C. Broyles and Craig A. Evans, VTSupp 70 (Leiden: Brill, 1997), 1:177–91.

in clarifying the movement of thought in Isaiah 38–55, the sixth section dealing with the transformation of Jerusalem in the old creation to Zion in the new creation.[11]

Isaiah 38–55: The Book of the Servant

A. Historical Prologue—Hezekiah's fatal choice	38:1–39:8
B[1]. Universal consolation	40:1–42:13
1. The consolation of Israel	40:1–41:20
2. The consolation of the Gentiles	41:21–42:13
C[1]. Promises of redemption	42:14–44:23
1. Release	42:14–43:21
2. Forgiveness	43:22–44:23
C[2]. Agents of redemption	44:24–53:12
1. Cyrus: liberation	44:24–48:22
2. Servant: atonement	49:1–53:12
B[2]. Universal proclamation	54:1–55:13
1. The call to Zion	54:1–17
2. The call to the world	55:1–13

First, the outline of the literary structure of Isaiah 38–55 shows that the return from exile involves two distinct issues and stages. This section looks further into the future, beyond the judgment of exile, to the comfort and consolation of Israel, i.e., bringing them back from exile. Then the Lord will establish Zion as the people/place where all nations will seek his instruction for social justice. This is described in the language of the exodus, so that the return from the Babylonian exile will be nothing less than a new

[11] See J. Alec Motyer, *The Prophecy of Isaiah: An Introduction and Commentary* (Downers Grove, IL: IVP Academic, 1993); J. Alec Motyer, *Isaiah: An Introduction and Commentary*, TOTC (Downers Grove, IL: InterVarsity, 1999); Gentry and Wellum, *Kingdom through Covenant*, 491–94.

exodus—indeed a greater exodus![12] This new exodus is also described by the term "redeem" (*gā'al*), which refers to the duties of the nearest relative. Since by virtue of the Israelite covenant Yahweh is Israel's nearest relative, he will "buy back" his people from exile as he once delivered them from bondage and slavery in Egypt. This is the first point in the unfolding canon of Scripture where the term "redeem" (*gā'al*) is transferred from the economic world to refer to deliverance from being enslaved by sin and death.

The return from exile, however, is not a momentary or short task. The promises of redemption are divided into two distinct events: release (Isa 42:18–43:21) and forgiveness (Isa 43:22–44:23). Release refers to bringing the people physically out of exile in Babylon and back to their own land; forgiveness entails dealing fully and finally with their sin and the broken covenant. It has been neatly expressed that you can take the people out of Babylon, but how do you get Babylon out of the people?[13] The books of Ezra and Nehemiah show that the people have returned from exile but have not changed at all in terms of their relationship to God: the failure to practice social justice remains a central problem in the community of the returned exiles. That is why, for a postexilic prophet like Zechariah, the return from exile is both a present reality and a future hope. The exile will be over only when God deals with the people's sin, renews the covenant, rebuilds the temple, and returns to dwell in their midst as king.

Second, key to the deliverance entailing the forgiveness of sin and restoration of the broken covenant relationship with God is the work of the servant of Yahweh, detailed in three panels: Isa 49:1–13; 50:4–11; and 52:13–53:12. The servant of Yahweh is a coming Davidic king who will

---

[12] For a discussion of exodus language and themes in Isaiah, see Bernhard W. Anderson, "Exodus Typology in Second Isaiah," in *Israel's Prophetic Heritage: Essays in Honor of James Muilenburg*, ed. Bernhard W. Anderson and Walter Harrelson (New York: Harper, 1962), 177–95.

[13] The vision in Zech 5:5–11 of the woman in a basket carried by flying women back to Babylon seems to symbolize the task of removing Babylon from the people.

fight the final battle on behalf of the nation. This final battle is not a military engagement with political overlords such as Rome but with slavery to sin, death, hell, and Satan. Just as David fought wars against the Philistines on behalf of Israel, so the coming king will fight the war against evil on behalf of his people. As I have demonstrated in a detailed exegetical treatment of Isa 52:12–53:12, the one (coming king) dies on behalf of the people, and with his resurrection the many (his people) share the victory of the one.[14] According to Isa 53:10, the king offers his life as an *ʾāšām*, normally a ram or male sheep. In the Old Testament, leaders and rulers are depicted as a ram or male sheep, so this fits the picture of a coming Davidic king giving his life for the nation. In Leviticus, the *ʾāšām* is a restitution offering bringing about the forgiveness of sins (see Lev 5:15–19).

As Isaiah 54 and 55 show, the atoning death of the king brings into effect a new covenant. This is a covenant of peace according to Isa 54:10 and is based upon the acts of loyal love performed by the new David in Isa 55:3.[15] These acts of loyal love are none other than his sacrificial death described in Isaiah 53. And as Isa 54:11–14a shows, the battlements and gates of the new city are sparkling jewels—symbolic of the righteousness and social justice characteristic of the new covenant community as v. 14a makes plain.

While Isaiah 54 constitutes an invitation to Israel to the new covenant community, Isaiah 55 extends the invitation to all the nations. The servant of Yahweh in the singular becomes the servants of Yahweh in the plural (Isa 54:17) for the first time in the plot structure of the book as a whole. It is the events of chapters 53–55 that form the foundation of Isaiah 56, where for the first time the word pairs "righteousness-salvation" and "justice-righteousness" are brought together, and the eunuch and foreigner

---

[14] Peter J. Gentry, "The Atonement in Isaiah's Fourth Servant Song (Isaiah 52:13–53:12)," *SBJT* 11, no. 2 (2007): 20–47.

[15] See Peter J. Gentry, "Rethinking the 'Sure Mercies of David' in Isaiah 55:3," *WTJ* 69 (2007): 279–304.

are integrated into the new Zion to such an extent that they are the priests offering sacrifices of praise and thanksgiving in the worship of the Lord.

Theological Formation and Implications

The exegesis and plot structure of Isaiah 38–55 just summarized are foundational for Christian theology, and the implications for current debates on social justice are profound.

First, in the book of Isaiah and among other prophets of the Old Testament, the term social justice, as a function of the Hebrew word pair "justice-righteousness," is directly tied to the obligations and requirements of the covenant between God and Israel and is defined by the behavioral standards that show what it means for humans to treat one another as bearers of the divine image. Ultimately, then, social justice is based on the character and righteousness of God himself.

People in North America are divided on how they define "fair" and "just." For some, fairness means proportionality, which means that people are getting benefits in proportion to their contributions. For others, fairness means equity in the sense that everyone gets the same. The third major definition of fairness is procedural fairness, which means that honest, open, and impartial rules are used to determine who gets what. A fourth definition is that funds and resources are allocated to people who have been disadvantaged in the past. People and politicians in North America, then, use the term social justice today in a wide variety of ways.

People are anxious to identify issues of social justice but not so willing to discuss the basis or foundations for the claims being made. Are the claims based on current cultural approval, majority rule, cultural Marxism, or varying notions of (bio-)diversity, equity, and tolerance? What are the epistemological underpinnings of these various views?

Second, not only is social justice defined by the covenant stipulations, it is directly tied to the new covenant/new creation community in its formation, life, and practice in the world. The original covenant made between

God and Israel at Sinai and Moab led to discipline and judgment. Beyond that judgment, God planned a new covenant and a new creation community, thus making the former covenant obsolete (Isaiah 54–55). The members of the new covenant community are not defined by ethnic Israel. The invitation in Isaiah 55 goes out to all the nations of the world to be included in the future Zion. This is clear as early as Isaiah 2 with all the nations streaming to the mountain of the Lord to receive Torah—and what is Torah but the instruction entailed in the new covenant? Torah is a covenant word. Towards the end of Isaiah, rebels in Israel are contrasted with the true servants of the Lord whose membership is defined by the new covenant.

Now, the righteousness of the new covenant community is not categorically different from what we find enshrined in the old covenant: loving and worshiping Jesus Christ as God and self-sacrificing love towards one another in the covenant community constitute its hallmarks, and so *ḥesed* and *'ĕmet* and "justice-righteousness" continue to summarize its obligations and requirements. Thus, social justice characterizes the new covenant/new creation community.

There is no aim in the plan of redemption to reform Israel or the nations through political or technological methods. In fact, Isaiah criticizes Israel for seeking to resolve her problems through alliances and politics. Revelation 13 warns Christians about combining politics and religion. This is the dragon-empowered beast from the sea and the beast from the land. The corollary of this point is that redemption entails dealing with the broken relationship with God. Isaiah 54 describes the new covenant as a covenant of peace. Unless there is reconciliation with God, there will be no social justice among humans. Put another way, reconciliation with God is fundamental and foundational to the practice of social justice in human relations. Thus, the calling of the church is to herald the good news about Jesus Christ and make disciples; we are not called to establish a Christian state.

Finally, in Isaiah's vision, the new covenant community is both "already" and "not yet" according to the interpretation of Jesus and the apostles. Jesus said, "You are the light of the world. A city set on a hill cannot be hidden"

(Matt 5:14). This is a direct allusion to Isaiah 60—a vision of the future city of Zion. The kings and rulers of the world bring the best of their culture and wealth into the city. This city is lighted by God himself and his righteousness. Thus, what is foundational to the church is to display to the rest of the world what a community exercising social justice looks like. Alas, the church is hardly different from the world and so fails in this regard. Christians should be focused on the social justice within the church and display this to the world in a winsome way, rather than on using politics to demand social justice of a world that has no covenant relationship with God and cannot by definition know real social justice.

Questions for Further Reflection

1. How does Jesus fulfill Isaiah's vision for the redemption of Zion?
2. How does Isaiah's definition of social justice differ from some current definitions, and how does Isaiah's vision for the restoration of justice differ from some current visions or proposals?
3. According to Isaiah, what is the relationship between the gospel and social justice?
4. How does the mission of the church relate to Isaiah's vision for social justice and its restoration?
5. Since the church as the inaugurated new covenant community is the place where social justice is to be manifested, what should social justice look like within the church?

Suggested Reading

Gentry, Peter J. *How to Read and Understand the Biblical Prophets*. Wheaton, IL: Crossway, 2017.

Gentry, Peter J. and Stephen J. Wellum. *God's Kingdom through God's Covenants: A Concise Biblical Theology*. Wheaton, IL: Crossway, 2015.

Gentry, Peter J. and Stephen J. Wellum. *Kingdom through Covenant: A Biblical-Theological Understanding of the Covenants.* 2nd ed. Wheaton, IL: Crossway, 2018.

Harman, Allan. *Isaiah: A Covenant to Be Kept for the Sake of the Church.* Focus on the Bible. Ross-shire, Scotland: Christian Focus, 2011.

Motyer, J. Alec. *The Prophecy of Isaiah: An Introduction and Commentary.* Downers Grove, IL: IVP Academic, 1993.

3

Justice in Amos

— Paul R. Raabe —

Introduction

Amos cried out:

> "And let *mišpāṭ* roll down like the waters
> and righteousness like an ever-flowing stream" (Amos 5:24).[1]

The Hebrew noun *mišpāṭ* is usually translated "justice." On the basis of a text like this, contemporary American preachers are tempted to immediately proceed to a sermon advocating for "justice" or "social justice" in America. But instead of going from zero to sixty in three seconds, let us slow down and ask some fundamental questions. Is *mišpāṭ* in Amos the same thing as what goes by the label "justice" or "social justice" in contemporary America? Can a preacher simply and directly move from Amos proclaiming to ancient Israel in 760 BC to America in the twenty-first century AD? Does this kind of sermon move from apples to apples? If not, how should a preacher proclaim Amos's message today? In order to get at these kinds of questions we first have to consider what Amos meant by *mišpāṭ* in his historical and written context. Then we need to follow the trajectory laid out in the book of Amos. After focusing on these two dimensions, we will then be equipped to consider how to move from this ancient prophecy to today's pulpit.

---

[1] Unless otherwise noted, all translations are by the author.

Biblical Texts and Exegesis

Mišpāṭ *and "Justice"*

The Hebrew noun *mišpāṭ* occurs frequently in the Hebrew Scriptures, 424 times in total. 301 are singular and 123 are plural. The plural is typically translated "judgments/ordinances/rules" and is collocated with "commandments" and "statutes." It is the singular usage that is important for our study.

This Hebrew noun is commonly translated "justice." Is that a good translation? In the context of North America we hear of many different types of "justice," such as "racial justice," "economic justice," "environmental justice," "earth justice," and the list continues to expand. In our linguistic context, what does the word "justice" even mean? Traditionally the noun "justice" denotes assigning merited rewards or punishments or adjudicating rights according to the rules of written law. With that traditional American understanding of "justice," we think of every human person's innate, God-given "rights" which are to be protected by the US government: the rights to life, liberty, and the pursuit of happiness, the rights to freedom of religion, freedom of speech, freedom of assembly, and the rights enumerated in the US Constitution. "Justice" is based on carrying out the written laws with their rewards and punishments, laws made by the legislative branch based on the Constitution. However, ancient Israel and the other ancient societies did not think of themselves as being governed by written laws rather than by people, and they did not separate the judicial power from the executive and legislative powers as three separate and coequal branches of government.[2] Should we translate *mišpāṭ* as "justice" or do the differences outweigh the similarities between ancient Israel and modern America?

With the noun *mišpāṭ* should we think of "social justice"? The label "social justice" is commonly used in American English. When we hear this phrase, we think of respecting the rights of minorities and the equitable distribution of wealth, privilege, and power in a society. In the current

---

[2] See Robert D. Culver, "*Shaphaṭ*," *TWOT* 2:947.

American debate, a common view of social justice holds that the government should ensure that everyone receives fair housing, medical care, and education. Michael A. Harbin discusses the definition:

> "In essence, social justice is a balance between benefits and burdens. As such, true social justice derives from balancing two questions that every individual should ask: 'Am I getting my fair share [the benefits]?' and also, 'Am I pulling my fair load [the burdens]?' Historically, it seems that these questions coupled together have guided the discussion."[3]

He contends that limiting "social justice" to everyone receiving a fair share raises two major problems. First is the definition of a "fair share." Second, it overlooks the reality of fallen human nature, that everyone is self-focused, including Christians. He argues that the Old Testament balances the two sides with priority given to the fair load side but also making provision for the benefit side.

> Consequently, while the OT concept of social justice begins with the premise that every individual should pull his or her fair share, it also provides a cultural safety net to catch individuals who encounter unexpected tragedies in life and to allow them to get back on their feet. The OT presents this safety net as woven into the social fabric of Israelite culture.[4]

In his study he demonstrates that the safety net was undergirded by Israelite culture, especially by the structure of the extended family and the demographics of the agrarian community.[5]

---

[3] Michael A. Harbin, "Social Justice for Social Outliers in Ancient Israel, Part 1: Cultural Background," *JETS* 64, no. 3 (2021): 473.

[4] Harbin, 475.

[5] See Harbin, 471–94; Michael A. Harbin, "Social Justice and Social Outliers in Ancient Israel, Part 2: Provision for Widows, Orphans, and Resident Aliens," *JETS* 64, no. 4 (2021): 681–701.

It seems to me that a translation of *mišpāṭ* as "justice" or even "social justice" is misleading. The Old Testament discourse for *mišpāṭ* does not concern judicial decisions in accord with written laws in contradistinction to the authority of persons. It does not deal with honoring or protecting the God-given natural rights of every individual or group. It does not deal with equitable distribution of the burdens and benefits of a society with the goal of producing a more egalitarian society. The overall biblical perspective focuses more on everyone's responsibility toward God for the well-being of others.[6] To Cain's cynical reply "Am I my brother's keeper?", God's response is "Yes, you are" (see Gen 4:9–10). It was not a matter of Abel's "rights" but of Cain's responsibility before God. To translate *mišpāṭ* as "justice" or "social justice" rings the wrong bells in American English.

Toward a Definition of *Mishpat*

What does the Hebrew noun mean? The noun *mišpāṭ* comes from the verb *shaphaṭ*, which means to do the activity of judging and to carry out that judgment. The texts do not distinguish between the act of deciding and the act of enacting or carrying out the decision. The noun *mišpāṭ* should be understood in connection with that verb. Both the verb and the noun pertain to interaction with others and responding to others, either God's response to humans or humans responding to other humans. Doing the activity of *shaphaṭ* or doing *mišpāṭ* is not the first initiating move but a response to the actions of others. Humans do not do this activity toward God or toward the rest of creation, such as animals and vegetation. The noun basically denotes the act of judging, the decision/verdict itself, and its being carried out in response to other persons. All

---

[6] For a helpful discussion of "human rights" from a biblical perspective, see Christopher J. H. Wright, *Walking in the Ways of the Lord: The Ethical Authority of the Old Testament* (Downers Grove, IL: IVP, 1995), 245–74.

three concepts belong together as a package. For this study I will translate the noun "rightly-distinguishing-judgment."

As an essential component of meaning, the action of doing *mišpāṭ* presupposes the activity of discerning and distinguishing between people. For example, Deut 17:8–9 speaks of rendering the "rightly-distinguishing-judgment" (*mišpāṭ*) between one sort of bloodshed and another, between one sort of lawsuit and another, between one sort of assault and another. Not every case should be treated the same. Another example is given in Jer 7:5, which speaks of doing *mišpāṭ* "between a man and his neighbor." Distinctions should be made, and they should be the proper distinctions.

What are the proper distinctions to be made? The distinctions of judgment (*mišpāṭ*) should not be based on status, importance, financial wherewithal, or even whether the person is an Israelite or Gentile (Lev 24:22). As we will see, the texts oppose making distinctions of judgment (*mišpāṭ*) based on whether persons are financially rich or poor, landowners or non-landowners, married women with a living husband or widows, children with fathers or fatherless, native Israelites or Gentile resident aliens. When it comes to *mišpāṭ*, the only proper distinctions of judgment are between the innocent and the guilty, between the righteous and the wicked.

We see this note of making the proper distinctions already in Genesis 18. When God threatens to destroy Sodom and Gomorrah, Abraham protests to God: "Far be it from you to do such a thing, to slay the righteous with the wicked, so that the righteous and the wicked are treated alike. Far be it from you! Shall the Judge (*šōpēṭ*) of all the earth not do rightly-distinguishing-judgment/*mišpāṭ*?" (Gen 18:25).

Another good illustration of the noun's meaning occurs in Malachi. In Mal 2:17 the prophet debates with his Israelite hearers: "You (plural) have wearied Yahweh with your words. Yet you say, 'How have we wearied him?' In that you say, 'Everyone who does evil is (treated as) good in the eyes of Yahweh, and he delights in them,' or (you say), 'Where is the God of *mišpāṭ*?'" Malachi's hearers were complaining that God was treating the evil as if they were good, that God was blessing and taking delight in those who were wicked, and that God was not discerning and rightly distinguishing between those who were evil and those who were good. Therefore they protested, "Where is the God of rightly-distinguishing-judgment/*mišpāṭ*?"

A third example occurs in the narrative about Solomon's wisdom. Solomon prayed to God to give him "a perceiving mind to judge (*shaphaṭ*) your people to discern between good and evil" (1 Kgs 3:9). Solomon prayed for "discernment to perceive rightly-distinguishing-judgment/*mišpāṭ*" (1 Kgs 3:11). God granted his prayer, and Solomon displayed it with his judgment between the two women who both claimed to be the boy's mother. He was able to distinguish properly between the two and return the boy to his true mother. The narrative concludes that all Israel "saw that the wisdom of God was in him to do/make rightly-distinguishing-judgment/*mišpāṭ*" (1 Kgs 3:28).

We can learn more about the noun when we consider what it is not. Rightly administering *mišpāṭ* entails not showing favoritism, being partial, or taking bribes.[7] It means that the righteous and the wicked should not be treated alike. Often the texts oppose "misdirecting" the judgment against the innocent.[8] When *mišpāṭ* is corrupted, then it does not practically exist at all (Hab 1:4).

In short, *mišpāṭ* denotes "rightly-distinguishing-judgment" and includes within its semantics making the decision, the decision itself, and its execution. The noun denotes rightly differentiating between the innocent and the guilty, between the righteous and the wicked. As we will see, it usually pertains to a law court setting. Moreover, it is to be done by persons in authority such as the town's elders and judges. The passages that speak to Israel as a whole should be understood this way. For example, Deut 16:18–20 directs

---

[7] See Lev 19:15; Deut 1:17; 10:18; 16:19.

[8] One common expression uses the *hiphil* of *nth*, "to misdirect, turn aside" plus *mišpāṭ* as the direct object. See Exod 23:6; Deut 16:19; 24:17; 27:19; 1 Sam 8:3; Prov 17:23; Lam 3:35 (cf. Job 8:3; 34:12; Isa 10:2; Amos 5:12; Hab 1:4).

Israel to appoint judges and officials to "judge" the people with "rightly-distinguishing-judgment of righteousness" (*mišpāṭ* of *ṣeḏeq*), judgments that are righteous and not corrupt. Moses commands the people of Israel not to misdirect the rightly-distinguishing-judgment or to take bribes. As Jeffrey H. Tigay comments, "Here, Moses may want to indicate that all Israelites are responsible to ensure that the judges act fairly. Or, he may address all Israelites because any of them might become a judge, either by virtue of being an elder or in some other way (Deborah, for example, was a judge by virtue of being a prophetess)."[9]

Mishpat *of the Needy*

Some texts use the noun *mišpāṭ* as a head noun followed by a genitive noun. Usually the semantic relationship between the two nouns is clear. For example, "*mišpāṭ* of death" means the rightly-distinguishing-judgment that condemns the guilty to death (Deut 19:6; 21:22; Jer 26:11, 16), or "*mišpāṭ* of righteousness" means the rightly-distinguishing-judgment that is most certainly righteous and not at all corrupt (Deut 16:18; Ps 119:160; cf. Ezek 18:8; Zech 7:9).

But there are other cases that deserve more attention. What does it mean when texts speak of "the *mišpāṭ* of the needy" (Exod 23:6; Ps 140:12; Jer 5:28), "the *mišpāṭ* of the afflicted" (Job 36:6; Isa 10:2), or "the *mišpāṭ* of the fatherless, widow, and resident alien" (Deut 10:18; 24:17; 27:19)? Does the expression mean "the legal claim and obligation of these persons on society"?[10] In my view that reads too much into the phrase. Rather it is simply a shorthand way of saying the rightly-distinguishing-judgment that will be made about even the most vulnerable

---

[9] Jeffrey H. Tigay, *Deuteronomy*, JPS Torah Commentary (Philadelphia: Jewish Publication Society, 1996), 160.

[10] G. Liedke says that in these cases the genitive means the legal claim and obligation that is due the poor. See G. Liedke, "*Shaphaṭ*," *TLOT* 3:1392–99.

in Israel, who can be easily exploited by others. Even they should receive rightly-distinguishing-judgment.

Mishpat in the Pentateuchal Legislation

The Mosaic legislation in the Pentateuch can help us understand what Amos meant. The noun *mišpāṭ* relates to the dimension of the law court and the decisions given by judges. Typically that judicial decision would be made in the city gate (Deut 17:8–9; 21:19; 22:15). In the Pentateuchal legislation, *mišpāṭ* denotes a fair, discerning judicial decision and not simply a judicial decision per se. Here are some examples of how it is used. I will add paraphrases to my translation to convey the sense from the Hebrew.

> You shall not misdirect the rightly-distinguishing-judgment (*mishpat*) of your needy Israelite brother in his judicial dispute. You shall keep far from a false charge, and you shall not kill the innocent and the righteous, for I will not declare the wicked to be righteous (*hiphil* of *tsadaq*). And you shall not take a bribe, for a bribe blinds the clear-sighted and distorts the words of the righteous ones (Exod 23:6–8).

> You shall not do unjust corruption in the rightly-distinguishing-judgment (*mišpāṭ*); you shall not lift up the face of the poor/be partial to the poor and you shall not honor the face of the great/defer to the great; in righteousness you are to judge (*shaphaṭ*) your neighbor (Lev 19:15).

These passages makes it clear that doing *mišpāṭ* should distinguish between the guilty and the innocent without regard for the person's status or economic condition. The judgment to be made must rightly distinguish.

> You shall not do unjust corruption in the rightly-distinguishing-judgment (*mišpāṭ*), in measurement, in the weight, and in the capacity. You shall have just balances, just weights, a just ephah,

> and a just hin. I am Yahweh your God who brought you out from the land of Egypt, and you shall keep all my statutes and all my judgments and do them; I am Yahweh (Lev 19:35–37).

As in Lev 19:15, here *mišpāṭ* refers to the act of rendering judicial decisions. There should be no corruption in the law court or in business dealings.

> And the one who kills an animal shall make it good, but the one who kills a man shall be put to death. There shall be one rightly-distinguishing-judgment/standard (*mišpāṭ*) for you; it shall be as with the resident alien as with the native, for I am Yahweh your God (Lev 24:21–22).

> And the cities shall be to you as a refuge from the avenger, so that the manslayer may not die until he stands before the congregation for the rightly-distinguishing-judgment/decision (*mišpāṭ*) (Num 35:12).

> Moses to Israel's judges: "Hear the cases between your Israelite brothers and judge (*shaphaṭ*) righteously between a man and his Israelite brother and his resident alien. You shall not show partiality in the rightly-distinguishing-judgment (*mišpāṭ*); you shall hear the small and the great alike. You shall not fear man, for the rightly-distinguishing-judgment (*mišpāṭ*) belongs to God. And the case that is too hard for you, you shall bring to me, and I will hear it" (Deut 1:17).

> For Yahweh your God is the God of gods and the Lord of lords, the great, the mighty, and the God to be feared who does not show partiality and does not take a bribe, doing rightly-distinguishing-judgment (*mišpāṭ*) of the fatherless and widow and loving the resident alien to give to him bread and clothing (Deut 10:17–18).

These verses are important for understanding Israel's God-given system. In their system, the judges were not to fear any man but to judge as God's servants, for "the rightly-distinguishing-judgment (*mišpāṭ*) belongs to God" (Deut 1:17). In fact, they were to imitate their God. The God of Israel cannot be bribed or coerced. He is no respecter of persons. In Egypt, Israel saw that God is no respecter of persons in his response to the high and mighty Pharaoh. Instead, God judges fairly, and this includes even those who are nobodies, who are easily exploited. Along with this judging activity he also shows love by giving bread and clothing.

> The judges and officers appointed in Israel's towns "shall judge (*shaphaṭ*) the people with rightly-distinguishing-judgment of righteousness (*mišpāṭ* of *ṣeḏeq*). You shall not misdirect a rightly-distinguishing-judgment (*mišpāṭ*); you shall not show partiality and you shall not take a bribe, for the bribe blinds the eyes of the wise and perverts the words of the righteous. Righteousness, (only) righteousness you shall pursue that you may live and possess the land which Yahweh your God is giving you" (Deut 16:18–20).

> "If any matter is too difficult for you for the rightly-distinguishing-judgment (*mišpāṭ*) between (one kind of) bloodshed and (another kind of) bloodshed, between (one kind of) lawsuit and (another kind of) lawsuit, between (one kind of) assault and (another kind of) assault, matters of cases in your city gates," then you shall go to the central sanctuary, to the Levitical priests and to the judge, and they will render the rightly-distinguishing-judgment (*mišpāṭ*), which you shall carry out (Deut 17:8–11).

> Cities of refuge should be established to prevent the avenger of blood from killing the manslayer, for "there was no rightly-distinguishing-judgment (*mišpāṭ*) of death decreed for him, since he was not hating him previously" (Deut 19:6).

> "And if a man has committed a sin receiving the rightly-distinguishing-judgment (*mišpāṭ*) of death, and he is put to death,

> and you hang him on a tree," then you shall bury him on the same day (Deut 21:22–23).
>
> You shall not misdirect the rightly-distinguishing-judgment (*mišpāṭ*) of a resident alien, a fatherless person; you shall not take a widow's garment in pledge. But you shall remember that you were a slave in Egypt, and that Yahweh your God ransomed you from there; therefore I am commanding you to do this thing (Deut 24:17–18).
>
> If there is a legal dispute between (two) men and they draw near to the rightly-distinguishing-judgment-seat (*mišpāṭ*), and they (the officials) judge (*shaphaṭ*) them and they declare the righteous one to be righteous and they declare the guilty one to be guilty (Deut 25:1).
>
> Cursed is the one who misdirects the rightly-distinguishing-judgment (*mišpāṭ*) of a resident alien, a fatherless person, and a widow (Deut 27:19).

What generalizations can be made from these texts? First, with respect to meaning, in the Mosaic legislation the noun *mišpāṭ* usually pertains to the domain of the law court and judicial decisions. It basically means "a just judicial verdict made by a judge which rightly distinguishes." It does not characterize an impersonal system but focuses on the response of human judges to other humans.

Second, the proper distinction to be made by the judges is between the righteous and the wicked, between the innocent and the guilty. The judges should show no partiality nor accept bribes. Very often, three types of persons are grouped together: the fatherless, widow, and resident alien.[11] The identification of these three types of persons calls for extra attention in the

[11] See Exod 22:20–21 MT (Eng. 22:21–22); Deut 14:29; 16:11, 14; 24:17–21; 26:12–13; 27:19; Jer 22:3.

legislation precisely because they are the ones most easily exploited (Exod 22:20–21 MT [Eng. 22:21–22]).

Third, these texts are all addressed to ancient Israel and concern how Israelites should deal with other Israelites. The non-Israelite "resident alien" (*ger*) is to come under the same judicial standard and in this respect is to be treated as a fellow Israelite (Lev 24:22).

Fourth, these are not secular laws meant for every nation based on "natural law."[12] They are stipulations given by Israel's own God who freed Israel from bondage to Egypt and made them his own covenant people.

Finally, they are based on the way Israel's God himself does *mišpāṭ* (Deut 10:17–18). Israel was to emulate the ways of the God of Israel, their own covenant God.

Doing Rightly-Distinguishing-Judgment and Righteousness

The nouns *mišpāṭ* and *ṣəḏāqāh* are commonly paired to form a stereotyped phrase (over twenty-five times). They often function as the direct object of the verb "doing." In Amos this word pair occurs in Amos 5:7, 24 where they are split up to fit the parallelism, which typically happens in Hebrew poetry.[13] In this word pair the first noun *mišpāṭ* seems to retain the standard sense of "rightly-distinguishing-judgment" pertaining to the law court and arbitration. This is clearly the case in Amos 5:15 and Ezek 18:8. Yet the second noun is used in a broader sense denoting "righteous conduct"

---

[12] For a concise discussion on the distinction between Israel's law and natural law, see David VanDrunen, *Natural Law: A Short Companion* (Brentwood, TN: B&H Academic, 2023).

[13] For example, see Isa 1:27; 5:7. On the device, see the standard work by E. Z. Melamed, "Breakup of Stereotype Phrases as an Artistic Device in Biblical Poetry," in *Studies in the Bible*, ed. C. Rabin, Scripta Hierosolymitana 8 (Jerusalem: Magnes, 1961), 115–53.

and encompassing a wide variety of activities.[14] I translate the expression as "doing rightly-distinguishing-judgment and righteousness."

The phrase denotes actions toward humans. These actions are grounded in the God of Israel and his activity in human history. He loves "rightly-distinguishing-judgment and righteousness" (Ps 33:5) and does it with his activity in Israel (Ps 99:4) and on earth (Jer 9:23 MT [Eng. 9:24]; cf. Job 37:23).

The word pair applies to the people of Israel, articulated already with respect to Abraham and his household (Gen 18:19). Yahweh desires that every individual Israelite act in ways that accord with "rightly-distinguishing-judgment and righteousness" (Prov 21:3; Isa 56:1). Ezekiel 18 lists the kinds of activities that contradict this idiom, such as idolatrous sacrificial meals, sexual transgressions, and financial exploitation of the poor and needy. In contrast, the positive behavior commended includes faithful arbitration between two men, giving food to the hungry, and covering the naked with clothing.[15]

The word pair can characterize the kind of rule that should be administered by the kings of Israel. Second Samuel 8:15//1 Chr 18:14 summarizes the rule of King David with these words: "And David ruled as king over all Israel, and David was doing rightly-distinguishing-judgment and righteousness." The Queen of Sheba blessed Yahweh for putting Solomon on the throne. In Yahweh's perpetual love for Israel "he made you (Solomon) into a king to do rightly-distinguishing-judgment and righteousness" (1 Kgs 10:9//2 Chr 9:8). The king is supposed to "do rightly-distinguishing-judgment and righteousness" (Jer 22:3, 15; Ezek 45:9).

Whereas ancient Israel's kings typically failed to live up to this standard, the prophets promised that it will characterize the future, ideal Davidic king

---

[14] Moshe Weinberg treats the phrase as a hendiadys. See Moshe Weinberg, *Social Justice in Ancient Israel and in the Ancient Near East* (Minneapolis: Fortress, 1995), 25. However, I am not so sure. It looks to me that the semantic domain and reach of *mishpat* is narrower than that of *tsedaqah*.

[15] For a discussion of Ezekiel 18, see Horace D. Hummel, *Ezekiel 1–20*, Concordia Commentary (St. Louis: Concordia, 2005), 520–47.

and his kingly reign. He will "do rightly-distinguishing-judgment and righteousness" (Jer 23:5; 33:15). His kingly rule and reign will be established and upheld by these constant activities (Isa 9:6 [Eng. 9:7]; 16:5).

Mišpāṭ in Amos

Amos from Tekoa in Judah was the first of the writing prophets, the prophets whose materials have been written down in their own books. Amos worked during the days of Uzziah the king of Judah (767–740 BC) and Jeroboam II the king of Northern Israel (782–753 BC). A date of about 760 BC for Amos seems reasonable. The opening verse calls the material "the words of Amos" and tells us that Amos spoke these words "two years before the earthquake" (Amos 1:1). That earthquake must have been particularly severe, given that it was remembered over 200 years later (see Zech 14:5). We should take the chronological notice of the earthquake seriously. While obviously the opening verse itself was written after the earthquake, the book contains the prophet's words spoken before the earthquake. Amos carried out his ministry of proclaiming God's Word to ancient Israel before this earthquake. The earthquake that came two years later gave God's testimony to the legitimacy of Amos as his truly called prophet. The prophet's words were preserved so that his words would be heard and cherished by succeeding generations as what they are: God's words spoken by this called prophet Amos.

What Activities Did Amos Oppose?

Amos protested that Israel was fundamentally corrupting "rightly-distinguishing-judgment and righteousness" (*mišpāṭ* and *ṣədāqāh*):

> Those who overturn rightly-distinguishing-judgment (*mišpāṭ*) into bitter wormwood, and righteousness (*ṣədāqāh*) they forcibly throw down to the ground (Amos 5:7).

> Yet you have overturned rightly-distinguishing-judgment (*mišpāṭ*) into poison, and the fruit of righteousness (*ṣəḏāqāh*) into bitter wormwood (Amos 6:12b).

What was meant to be "the fruit of righteousness," the refreshing fruit that would give blessing to the nation of Israel, the Israelites were "overturning" and changing into "poison" (*rōš*) and "bitter wormwood" (*la'ănāh*). The former is a poisonous plant, possibly hemlock, and the latter an extremely bitter shrub.[16] What kinds of actions were the focus of the prophet's complaints? By surveying the activities condemned by Amos, we can get a sense of what kinds of God-pleasing behavior Amos was urging.

Amos condemned the Israelites for what he labeled "transgressions/ rebellions" (Amos 2:6; 3:14; 4:4; 5:12), "iniquities" (Amos 3:2), and "sins" (Amos 5:12). Israel was fundamentally "a sinful kingdom" (Amos 9:8), and the stubborn "sinners" of Israel would die by the sword (Amos 9:10). These three terms for "sin" are commonly associated in the Hebrew Scriptures. They provoke God to anger and bring down upon the guilty God's righteous punishment. What were the specific activities condemned by Amos?

In Amos 2:6–8 he gives a list of seven charges: 1) They sell the innocent for silver; 2) they sell the needy for merely a pair of sandals; 3) they trample the heads of the poor as though they were stepping on the dust; 4) they thrust the humble out of the road; 5) a man and his father cohabit with the same young woman; 6) they stretch themselves out beside every altar on garments seized in distraint; 7) and in the sanctuary they drink the wine of those they fined.[17]

In Amos 3:9–10 he asserts that the Israelites' conduct is worse than the godless Gentiles, who would be appalled if they saw the oppression, violence, and devastation against property in Samaria. Such sin shows that the Israelites do not know how to do what is right.

---

[16] See Irene Jacob and Walter Jacob, "Flora," *ABD* 2:816; Mitchell G. Reddish, "Wormwood," *ABD* 6:973.

[17] While there is some debate, it seems probable that Amos itemized seven charges. See Shalom M. Paul, *Amos*, Hermeneia (Minneapolis: Fortress, 1991), 76–87.

In Amos 4:1 he complains that the aristocratic women of Samaria also oppress the poor and crush the needy by pressuring their husbands to greedily exploit the disadvantaged in order to maintain their "lifestyle of the rich and famous."

In Amos 5:10–12 he accuses the Israelite rulers of hating the one who justly reproves the guilty and speaks the truth during the court proceedings in the city gate. He charges that they impose heavy rent on the financially poor and exact from them a tribute of grain. They distress the innocent, accept bribes, and turn aside the innocent poor during their judicial proceedings in the city gate.

In Amos 6:1–8 he indicts the aristocratic leaders of Zion and especially Samaria, his principal target, for their callous and arrogant indifference to the people. They enjoy their luxurious lifestyle but "do not grieve over the upcoming ruin facing Northern Israel" (Amos 6:6). Therefore the leaders will be the first of the exiles going into exile.

In Amos 8:4–6 Amos condemns those who cheat with dishonest scales in the marketplace, with the result that they "buy the helpless for money and the needy for a pair of sandals" and even "sell the refuse of the wheat."

Amos 5

In particular, Amos 5 powerfully and memorably expresses Amos's call for justice in Israel. As such, it deserves a closer analysis here. In contrast to the way Israel was acting at the time, Amos instead wanted to see the opposite:

> Begin to seek what is good and not what is bad. . . . Begin to hate what is bad and love what is good, and begin to establish rightly-distinguishing-judgment" (*mišpāṭ*) in the city-gate! (Amos 5:14–15).

> And let rightly-distinguishing-judgment (*mišpāṭ*) roll down like the waters and righteousness (*ṣəḏāqāh*) like an ever-flowing stream (Amos 5:24).

In order to see how this kind of exhortation fits into the overall message of Amos, we should examine Amos 5 in a holistic way. Here I will give my own summary and paraphrase of the material to show how the thought flows.[18]

Amos 5:1–27

1–2 Amos takes up a funeral dirge for the house of Israel, which in his vision of the future has already died.

3 Amos states the message of future doom in literal language: the military of each Israelite town will suffer defeat, and each town's numbers will dwindle.

4–6 Amos calls Israel to seek Yahweh and live, that is, survive the coming disasters, but they should not go to their sanctuaries, because the worshipers in those sanctuaries will go into exile (cf. Amos 3:13–14; 7:9). Disaster is definitely coming to the nation of Israel, but Amos exhorts his hearers to repent, seek Yahweh in a truthful way, and become part of the remnant.

7 "Those who turn upside down rightly-distinguishing-judgment (*mišpāṭ*) into poisonous wormwood, and righteousness (*ṣəḏāqāh*) they forcibly throw down to the ground . . ." Amos continues this thought in v. 10 but first makes a digression by working with the catchword "turn."

8–9 Yahweh the Creator can "turn" things upside down as well. The One who makes the Pleiades and Orion can "turn upside down" deep darkness into morning and can darken day into night. He can destroy strong fortresses. The

[18] See the fuller discussions given in Francis I. Andersen and David Noel Freedman, *Amos: A New Translation with Introduction and Commentary*, Anchor Bible 24A (New York: Doubleday, 1989); Gary V. Smith, *Amos: A Commentary*, Library of Biblical Interpretation (Grand Rapids: Regency Reference Library, 1989); Paul, *Amos*; R. Reed Lessing, *Amos*, Concordia Commentary (St. Louis: Concordia, 2009).

Israelite hearers should fear their God who can do reversals and change their good fortune into tragedy.

10 Amos continues the thought started in v. 7 about those who turn upside down rightly-distinguishing-judgment into wormwood and throw righteousness to the ground. "They hate the one who reproves in the city gate, and they abhor the one who speaks with truthfulness." Amos focuses on the judicial proceedings that take place in the city gate.

11 "Therefore because your judges and leaders impose heavy rent on the financially poor and exact a tribute of grain from them, you who have built your own houses of well-hewn stone, you will no longer continue to live in them but will have to go into exile. You who have planted pleasant vineyards will no longer be able to enjoy your wine but will have to go into exile."

12 Why do I, Yahweh, say this? "For I know your transgressions are many and your sins are great, you who distress the righteous and accept bribes and turn aside the innocent poor in the judicial proceedings in the city gate."

13 "Therefore at that time a prudent person will remain silent in grief, for it is such an evil and oppressive time."[19]

14–15 You Israelites, "begin to seek what is good and not evil that you may live and survive the upcoming disasters. Then Yahweh the God of Hosts will be with you as you say he is. Begin to hate evil and love what is good, and 'establish rightly-distinguishing-judgment' (*mišpāṭ*) in the city gate!" Perhaps Yahweh the God of Hosts may be gracious to the future remnant of Joseph/Northern Israel, including you who repent now.

---

[19] The meaning of Amos 5:13 is difficult. I take the verb *dmm* to mean "remain silent in grief" in that the evil times will render the prudent person speechless (cf. Lam 2:10; 3:28). See BDB *dmm* I, 198; A. Baumann, "*damah* II," *TDOT* 3:263.

16–17 Because of Israel's transgressions and sins, Yahweh will come to them in judgment and condemnation, and Israel will wail in grief in their towns and fields.

18–20 You, O Israel, suppose that your future is bright and promising. On the contrary, the coming day of Yahweh will bring great distress and darkness, and it is inescapable.

21–27 Israel's worship practices were hypocritical. Without repentance and faith they were simply going through the motions and thinking that their God was pleased and would bless them. They were not truly "seeking Yahweh." Because of this worship practice Yahweh responded in a startling way (in first person), "I hate, I reject your festivals." Instead, he called for repentance and faith, which would be reflected in their conduct. "But let rightly-distinguishing-judgment (*mišpāṭ*) roll down like waters and righteousness (*ṣəḏāqāh*) like an ever-flowing stream" (v. 24). Then Yahweh returns to his complaint with their worship practices, including idolatry. Yahweh concludes with this condemnatory sentence: "Therefore I will make you go into exile beyond Damascus" (v. 27). The disaster of exile is definitely coming to the entire nation of Israel.

Following the Trajectory Given by Amos

The Hebrew Scriptures come to us as a collection of books. To write that is to belabor the obvious, but sometimes the obvious needs to be belabored. The methods of source, form, tradition, and redaction criticism have taught and trained readers to see each book as a collection of bits and pieces, layers and strata, traditions, and redactional seams, each of which needs to be identified, separated out, and studied on its own. These methods are called "diachronic" meaning "through time," because they attempt to uncover a book's prefinal stages of composition through time. Readers trained in these diachronic methods tend to treat each prophetic book as an archaeological tell whose layers need to be separated out, or as an old farmhouse constructed over the years with additions, updates, and reuse of older materials.[20] The goal of these approaches then is to identify each layer or piece of the old farmhouse to determine how the prophetic book was constructed over the years or even over the centuries.[21]

This is not the place to engage in a lengthy discussion of diachronic reading methods. I bring it up only to make one simple and straightforward point: The book of Amos should be heard and read as a whole book as it is now laid out, beginning with the first verse and proceeding to the last. We should respect the way the book stands and study it in that way. Instead of helicoptering down and lifting up a verse or paragraph out of its written context, we should follow the trajectory laid out in the book and see how the verses and paragraphs build.[22] When we do this, we see that the book of Amos reaches a final climax in chapter 9.

Consider the analogy of waves. Each book of the Latter Prophets exhibits a series of waves with some sections building up to a crest and other sections displaying a crest or climactic depiction. In keeping with this convention, each book of the Latter Prophets reaches a climactic crest and strikes a dominant note at the very end of the book. This is true for the books of Isaiah (chapters 65–66), Ezekiel (chapter 48), Hosea (chapter 14), Joel (chapters 3–4 MT [Eng. 2:28–3:21]), Obadiah (v. 21), Jonah (chapter 4), Micah (chapter 7), Nahum (chapter 3), Habakkuk (chapter 3), Zephaniah (chapter 3), Haggai (chapter 2), Zechariah (chapter 14),

[20] The analogy of an old farmhouse comes from Christopher R. Seitz, "Isaiah 1–66: Making Sense of the Whole," in *Reading and Preaching the Book of Isaiah*, ed. Christopher R. Seitz (Philadelphia: Fortress, 1988), 108–9.

[21] For a recent example of a diachronic approach to the compositional prehistory of Amos, see Göran Eidevall, *Amos: A New Translation with Introduction and Commentary*, Anchor Yale Bible 24G (New Haven: Yale University Press, 2017).

[22] The analogy of helicoptering down and lifting comes from James W. Voelz.

and Malachi (chapter 3 MT [Eng. 3:1–4:6]).[23] It is certainly the case with Amos 9.

Destruction—Remnant—Future Restoration

Like other prophets, Amos saw the future as developing in two stages.[24] First, destructive judgment from God will most certainly fall with no "ifs, ands, or buts" about it. God stresses this note through Amos in the opening section of the book (Amos 1:3–2:16): "For three rebellions and for four I will not reverse it," namely "his voice" with its pronouncements of doom (Amos 1:2).[25] This refrain is repeated six times against the surrounding Gentile nations, then against Judah for a seventh occurrence, and then zeroes in on Northern Israel for the eighth occurrence. The book establishes at the beginning that disaster is definitely coming from Yahweh. Amos portrays these impending disasters in various ways: consuming fire from God, taking populations into exile, defeat in warfare, the destruction of various towns, the coming of a conquering nation, and the coming earthquake and darkening of the sun. This destruction is coming to Northern Israel and Judah because of their sins, iniquities, and rebellions against their God. As we have seen, one of the chief causes for the coming wrath is their perversion of "rightly-distinguishing-judgment and righteousness" toward one another, especially on the part of the leaders in authority.

---

[23] The book of Jeremiah is more of an exception given that the MT has an ending identical with the ending of the book of Kings and that the LXX has a different arrangement.

[24] See Paul R. Raabe, "Why Oracles Against the Nations?" in *Fortunate the Eyes That See: Essays in Honor of David Noel Freedman in Celebration of His Seventieth Birthday*, ed. Astrid B. Beck, Andrew H. Bartelt, Paul R. Raabe, and Chris A. Franke (Grand Rapids: Eerdmans, 1995), 236–57, esp. 244–47.

[25] While commentators usually take the antecedent of the pronoun "it" in Amos 1:3 as cataphoric, referring to the following punishment, I consider it more probable grammatically to identify it as the preceding "voice" of Amos 1:2. See Andersen and Freedman, *Amos*, 234–35.

Given this impending doom, God through Amos exhorted the individual Israelites to turn away from their evil ways and toward Yahweh:

> "Seek me and survive" but do not go to your usual sanctuaries, for they will be destroyed (Amos 5:4–5).
>
> "Seek Yahweh that you may survive," lest he completely consume Northern Israel/"the house of Joseph" (Amos 5:6).
>
> "Seek good and not evil, that you may survive, and thus may Yahweh the God of Hosts be with you as you have said he is. Hate evil, love good, and establish rightly-distinguishing-judgment (*mišpāṭ*) in the city gate. Perhaps Yahweh the God of Hosts may be gracious to the remnant of Joseph" (Amos 5:14–15).
>
> "But let rightly-distinguishing-judgment (*mišpāṭ*) roll down like waters and righteousness (*ṣədāqāh*) like an ever-flowing stream" (Amos 5:24).

There are a few things to note about these exhortations. First, the imperatives are plural, addressed to the individual Israelites. Second, the appeal is to turn away from their current sinful behavior and instead to "seek Yahweh" in true repentance and faith. From this turning and "seeking Yahweh" will flow doing "rightly-distinguishing-judgment and righteousness." Amos was not calling for secular "social justice" but for God-pleasing actions that flow from repentance and faith in the God of Israel. Finally, these exhortations presuppose that disaster from God is definitely coming. By seeking Yahweh these individual Israelites may "survive" the upcoming devastation.

Is the upcoming destruction the final end? An older generation of historical-critical scholars often supposed that the historical Amos preached only "fire and brimstone" with no hope at all. Any statement revealing a hopeful future must have been added later. Working with this assumption, many older critics dated the composition of Amos 9:11–15 to the postexilic period after the 587 BC destruction of Jerusalem.[26] One needs to ask, however: Would Amos foresee only death as the ultimate end? As Gerhard Hasel observes:

> Did Yahweh have really only an end to proclaim through Amos without any kind of a future for anyone or any entity? Why would only later editors/redactors be able to have a message of hope? There is no compelling reason why the final section of Amos could not derive from the historical Amos himself.[27]

In fact, every book of the Latter Prophets has hopeful passages about the future, and there is no reason to deny such a possibility to Amos. The prophet Amos knew that destruction was coming, but he also foresaw a future with God beyond the upcoming disasters.

The end of the book affirms that there will be a remnant, that God "will not totally destroy the house of Jacob" (Amos 9:8). God will sift Israel and separate the remnant from the stubborn sinners who will perish (Amos 9:9–10). In the age to come God will build upon that remnant and restore his people and include Gentiles.

> In that day I will raise up the booth/hut of David about to fall,
> and I will wall up the breaches of them (of the two kingdoms of north and south),
> and his (David's) ruins I will raise up,
> and I will build her (the booth/hut) as in the days of old,
> to the end that they will possess the remnant of Edom and all the Gentiles
> upon whom my name has been pronounced—the utterance of Yahweh

---

[26] For a discussion of various views, see Gerhard F. Hasel, *Understanding the Book of Amos: Basic Issues in Current Interpretations* (Grand Rapids: Baker, 1991), 105–20.

[27] Hasel, 118.

who is about to do this (Amos 9:11–12).

The book ends with a promise from God for the future beyond the time of Amos. It invites us to leave the book of Amos and follow the promise's trajectory. The God of Israel did bring destruction upon Israel. In 732 BC Assyria brought ruin upon Northern Israel and then in 720 BC destruction upon Samaria the capital. In 701 BC Assyria devastated Judah, and then in 587 BC Babylon destroyed Jerusalem. Both the Assyrians and the Babylonians took the Israelites into exile. The threats pronounced by Amos came to pass in subsequent history.

Then in 538 BC exiles began to return to Jerusalem and additional returnees in the fifth century BC. During the post-exilic period they rebuilt the temple and the city which remained during the Persian, Greek, and Roman periods. Then in the fullness of time the God of Israel brought the promise of Amos to its fulfillment.

Theological Formulation

Jesus as the Righteous Davidic King and Judge

Through Amos, the God of Israel promised to raise up the booth/hut of David about to fall and to build it up as in the days of old (Amos 9:11). This statement is best taken as referring to the Davidic dynasty, "the house of David," which Amos considered more like a flimsy hut about to fall. Through Amos and elsewhere, the God of Israel promised that there would be a new and greater Davidic king.[28] The entire New Testament proclaims that Jesus of Nazareth is this promised son of David, the Messianic king of Israel. The promise of Amos 9:11–12 is repeated by James at the Jerusalem

---

[28] See, for example, Stanley E. Porter, ed., *The Messiah in the Old and New Testaments* (Grand Rapids: Eerdmans, 2007); Andrew T. Abernethy and Gregory Goswell, *God's Messiah in the Old Testament: Expectations of a Coming King* (Grand Rapids: Baker Academic, 2020).

Council recorded in Acts 15:15–18. In the context of his Gospel and the Acts of the Apostles, Luke sees the restoration of the Davidic dynasty as fulfilled by God raising Jesus up from the dead.[29]

While Amos did not explicitly articulate what the future Davidic king would do, we can assume based on the other prophets that the expectation included "rightly-distinguishing-judgment and righteousness" (cf. Isa 11:3–5; Jer 23:5; 33:15). This type of activity will characterize the expected rule of the coming Davidic king (see the previous section "Doing Rightly-Distinguishing-Judgment and Righteousness").

The New Testament uses this kind of language to characterize Jesus of Nazareth. In the LXX the Hebrew verb *shaphaṭ* is typically translated with *krinō* ("to judge") and the noun *mišpāṭ* with *krisis* ("decision, judgment") or with *krima* ("fair dealing, impartiality").[30] The New Testament often speaks of Jesus as the one who will come again in glory to "judge" the living and the dead (e.g., Acts 10:42; 2 Tim 4:1). Jesus the Davidic king will give the final "rightly-distinguishing-judgment."

At the same time, with his first advent Jesus has come to bring "judgment" (*krima*, John 9:39). The Gospel of John emphasizes this "now" of judgment. Jesus said: "This is the judgment (*krisis*)," the indictment against people, that "the light has come into the world and people loved the darkness rather than the light" (John 3:19). Concerning his crucifixion Jesus stated: "Now is the judgment of this world; now the ruler of this world shall be cast out," and Jesus will draw all people to himself (John 12:31–33; cf. 16:8–11). Whoever hears the word of Jesus and believes in God the Father who sent the Son already has eternal life and "does not come into judgment (*krisis*)," the judgment of eternal death. At the final judgment to be executed by Jesus they will receive the resurrection unto life, because the judgment of Jesus is just (John 5:22–30; 8:15–16).

---

[29] For a discussion, see Brandon D. Crowe, *The Hope of Israel: The Resurrection of Christ in the Acts of the Apostles* (Grand Rapids: Baker Academic, 2020), 87–94.

[30] See under "*krinō*" in *NIDNTTE* 2:744–50.

Christians Called to "Rightly-Distinguishing-Judgment"

How does "judging" language relate to Christians? On the one hand, followers of Jesus are not to "judge/condemn" lest we too be "judged/condemned" (Matt 7:1–5). Because we are all guilty sinners before God, none of us has the right to judge another. We should take the speck out of our own eye first. The final judgment belongs to God.

On the other hand, there are some New Testament passages that bid Christians to "judge" in a positive way. We should "judge with right judgment" and not according to mere appearances (John 7:24). Jesus told his twelve disciples that they will "sit on twelve thrones, judging the twelve tribes of Israel" (Matt 19:28; cf. Luke 22:30; Rev 20:4). Christian churches are to judge their own members (1 Cor 5:12). In the future eschaton believers will judge the world and the angels, and therefore Christians should be able to settle disputes between Christians (1 Cor 6:1–11).[31] In light of the New Testament, the exhortations by Amos apply to Christians and their dealings with fellow Christians within the context of the church.

Implications

Protestant preaching in America has often moved from a text like Amos 5:24 to a sermon advocating for "justice" or "social justice." I submit that such a move is unwarranted and misguided. The preacher should keep in mind at least six considerations or implications.

First, America is not the AD equivalent to BC Israel. America is not the covenant people of God. The God of Israel did not say to America what he said to ancient Israel through Amos, "You only have I known from all the families of the earth" (Amos 3:2).

Second, Amos was not calling for secular "justice" or "social justice," for equitable distribution of power and wealth. We have seen that the

[31] See "*krinō*," *NIDNTTE* 2:749–50.

translation of "justice" is misleading for the Hebrew noun *mišpāṭ*. Moreover, Amos was calling for righteous conduct toward others that flows from faith in the God of Israel, as indicated by the message of Yahweh—"Seek me and survive"—and Amos—"Seek Yahweh and survive" (Amos 5:4, 6). The call for doing *mišpāṭ* and righteousness in Amos 5:24 should not be separated from these exhortations in the same chapter that call for repentance and seeking Yahweh. The God of Amos was the specific God of ancient Israel, not the "anonymous God" of American civil religion and culture.[32]

Third, the preacher should not helicopter down and lift Amos 5:24 out of its written context. Instead, he should follow the trajectory of the book of Amos through the promise given in Amos 9. Do not preach as if Amos's promise of a new Davidic king has not been fulfilled, as if Jesus and his work did not take place in history. In the fullness of time, the God of Israel sent his Son to become the new and greater Davidic king (Rom 1:2–3). As he said he would do through Amos, the God of Israel has raised up the fallen house of David by raising up Jesus the Davidic Messiah from the dead. Jesus now rules, and he is the offspring of David (Rev 22:16) and David's Lord (Ps 110:1). Preaching on Amos 5 should not bypass Amos 9:11 and Jesus as the fulfillment.

Fourth, Amos's call to ancient Israel in 5:24 to "let rightly-distinguishing-judgment roll down like the waters and righteousness like an ever-flowing stream" was perfectly fulfilled by Jesus the Davidic Messianic king and Israel-reduced-to-one.[33] As noted above, the language of "rightly-distinguishing-judgment" applies to Jesus with both his first and second advent.

Fifth, God's call to ancient Israel through Amos is now God's call to us as the followers of Jesus the Davidic king. Jesus who was crucified, raised,

---

[32] See David L. Adams and Ken Schurb, *The Anonymous God: The Church Confronts Civil Religion and American Society* (St. Louis: Concordia, 2005).

[33] The language of Jesus as "Israel-reduced-to-one" comes from Horace D. Hummel, *The Word Becoming Flesh: An Introduction to the Origin, Purpose, and Meaning of the Old Testament* (St. Louis: Concordia, 1979), 17, 224, 296.

and exalted sends his Holy Spirit to conform us, his followers, into his image so that we too live a life that reflects God's will for rightly-distinguishing-judgment and righteous conduct toward others. In light of New Testament usage, the call for "rightly-distinguishing-judgment" applies especially to churches and the conduct of Christians toward each other. Christians should be able to settle their disputes in a God-pleasing way (1 Corinthians 5–6). The call for *mišpāṭ* from Amos moves to the Christian life and the internal conduct of churches, not to the governmental and economic systems of America.

Finally, the call of Amos 5:24 awaits its full consummation when Jesus the Davidic king comes again in visible glory to judge the living and the dead. As the perfect Judge he will carry out rightly-distinguishing-judgment. Then perfect righteousness will characterize his resurrected and glorified followers in the new heavens and new earth where righteousness will dwell as its permanent home (2 Pet 3:13).

The question of "social justice," of equitable distribution of wealth and power and influence, should be considered on the basis of human reason and political-economic wisdom. But that is not what Amos was talking about. The message of Amos 5:24 needs to be heard but proclaimed only in the right way, making the right moves and connecting the right dots with each other. When proclaimed properly, it is truly an important message: "Let rightly-distinguishing-judgment roll down like the waters and righteousness like an ever-flowing stream."

Questions for Further Reflection

1. What does American English mean by "justice" and "social justice"? How does this compare or contrast with Amos's call for justice?
2. According to the literary context of Amos 5, what kinds of actions did Amos 5:24 seek in ancient Israel?
3. How does God's promise of a rebuilt booth of David in Amos 9:11–12 relate to the mandate for justice in Amos 5:24?

4. How does Amos 5:24 relate to Jesus of Nazareth? How does James's citation of Amos 9:11–12 in Acts 15:15–18 help us answer this question?
5. How does Amos 5:24 relate to Christians and churches today? How should pastors preach Amos 5:24 today?

Suggested Reading

Andersen, Francis I. and David Noel Freedman. *Amos: A New Translation with Introduction and Commentary*. Anchor Bible 24A. New York: Doubleday, 1989.

Harbin, Michael A. "Social Justice for Social Outliers in Ancient Israel, Part 1: Cultural Background." *JETS* 64, no. 3 (2021): 471–94.

———. "Social Justice and Social Outliers in Ancient Israel, Part 2: Provision for Widows, Orphans, and Resident Aliens." *JETS* 64, no. 4 (2021): 681–701.

Lessing, R. Reed. *Amos*. Concordia Commentary. St. Louis: Concordia, 2009.

Paul, Shalom M. *Amos: A Commentary on the Book of Amos*. Hermeneia. Minneapolis: Fortress, 1991.

Smith, Gary V. *Amos: A Commentary*. Library of Biblical Interpretation. Grand Rapids: Regency Reference Library, 1989.

Wright, Christopher J. H. *Walking in the Ways of the Lord: The Ethical Authority of the Old Testament*. Downers Grove, IL: IVP, 1995.

4

Justice in Luke–Acts

— Brian J. Tabb —

Introduction

Jesus tells a parable of an unjust judge and an insistent widow who appeals, "Give me justice!" He explains that God will swiftly grant justice to his praying people (Luke 18:1–8). Yet Jesus himself does not experience just treatment but consummate injustice as he is convicted and crucified, even though he is truly righteous (Luke 23:4, 47; Acts 8:33). His followers likewise speak about "righteousness, self-control, and the judgment to come"[1] (Acts 24:25) even as they are unfairly maligned, maltreated, and imprisoned.

Justice may be defined as just, fair, and reasonable behavior towards others. To be just is to give people their due. Aristotle explains that a just person is both lawful and fair, while an unjust person is not. Justice is inherently social since the just person exercises virtue "towards others and not merely by himself."[2] The phrase *social justice*, first used in the nineteenth century, refers generally to equitable distribution of advantages and disadvantages within a society.[3] While "the notion of social justice is based on

[1] Unless otherwise noted, Scripture citations in this chapter come from the Christian Standard Bible.

[2] Aristotle, *Nichomachean Ethics* 5.1.8, 15, trans. H. Rackham (LCL).

[3] Michael Novak, "Social Justice: Not What You Think It Is," *The Heritage Foundation,* December 29, 2009, https://www.heritage.org/poverty-and-inequality

the Christian doctrine of helping less fortunate people—the weak, sickly, and oppressed,"[4] some contemporary varieties of "social justice" reflect worldviews and ideologies that are fundamentally opposed to traditional Christian doctrine.[5] Westfall and Dyer explain,

> The call to implement God's justice here on earth, what we might deem "social justice," remains vital to the church in its present context, but it needs definition and further discussion. In recent years, the term *social justice* has become politicized, criticized, and often used with a variety of meanings and for a variety of causes.[6]

According to the Scriptures, the sovereign God is the supreme standard and source of justice. The Lord loves and executes justice, particularly for the oppressed and exploited (Pss 37:28; 103:6; 146:7). As Abraham declares, "Won't the Judge of the whole earth do what is just?" (Gen 18:25). The God of justice also commands his people to practice justice and righteousness and condemns those who fail to do so. According to Isa 5:7, the Lord "expected justice" in Israel and Judah "but saw injustice; he expected righteousness but heard cries of despair." So the prophets announce that God himself will shepherd his scattered people with justice (Ezek 34:16) and send a coming king and servant who will establish and sustain enduring justice and righteousness (Isa 9:7; 11:3–5; 42:1–4).

/report/social-justice-not-what-you-think-it#.

[4] Allan C. Ornstein, "Social Justice: History, Purpose and Meaning," *Social Science and Public Policy* 54 (2017): 545.

[5] See Chapter 1 by Cory Higdon in this volume, as well as the extended discussion of Social Justice A and Social Justice B in Thaddeus J. Williams, *Confronting Injustice without Compromising Truth: 12 Questions Christians Should Ask about Social Justice* (Grand Rapids: Zondervan Academic, 2020).

[6] Cynthia Long Westfall and Bryan R. Dyer, "Introduction," in *The Bible and Social Justice: Old Testament and New Testament Foundations for the Church's Urgent Call*, ed. Cynthia Long Westfall and Bryan R. Dyer, McMaster New Testament Studies (Eugene, OR: Pickwick, 2016), xvii, emphasis original.

This chapter offers exegetical and theological reflections on concerns related to justice and mercy in the Gospel of Luke and the book of Acts. The Gospel stresses that God humbles the proud and lifts up the lowly (Luke 1:52; cf. 1 Sam 2:8) and that would-be disciples must "produce fruit consistent with repentance" (Luke 3:8). Jesus brings good news for the poor (Luke 4:18), heals the oppressed (Acts 10:38), and searches for the lost (Luke 19:10). Acts depicts Christians unified in heart and soul and holding "everything in common" such that there are no needy people among them (Acts 4:32, 34), echoing Deut 15:4 (LXX) and eclipsing Greco-Roman ideals for friendship and community.[7] The apostles proclaim that Jesus is "Lord of all" (Acts 10:36), and they turn the world upside down by declaring their supreme allegiance to "another king—Jesus" (Acts 17:6–7).

Justice and mercy characterize Christ's teaching and activity as the promised king. Likewise, his people should perform deeds of justice, love, and mercy that reflect the reality of Christ's reign while they prioritize gospel proclamation and prayerfully wait for perfect justice.

Biblical Texts and Exegesis

This section reflects on representative passages in Luke's Gospel and Acts related to justice and mercy. I focus significant attention on Christ's own summaries of his ministry priorities (especially Luke 4:16–27 and 19:10), his chastisement of those who neglect justice (Luke 11:42), and his teachings that emphasize justice and mercy (esp. Luke 6:36; 10:25–37; 18:1–8). I then consider examples in Acts in which followers of Jesus practice justice and mercy while confronting and experiencing injustice.

---

[7] For example, Seneca writes about an earlier age when human beings "enjoyed all nature in partnership" and "you could not find a poor person among them" (*Epistle* 90.38, trans. Richard M. Gummere [LCL]). See the discussion in Steve Walton, "Primitive Communism in Acts? Does Acts Present the Community of Goods (2:44–45; 4:32–35) as Mistaken?," *EvQ* 80, no. 2 (2008): 99–111.

Justice and Mercy in Jesus's Ministry

Luke's Gospel includes many examples of Jesus's deeds of justice and mercy. He heals the sick, raises the dead, and drives out demons to reveal that he is the incarnate Lord who brings near the kingdom of God (cf. Luke 9:11; 11:20). Jesus insists on doing good (*agathopoiēsai*) on the Sabbath, then restores a man's shriveled hand (Luke 5:9–10). The Lord is moved with compassion (*esplanchnisthē*) for a bereaved widow and raises her lifeless son (Luke 7:13–15). For the woman whose perpetual menstrual bleeding rendered her ritually unclean, financially destitute, and socially excluded (Luke 8:43; Lev 15:25), Jesus brings full-orbed salvation (note *sōzō* in Luke 8:48). He stops her bleeding as no physician could, brings her into restored relationship by calling her "daughter," and sends her away in peace (Luke 8:46–48). He also frees a "daughter of Abraham" from her long-term disability due to spiritual oppression (Luke 13:10–16). As Peter explains, the Lord Jesus "went about doing good [*euergetōn*] and healing all who were under the tyranny of the devil, because God was with him" (Acts 10:38).

Good News to the Poor (Luke 4)

Jesus's public ministry in Luke's Gospel begins with his synagogue sermon in Nazareth, which programmatically summarizes his messianic identity and his vocation to preach good news to the poor, oppressed, and marginalized.[8] In Luke 4:18–19, Jesus defines his mission according to the prophecy of Isaiah:

> The Spirit of the Lord is on me,
> because he has anointed me
> to preach good news to the poor.
> He has sent me

---

[8] This exposition of Luke 4 condenses a lengthier discussion in Brian J. Tabb, *After Emmaus: How the Church Fulfills the Mission of Christ* (Wheaton, IL: Crossway, 2021), 94–101.

to proclaim freedom to the captives[9]
and recovery of sight to the blind,
to set free the oppressed,
to proclaim the year of the Lord's favor.

Jesus emphatically announces that the prophet's words are fulfilled "today" (Luke 4:21).

This quotation draws upon Isa 61:1–2a (LXX), combined with a line from Isa 58:6 to underscore the emphasis on "freedom" (*aphesis*) for those on the margins. As J. Daniel Hays explains, "The theme of justice hovers just below the surface" in this citation.[10] Several verses after the passage Jesus quotes, God declares emphatically, "I the Lord love justice; I hate robbery and injustice" (Isa 61:8). The call for justice and mercy is especially clear in Isaiah 58.

The prophet presents the standard of "a nation that does what is right [*tsedaqah*] and does not abandon the justice [*mišpāṭ*] of their God" (Isa 58:2). The Lord then rebukes the people for their hypocritical fasting (Isa 58:3–5) and calls for true fasting that seeks justice and the well-being of others:

Isn't this the fast I choose:
To break the chains of wickedness,
to untie the ropes of the yoke,
to set the oppressed free,
and to tear off every yoke?
Is it not to share your bread with the hungry,
to bring the poor and homeless into your house,
to clothe the naked when you see him,
and not to ignore your own flesh and blood? (Isa 58:6–7)

---

[9] The CSB renders *aphesis* "release" but offers "freedom" and "forgiveness" as marginal readings.

[10] J. Daniel Hays, "'Sell Everything You Have and Give to the Poor': The Old Testament Prophetic Theme of Justice as the Connecting Motif of Luke 18:1–19:10," *JETS* 55, no. 1 (2012): 45.

The opening line of Isaiah 61:1—"The Spirit of the Lord is upon me" (Luke 4:18)—fittingly summarizes what the early chapters of Luke's Gospel recount in detail: the Holy Spirit comes upon the virgin Mary (Luke 1:35), rests on Jesus at his baptism (Luke 3:22), and leads Jesus through his wilderness temptation (Luke 4:1, 14). According to Acts 10:38, "God anointed Jesus of Nazareth with the Holy Spirit and with power."

The remainder of Jesus's quotation from Isaiah sums up the aims of his Spirit-anointed ministry. God sent Christ to preach (1) good news to the poor, (2) freedom for the captives and the oppressed, (3) recovery of sight to the blind, and (4) the Lord's favor. Luke's Gospel develops each of these four emphases.

First, Jesus is anointed "to preach good news to the poor" (Luke 4:18). Angels announce joyous good news (Luke 1:19; 2:10), and the prophet John exhorts the people with good news (Luke 3:18). Following his Nazareth sermon, Jesus casts out demons and heals the sick in Capernaum, then he asserts his calling "to proclaim good news about the kingdom of God to the other towns also" (Luke 4:43). This good news about God's kingdom reflects prophecies announcing the "good news" of salvation and God's reign (Isa 40:9–11; 52:7).

In Luke 7:18–20, John sends his disciples to Jesus to ask, "Are you the one who is to come, or should we expect someone else?" Jesus heals many people at that time and then says, "Go and report to John what you have seen and heard: The blind receive their sight, the lame walk, those with leprosy are cleansed, the deaf hear, the dead are raised, and the poor are told the good news, and blessed is the one who isn't offended by me" (Luke 7:22–23). Christ's actions and his response to John's question clearly recall his earlier quotation of Isa 61:1–2, along with other restoration prophecies (e.g., Isa 35:4–6).

Luke 4:18 and 7:22 focus on *the poor* receiving good news, reflecting this Gospel's frequent discussion of the poor and lowly (cf. Luke 1:52), terms that have both material and spiritual connotations.[11] The rich and

---

[11] Christopher M. Hays, *Luke's Wealth Ethics: A Study in their Coherence and Character*, WUNT 2/275 (Tübingen: Mohr Siebeck, 2010), 111.

proud typically resist Jesus's message, while humble, needy, and marginalized people humbly receive mercy.[12] For example, Jesus declares, "Blessed are you who are *poor*, because the kingdom of God is yours" (Luke 6:20). He instructs those hosting a banquet to invite the "poor, maimed, lame, or blind," rather than those who can reciprocate the offer (Luke 14:13, 21). He praises "a poor widow" for her consummate generosity (Luke 21:1–4). Moreover, the wealthy tax collector's eagerness to give away half of his possessions to the poor demonstrates the saving power of his encounter with Christ (Luke 19:8–9). Zacchaeus's actions also contrast sharply with the rich man who feasts lavishly while Lazarus suffers at his gate (Luke 16:19–21) and the ruler whose great wealth hinders him from following Jesus (Luke 18:18–25). The Gospel's repeated focus on the poor signals that "the gospel is truly for everyone."[13]

Second, Jesus is sent "to proclaim freedom to the captives" and "to set free the oppressed" (Luke 4:18). The repeated term *aphesis* means "the act of freeing and liberating" from confinement, obligation, or punishment.[14] It occurs only twice in the Greek text of Isaiah (Isa 58:6; 61:1, LXX)—the precise texts cited in Luke 4:18.[15] The other eight uses of *aphesis* in Luke and Acts explicitly refer to "the forgiveness of sins" (*aphesis [tōn] hamartiōn*) for those who repent and receive God's salvation.[16] This usage clarifies the meaning of Jesus's programmatic reference to *aphesis* in Luke 4:18. Jesus does not simply proclaim "freedom" or "release" from physical captivity or oppression

[12] Michael Ovey contrasts the repentant and unrepentant in *The Feasts of Repentance: From Luke–Acts to Systematic and Pastoral Theology*, NSBT 49 (Downers Grove, IL: IVP Academic, 2019), 11–34.

[13] Darrell L. Bock, *A Theology of Luke and Acts*, Biblical Theology of the New Testament (Grand Rapids: Zondervan, 2012), 352.

[14] BDAG, s.v. "*aphesis*," 155.

[15] On the verbal analogy between Isa 58:6 (LXX) and 61:1 (LXX) (*apostellō . . . aphesis*), see David W. Pao and Eckhard J. Schnabel, "Luke," in *Commentary on the New Testament Use of the Old Testament*, ed. G. K. Beale and D. A. Carson (Grand Rapids: Baker Academic, 2007), 289.

[16] See Luke 1:77; 3:3; 24:47; Acts 2:38; 5:31; 10:43; 13:38; 26:18.

but from spiritual bondage to sin and Satan's tyranny (cf. Luke 13:16; Acts 10:38; 26:18). Further, Jesus not only announces this freedom (like John and other prophets), he also achieves it as the anointed Savior. Jesus's declaration of "freedom" in his Nazareth sermon anticipates his climactic teaching that "repentance for forgiveness of sins will be proclaimed in his name to all the nations, beginning at Jerusalem" (Luke 24:47). Thus, the repetition of *aphesis* links Christ's own message and mission to that of his disciples.[17]

Third, Jesus proclaims restored sight for the blind, reflecting Old Testament expectation of the coming era of salvation when "the eyes of the blind will be opened" (Isa 35:5). However, Isaiah also rebukes his hearers for their metaphorical blindness and deafness toward the Lord and his word—they see yet do not perceive and hear without understanding (Isa 6:9–10), thus resembling the idols they worship that are blind, deaf, mute, and powerless to save.[18] Malfunctioning eyes and ears signify the people's true spiritual state before the Lord; only God can lead them out of darkness and offer them genuine sight and hearing (Isa 29:18). Jesus restores sight to the blind on multiple occasions (e.g., Luke 7:21–22; 18:42–43), which shows that the promised age of salvation has dawned.[19] Yet Jesus also speaks in parables "so that seeing they may not see" (Luke 8:10; cf. Isa 6:9). Even his own disciples cannot perceive what sort of Messiah he really is (Luke 18:31–34) until he "opens their minds to understand" after his resurrection (Luke 24:45).

Fourth, Jesus is sent "to proclaim the year of the Lord's favor" (Luke 4:19). Isaiah's prophecy may recall the proclamation of "freedom in the land" in the Year of Jubilee (Lev 25:10), when the Lord instructed Israel

---

[17] Similarly, Thomas S. Moore, "The Lucan Great Commission and the Isaianic Servant," *BibSac* 154 (1997): 51–52.

[18] See Isa 29:9–10; 42:18–20; 43:8; 59:10; and the persuasive discussion in G. K. Beale, *We Become What We Worship: A Biblical Theology of Idolatry* (Downers Grove, IL: IVP Academic, 2008), 41–51.

[19] Thus, according to Thomas R. Schreiner, "the sight promised to the blind is both literal and spiritual." *New Testament Theology: Magnifying God in Christ* (Grand Rapids: Baker Academic, 2008), 760.

to cancel debts, release bondservants, and restore property to its original owners.[20] In Isa 49:8, the Lord also promises to answer his people "in a time of favor" (*kairō dektō*) and help them "in the day of salvation."[21] Isaiah evidently employs Jubilee imagery to portray the comprehensive freedom in the new age of restoration.[22] In Luke 4:19, "the year of the Lord's favor" does not mean that the people of Nazareth must return land and cancel debts; rather, it pictures "what God is doing spiritually and physically through his commissioned agent, Jesus."[23]

Strikingly, after proclaiming the year of the Lord's favor (*dektos*), Christ does not find favor (*dektos*) in his hometown like the prophets before him (Luke 4:24). He illustrates this point from the ministries of Elijah and Elisha (Luke 4:25–27).[24] God sent Elijah to serve a widow in Sidon—not in Israel—during a time of great famine (1 Kgs 17:8–24). The prophet Elisha healed and cleansed the Syrian commander Naaman (2 Kgs 5:1–14) yet did not heal any of Israel's many lepers. These familiar biblical accounts anticipate aspects of Jesus's ministry in Luke's Gospel. The Lord raises a widow's only son, just as Elijah did in Zarephath, which prompts onlookers to call him "a great prophet" and exclaim that "God has visited his people" (Luke 7:11–16). Jesus tells John's followers that "those with leprosy are cleansed . . . the dead are raised, and the poor are told good news" (Luke 7:22), reflecting

---

[20] Paul R. House, *Isaiah, Volume 2: Chapters 28–66*, Mentor Commentary (Ross-Shire, UK: Christian Focus, 2019), 637–38.

[21] Cf. Paul's citation of Isa 49:8 in 2 Cor 6:2.

[22] Chris Bruno, "Jesus Is Our Jubilee . . . But How? The OT Background and Lukan Fulfillment of the Ethics of Jubilee," *JETS* 53, no. 1 (2010): 94, 98.

[23] Darrell L. Bock, *Luke 1:1–9:50*, BECNT (Grand Rapids: Baker Academic, 1994), 410. Scholars have often recognized that Jesus's citation of Isa 61:1–2 does not include "the day of our God's vengeance." Most likely, the quotation ends with "the Lord's favor" to emphasize the aspects of Isaiah's prophecy that Jesus "fulfills" in his first coming (note Luke 4:21).

[24] Luke 4:25–27 are the "hermeneutical key" for interpreting Jesus's earlier Isaiah citation, according to Jeffrey S. Siker, "'First to the Gentiles': A Literary Analysis of Luke 4:16–30," *JBL* 111, no. 1 (1992): 83.

his foundational quotation of Isa 61:1–2 and his miraculous deeds that parallel Elijah and Elisha. Moreover, these great Israelite prophets ministered to non-Israelites in need, which recalls the Old Testament hope that God would save Gentiles and count them among his people.[25] Jesus also heals ten lepers, including a Samaritan "foreigner" whose actions demonstrate real faith (Luke 17:11–19). Christ offends his hometown crowd with these examples of God sending prophets to foreigners, yet this reflects his role as "a light for revelation to the Gentiles" (Luke 2:32; cf. Isa 49:6) and anticipates the coming mission to the Gentiles after Pentecost.

Thus, the Nazareth scene offers a programmatic summary of Christ's identity and mission. He fulfills Isaiah's prophecy as the Spirit-anointed agent who comes to preach good news to the poor and freedom to captives (Luke 4:18–19). Jesus offers favor and forgiveness to the poor, the afflicted, and the marginalized, while he does not find favor among his Nazareth neighbors (Luke 4:22–29). Jesus's message of *aphesis* anticipates his followers' mission to proclaim forgiveness of sins in his name among all nations (Luke 24:47). Luke 4 also prepares for Christ's further explanation of his mission to seek and save those who are lost (Luke 19:10).

Seeking the Lost (Luke 19)

The theme of seeking frames Christ's encounter with Zacchaeus in Luke 19:1–10: the tax collector "was seeking [*ezētei*] to see who Jesus was" (Luke 19:3 ESV), but finally the Lord declares that he comes "to seek [*zētēsai*] and to save the lost" (Luke 19:10).[26] Luke identifies Zacchaeus as "rich" (*plousio*, Luke 19:2), which recalls Jesus's chastisement of the rich who have already received comfort in this life (Luke 6:24; cf. 16:19, 25) and his warnings about the difficulties for the wealthy to enter the kingdom (Luke 18:25). Zacchaeus is also "a chief tax collector," whom the people dismiss as "a sinful

---

[25] David W. Pao, *Acts and the Isaianic New Exodus*, BSL (Grand Rapids: Baker Academic, 2002), 78–84.

[26] For additional discussion of Luke 19, see Tabb, *After Emmaus*, 101–5.

man" (Luke 19:2, 7). While "tax collectors were despised and hated"[27] by Jews and Gentiles alike in the first century, Luke presents them as models of true repentance and discipleship (Luke 5:27–32; 18:9–14). Indeed, Zacchaeus welcomes Christ gladly and declares his intention to give away half of his possessions to the poor and to restore fourfold what he has extorted from others (Luke 19:8). Jesus then identifies this tax collector as "a son of Abraham" and says, "Today salvation has come to this house" (Luke 19:9).

Zacchaeus typifies Jesus's mission to seek and save those who are lost and outcasts.[28] In Luke 15, Christ tells three parables in which people search for and find what is lost: a sheep, a coin, and finally a son. Christ's summary aim to seek and save the lost also alludes to Ezekiel's prophecy in which the Lord condemns Israel's harsh and worthless leaders and commits to shepherd his lost people with justice:

> I will seek the lost [LXX: *to apolōlos zētēsō*], bring back the strays, bandage the injured, and strengthen the weak . . . I will shepherd them with justice . . . I will save my flock [LXX: *sōsō ta probata mou*] (Ezek 34:16, 22).

Thus, in Luke 19:10, Jesus asserts his plan to carry out what God himself resolved to do for his people.[29] In Luke 19:1–10, the Lord Jesus sees,

---

[27] James R. Edwards, *The Gospel according to Luke*, PNTC (Grand Rapids: Eerdmans, 2015), 112; cf. T. E. Schmidt, "Taxation, Jewish," in *Dictionary of New Testament Background*, ed. Craig A. Evans and Stanley E. Porter (Downers Grove, IL: InterVarsity, 2000), 1165.

[28] Ovey, *The Feasts of Repentance*, 31. Luke 19:1–10 is not a conversion story, according to Joel B. Green, *The Gospel of Luke*, NICNT (Grand Rapids: Eerdmans, 1997), 672. However, the close link between vv. 9 and 10 shows that "salvation" has come to Zacchaeus's house because Jesus is there, and he has come to seek and save "lost" people just like this tax collector. Cf. Monique Cuany, "'Today, Salvation Has Come to This House': God's Salvation of God's People in Luke's Gospel," *CurTM* 45, no. 4 (2018): 15n10.

[29] Similarly, Michael Wolter, *Das Lukasevangelium*, HNT 5 (Tübingen: Mohr Siebeck, 2008), 616.

seeks, and saves even the most despised sinners, and Zacchaeus demonstrates the marks of a genuine disciple by using his wealth to help the poor and restore what has been wrongfully taken.

Justice and Mercy in Jesus's Teaching

Themes of justice and mercy feature prominently in Jesus's teaching. He summons disciples to do good and be merciful as true children of their Father (Luke 6:35–36). He insists that those who hear and keep God's word are blessed (Luke 11:28). He rebukes the Pharisees for bypassing justice and love for God as they seem to carry out the law's precepts while neglecting matters of first importance (Luke 11:42). The Lord also showcases neighborly love and concern for justice in several parables unique to Luke's Gospel (Luke 10:25–37; 18:1–8).

Blessed are the Poor (Luke 6)

The summary of Jesus's teaching recorded in Luke 6 "heralds the way of the kingdom of God as a radical antithesis to the ways of the world."[30] Jesus reassures those who are poor, hungry, weeping, and hated on his account and warns those who are rich, satisfied, jovial, and popular (Luke 6:20–26). True blessing is found by aligning with the reality and values of the coming kingdom of God, associating with the Son of Man, and seeking a heavenly reward above consolation in the here and now.

---

[30] Edwards, *The Gospel according to Luke*, 192. Luke 6:20–49 is typically called "the Sermon on the Plain" to differentiate it from the longer "Sermon on the Mount" in Matthew 5–7. For extensive discussion of Luke's sources and relationship to Matthew, see Bock, *Luke 1:1–9:50*, 549–57. Contrary to conventional scholarship, Edwards contends that Luke 6 represents "an earlier anthology of Jesus' ethical teaching that was widely known and variously quoted in the early church," rather than an adaptation of Matthew's Sermon (*The Gospel according to Luke*, 192).

Jesus then applies these kingdom indicatives with a series of imperatives: "*Love* [*agapate*] your enemies, *do what is good* [*kalōs poieite*] to those who hate you, *bless* [*eulogeite*] those who curse you, *pray* [*proseuchesthe*] for those who mistreat you" (Luke 6:27–28). These commands express generally applicable ethical instructions that should characterize Christ's disciples.[31] In contrast to conventional thinking rooted in reciprocity and personal benefit, Jesus summons his people to love, do good, lend without expecting a return in kind, and show mercy. Those who act in this countercultural way demonstrate that they are "children of the Most High" and anticipate a heavenly reward (Luke 6:35–36). In other words, the disciples' conduct is not guided by societal norms but the character and actions of God the Father, who is kind [*chrēstos*] and merciful [*oiktirmōn*] to ungrateful, evil people. This reflects the Lord's foundational self-revelation in Exod 33:19 and 34:6 and the psalmist's praise in Ps 145:8–9 (144:8–9 LXX): "The Lord is gracious and compassionate [*oiktirmōn kai eleēmōn*], slow to anger and great in faithful love. The Lord is good [*chrēstos*] to everyone; his compassion [*hoi oiktirmoi*] rests on all he has made." Thus, love and mercy are signature marks of the people who belong to the supremely compassionate Creator God, as good trees produce good fruit (Luke 6:43).

God's character and the reality of his coming kingdom similarly shape Jesus's teaching in Luke 6:37–38a: "Do not judge, and you will not be judged. Do not condemn, and you will not be condemned. Forgive, and you will be forgiven. Give, and it will be given to you." The oft-misunderstood command "do not judge" (*mē krinete*) does not prohibit discerning, moral evaluation but warns against judgmental, self-righteous words and deeds that lack mercy and effectively place oneself in God's stead. Jesus warns that God will judge those who judge wrongly, and the promise of divine forgiveness and generosity motivates disciples to forgive and be generous to others in the present.

---

[31] On the imperfective aspect of Greek present imperatives, see Constantine R. Campbell, *Basics of Verbal Aspect in Biblical Greek* (Grand Rapids: Zondervan, 2008), 70.

The closing parable of the builders in Luke 6:46–49 distinguishes between true faith and empty profession. Genuine disciples come to Christ and heed his teaching, in contrast to those who call him *kyrios* (Lord) yet fail to do what he says. As Jesus says elsewhere, "Blessed are those who hear the word of God and keep it" (Luke 11:28).

Woe to Those Who Neglect Justice (Luke 11:42)

Jesus denounces the hypocrisy and spiritual negligence of the Jewish leaders, who appear righteous and clean yet inside "are full of greed and evil" (Luke 11:39). He charges them instead to "give from what is within to the poor" (Luke 11:41), as almsgiving [*eleēmosynē*] is antithetical to greed and reflects a pure heart concerned with God's priority on justice and mercy.[32] Christ's blistering rebuke in v. 42 offers one of the Gospel's clearest statements about true justice: "But woe to you Pharisees! You give a tenth of mint, rue, and every kind of herb, and you bypass justice and love for God [*parerchesthe tēn krisin kai tēn agapēn tou theou*]. These things you should have done without neglecting the others."

The law of Moses stipulates that every tenth of the land's produce is holy to the Lord (Lev 27:30; Deut 14:22). Significantly, these tithes provided for the Levites who depended on the contributions of the other tribes, as well as for the resident alien, the orphan, and the widow (Deut 14:28–29; 26:12). Thus, the tithe offerings reflect God's concern for the ministry of the tabernacle as well as his compassionate care for the most vulnerable people in the community. The Mishnah explained that the law of tithes applied to "anything which is (1) food, (2) cultivated, (3) and which grows from the earth" (*Maaserot* 1:1). In Jesus's parable of the Pharisee and the tax collector, the Pharisee boasts, "I give a tenth of everything I get" (Luke 18:12). However, it is the humble tax collector calling out for divine mercy who is justified rather than the Pharisee who exalts himself and treats others with disdain (Luke 18:9, 14).

---

[32] Cf. Edwards, *The Gospel according to Luke*, 355.

Jesus chides the Pharisees for neglecting justice and love for God, which are foundational concerns in the Law and Prophets (Luke 11:42; cf. Deut 6:5; Mic 6:8). As noted above, the OT laws about tithes were intended to promote justice and mercy towards the needy in Israel. However, Luke characterizes the Pharisees as greedy and lovers of money (Luke 11:39; 16:14), and their neglect of justice and generosity to the poor reveals that their scrupulous tithing is fundamentally misguided and devoid of the practice's true purpose.

The Parable of the Good Samaritan (Luke 10)

Jesus's parable of the Good Samaritan expounds the foundational command in Lev 19:18 while clarifying the meaning of neighbor love (Luke 10:27). A legal scholar poses a self-justifying question: "And who is my neighbor?" (Luke 10:29). Jesus replies with a brief story about a man traveling to Jericho who is attacked by robbers and left half dead (Luke 10:30–35). A priest and Levite each see the hurting man yet pass by on the other side, then a third traveler comes to his aid. Help comes from a most unlikely source—a despised Samaritan. The brief explanation in John 4:9—"Jews do not associate with Samaritans"—sums up centuries of hostility between these neighboring groups.[33] For example, during Antiochus IV's bitter persecution of the Jews, Josephus explains, "But when the Samaritans saw the Jews suffering these misfortunes, they would no longer admit that they were their kin or that the temple on Garizein was that of the Most Great God."[34] However, the Samaritan in Luke 10:33

[33] Cf. H. G. M. Williamson and M. Kartveit, "Samaritans," in *Dictionary of Jesus and the Gospels*, ed. Joel B. Green, Jeannine K. Brown, and Nicholas Perrin, 2nd ed. (Downers Grove, IL: InterVarsity, 2013), 832–36.

[34] Josephus, *Antiquities of the Jews* 12.257, trans. Ralph Marcus (LCL). However, 2 Chr 28:12–15 recounts an occasion of remarkable kindness of Samaritan soldiers towards their prisoners from Judah. Luke 10 may allude to this account in 2 Chronicles 28, according to Klyne Snodgrass, *Stories with Intent: A Comprehensive Guide to the Parables of Jesus*, 2nd ed. (Grand Rapids: Eerdmans, 2018), 358.

is moved with compassion (*esplanchnisthē*) when he sees the man by the road. The Samaritan bandages and treats the man's wounds with oil and wine (cf. Isa 1:6), sets him on his own animal, checks him into an inn, and promises to cover all his expenses.

Some scholars have recently claimed that this parable's central point "is not ethical but ecclesiological."[35] While passages such as Acts 8 reflect the prophetic hopes for the inclusion of Samaria under the rule of the Davidic king,[36] this is at most an implication of Luke 10:25–37, not its chief concern. The concluding exchange in vv. 36–37 distills the parable's ethical focus. Jesus asks, "Which of these three . . . proved to be a neighbor to the man?" The lawyer answers, "The one who showed mercy to him." Jesus responds, "Go, and you do likewise" (my translation). The final command in Greek is emphatic—(*sy poiei homoiōs*). It recalls Jesus's earlier charge to the lawyer in v. 28—"Do [*poiei*] this and you will live"—and reflects the scholar's own description of the compassionate Samaritan as *ho poiēsas to eleos*, the one who practices mercy. Thus, "The emphasis throughout is on action and especially on 'doing'" (*poiein*).[37] Rather than carefully defining the boundaries of who does or does not count as a "neighbor," this parable illustrates what it looks like to *act* as a neighbor (*plēsion . . . gegonenai*, v. 36). The Samaritan's neighbor-love is characterized by compassion (v. 33), mercy (v. 37), and tangible and costly service for someone in need (vv. 34–35), regardless of racial, ethnic, or religious barriers or cultural norms.[38]

---

[35] Jeannine K. Brown and Kazuhiko Yamazaki-Ransom, "The Parable of the Good Samaritan and the Narrative Portrayal of Samaritans in Luke-Acts," *JTI* 15, no. 2 (2021): 235. Cf. Matthew Chalmers, "Rethinking Luke 10: The Parable of the Good Samaritan Israelite," *JBL* 139, no. 3 (2020): 543–66.

[36] Alan J. Thompson, *The Acts of the Risen Lord Jesus: Luke's Account of God's Unfolding Plan*, NSBT 27 (Downers Grove, IL: InterVarsity, 2011).

[37] Snodgrass, *Stories with Intent*, 344. Note also the lawyer's opening question in Luke 10:25.

[38] Edwards, *The Gospel according to Luke*, 323–24.

The Parable of the Persistent Widow (Luke 18:1–8)

Following an extended discussion about the importance of faith (Luke 17:5–6) and the coming of the Son of Man (Luke 17:20–37),[39] Jesus tells the parable of the persistent widow to encourage enduring prayer and faith while awaiting divine justice and vindication (Luke 18:1, 8).

The contrast between the parable's two characters is striking: an unjust judge and a widow seeking justice. Weaver comments, "If the judge is the symbol of power and authority, the widow symbolizes powerlessness and vulnerability."[40] This judge neither fears God nor respects people, and he is reluctant to grant the widow's request for justice (Luke 18:2–5).

This parable's focus on justice is reflected in the repeated use of terms related to the *dikē* and *krinō* word groups:

- *kritēs*, "judge"; 18:2, 6
- *ekdikeō*, "to grant justice"; 18:3, 5
- *antidikos*, "adversary"; 18:3
- *adikia*, "injustice"; 18:6
- *ekdikēsis*, "justice"; 18:7–8.

Indeed, Hays proposes that the Old Testament prophets' vision for "justice" is central to not only this parable but to the larger section of Luke 18:1–19:10.[41]

Scholars have proposed various interpretations of the parable of the persistent widow related to seeking justice. For example, Reid calls this parable "an effective example of nonviolent confrontation in the pursuit of justice" that "underscores the paradoxical power of seeming weakness,"[42] while

---

[39] The parable's thematic links to the preceding and following sections of Luke's Gospel are noted by Snodgrass, *Stories with Intent*, 453.

[40] Dorothy Jean Weaver, "Luke 18:1–8," *Int* 56, no. 3 (2002): 317.

[41] Hays, "Sell Everything," 43.

[42] Barbara E. Reid, "A Godly Widow Persistently Pursuing Justice: Luke 18:1–8," *BR* 45 (2000): 32. Reid's claim that the widow in Luke 18 "recovers a crucial

Cotter claims that it challenges listeners "about the power for justice wielded by those who remain independent, refusing to conform to the dominating social codes so convenient to the elite."[43] However, vv. 6–8 clearly relate the parable to the character of *God*, who will surely vindicate his waiting people. Jesus's logic moves from the lesser to the greater: If even a powerless, pesky widow can eventually prevail upon a powerful, immoral judge, how much more will the supremely righteous divine Judge respond to his chosen people's prayers for justice?[44]

Justice and Mercy in Acts

Luke's second volume covers all that the risen Lord Jesus *continues* to do and teach after his ascension through his Spirit-empowered apostles (Acts 1:1–2). The narrative focuses on the fulfillment of Old Testament prophecy and Jesus's own promise in Acts 1:8: "But you will receive power when the Holy Spirit has come on you, and you will be my witnesses in Jerusalem, in all Judea and Samaria, and to the ends of the earth." Many souls call on the name of the Lord Jesus and are added to the church (Acts 2:21, 41), and the word goes forth from Jerusalem (Isa 2:3) such that those who are far off—even Samaritans and Gentiles—turn from darkness to light and join with those sanctified by faith (Acts 26:18; cf. 2:39; 8:15–17; 10:45). The summary statements highlighting the advance of the gospel message

---

biblical presentation of God in a female image" (32) fundamentally confuses the parable's logic and referents.

[43] Wendy Cotter, "The Parable of the Feisty Widow and the Threatened Judge (Luke 18:1–8)," *NTS* 51, no. 3 (2005): 343. To reach this conclusion, Cotter focuses on the "core" of the parable (Luke 18:2–5) while regarding vv. 1, 6–8 as redactional additions (328–31).

[44] This interpretation assumes that a parable can have more than one main point—in this case, it teaches us about both prayer and justice. For a discussion of this question, see Craig L. Blomberg, *Interpreting the Parables* (Downers Grove, IL: IVP Academic, 1990), 166; Zoltan L. Erdey, "Interpreting Parables: One Point or Many?" *Conspectus* 10 (2010): 5–24; Robert L. Plummer, *40 Questions about Interpreting the Bible*, 2nd ed. (Grand Rapids: Kregel, 2021), 289–96.

and the growth of the church in Jerusalem and beyond reflect the book's primary storyline (Acts 6:7; 9:31; 12:24; 19:20). As Rosner notes, "It would be difficult to imagine a theme that is more comprehensive in scope."[45] As the word spreads and the church is strengthened, Acts offers multiple examples of believers in Christ pursuing and practicing justice and mercy. This section examines Luke's descriptions of the early church's unity and supernatural generosity and examines the emphasis in Acts on almsgiving and good works. Throughout, we see that how people handle possessions offers a crucial window into their relationship with God.

A Unified and Generous Community (Acts 2:42–47; 4:32–37; 11:27–30)

Those who call on the name of the Lord Jesus for salvation are added to the community of disciples devoted to the apostles' teaching, table fellowship, and prayers (Acts 2:41–42). Verses 43–47 elaborate on this summary portrait by emphasizing the amazed response to God's work through the apostles and the radical unity, generosity, joy, and growth of the early church in Jerusalem. Acts 2:44 and 4:32 present the believers being together in the same place (*epi to auto*), holding all things in common (*eichon hapanta koina*), and sharing "one heart and soul" (*kardia kai psychē mia*). These descriptions parallel Greco-Roman writings about ideals of friendship and society,[46] though the community of disciples also reflects biblical expectations for the people of God.[47] This is particularly evident in Acts 4:34: "For there was not a needy person among them" (*oude gar endeēs tis ēn en autois*),

---

[45] Brian Rosner, "The Progress of the Word," in *Witness to the Gospel: The Theology of Acts*, ed. I. Howard Marshall and David G. Peterson (Grand Rapids: Eerdmans, 1998), 233.

[46] For various primary source references, see Charles H. Talbert, *Reading Acts: A Literary and Theological Commentary on the Acts of the Apostles*, rev. ed. (New York: Crossroad, 2005), 47–49; Hays, *Luke's Wealth Ethics*, 202–8.

[47] Walton, "Primitive Communism in Acts?," 104–5; Daniel Marguerat, *Les Actes des Apôtres (1–12)*, CNT 5A (Genève: Labor et Fides, 2007), 170.

which clearly alludes to Deut 15:4 (LXX), "For there will not be a needy person among you" (*hoti ouk estai en soi endeēs*, my translation). Elsewhere in Deuteronomy 15 the Lord promises to bless his people as they cancel the debts of their neighbors and open their hearts and their hands to the needy and poor in the land (Deut 15:1, 7, 11). Thus, the early church shows itself to be the true people of God by fulfilling God's standards for meeting needs in the community.[48]

The summaries in Acts 2:42–47 and 4:32–37 reflect the Lord's teaching in Luke 12:34: "For where your treasure is, there your heart will be also." Walton states, "As is often the case in Luke-Acts, how possessions are handled is an index of a person's standing with God."[49] Luke's description suggests that the early believers retained personal possessions (*tōn hyparchontōn*) as they regularly met in one another's homes (Acts 4:32; cf. 2:46; 12:12; 18:7; 21:8). They were not compelled to renounce all their belongings (Acts 5:4), yet their unity of heart and soul prompted them periodically to sell property and share what they had as needs arose (Acts 4:32, 34).[50] The narrative thus depicts a "community of unity," not a "community of goods."[51] Said another way, Luke describes the church's "shared *use*, not the shared *ownership*, of private goods."[52] Barnabas illustrates this generous sharing as he sells a field and gives the proceeds to the apostles to distribute to those in need (Acts 4:36–37). He stands in sharp contrast to Ananias and Sapphira, who lie to the apostles and to God about their contributions (Acts 5:1–4).

---

[48] Jacob Jervell, *Die Apostelgeschichte*, KEK 17 (Göttingen: Vandenhoeck & Ruprecht, 1998), 191.

[49] Steve Walton, "What Does 'Mission' in Acts Mean in Relation to the 'Powers that Be'?," *JETS* 55, no. 3 (2012): 555–56.

[50] Craig L. Blomberg, *Neither Poverty nor Riches: A Biblical Theology of Material Possessions*, NSBT 7 (Downers Grove, IL: InterVarsity, 1999), 164.

[51] Thompson, *The Acts of the Risen Lord Jesus*, 162n63; against Brian Capper, "Reciprocity and the Ethic of Acts," in *Witness to the Gospel: The Theology of Acts*, ed. I. Howard Marshall and David G. Peterson (Grand Rapids: Eerdmans, 1998), 499–518.

[52] Hays, *Luke's Wealth Ethics*, 200, emphasis original.

Remarkably, "the 'original sin' of the church is portrayed in terms of the misuse of money and possessions!"[53] In Acts 6:1, the neglect of the Hellenistic widows threatens the church's continued growth and requires decisive action. Nevertheless, the portraits of the early church in Acts 2 and 4 illustrate the remarkable grace of God (Acts 4:34) on display through the community's heartfelt love and openhanded generosity.

In response to a severe famine, the disciples in Antioch "determined to send relief to the brothers and sisters who lived in Judea" (Acts 11:29). This passage demonstrates at least two important points related to Luke's treatment of justice and mercy. First, the Judean church's acute need provides the occasion for the largely Gentile church in Antioch to show solidarity with and genuine care for fellow believers beyond their local community or ethnic background. Second, it is remarkable that all the disciples were involved in this effort, "as each one was able" (Acts 11:29, NIV). This contrasts sharply with the conventional Greco-Roman practice of the wealthy taking responsibility for the community's supply of grain and reveals that "the role of benefactor was assigned not only to the Christian of substance but to *all* members of the community who could work. All were to do good."[54]

Good Works and Acts of Charity

The book of Acts frequently highlights believers' acts of charity and good works as concrete expressions of their genuine faith.[55] Ten of the New Testament's thirteen uses of *eleēmosynē* ("alms" or "charitable giving")

---

[53] David G. Peterson, *The Acts of the Apostles*, PNTC (Grand Rapids: Eerdmans, 2009), 209; cf. Daniel Marguerat, *The First Christian Historian: Writing the 'Acts of the Apostles'*, trans. Richard Bauckham, SNTSMS 121 (Cambridge: Cambridge University Press, 2002), 155–78.

[54] Bruce W. Winter, "Acts and Food Shortages," in *The Book of Acts in Its Graeco-Roman Setting*, ed. David W. Gill and Conrad H. Gempf (Grand Rapids: Eerdmans, 1994), 2:75–76, emphasis original.

[55] Cf. Marguerat, *Les Actes des Apôtres (1–12)*, 355.

occur in Luke's writings, and the disciples' exemplary generosity reflects the Lord's instruction to "give alms" (*dote eleēmosynēn*) in Luke 11:41 and 12:33.[56]

In Acts 3:1–10, Peter and John encounter a lame beggar seeking alms (*eleēmosynē*) as they go to the temple for prayer. The apostles pay attention to the man and go beyond his immediate request for money, calling him to rise and walk in the name of Jesus Christ (Acts 3:6). This scene not only demonstrates concern for those in need but also the matchless power of Jesus the Messiah (cf. Luke 7:22) and the invitation for the poor and the lame to share in the blessings of the kingdom (Luke 14:13, 21).

Acts 9:36 introduces a disciple named Tabitha, who "was always doing good works and acts of charity" (*hautē ēn plērēs ergōn agathōn kai eleēmosynōn hōn epoiei*). These good works include making clothes for widows (Acts 9:39). Tabitha's miraculous healing not only offers great joy to the saints but leads to the advance of the word throughout Joppa, as "many believed in the Lord" (Acts 9:42).

Luke presents the centurion Cornelius as a devout man (*eusebēs*) who "did many charitable deeds" (*poiōn eleēmosynas pollas*) and constantly prayed to God (Acts 10:2). Employing Old Testament sacrificial imagery,[57] an angel calls Cornelius's prayers and almsgiving "a memorial offering before God" and directs him to send for Peter (Acts 10:4–5, 31–32). Barrett reasons that the centurion's piety and charity demonstrate that he "deserves" to receive the apostle's message.[58] More likely, God commends this Gentile's genuine faith expressed through pious generosity,[59] demonstrating that "in every nation the person who fears him and does what is right is acceptable to him" (Acts 10:35).

---

[56] Cf. *eleēmosynē* in Acts 3:2–3, 10; 9:36; 10:2, 4, 31; 24:17.

[57] Cf. Lev 6:8 (LXX); Luke Timothy Johnson, *The Acts of the Apostles*, SP 5 (Collegeville, MN: Liturgical, 1992), 183.

[58] C. K. Barrett, *Acts 1–14*, ICC (London: T&T Clark, 1994), 503.

[59] Peterson, *The Acts of the Apostles*, 328.

Paul also commends generosity and good works in his teaching and example in the book of Acts. He heals a lame man in Lystra (Acts 14:8–10) and various people in Malta (Acts 28:8–9), and he frees an enslaved woman in Philippi from a "spirit of divination" (Acts 16:16–18).[60] In his address to the Ephesian elders, the missionary recounts his blameless conduct throughout his time in Asia (Acts 20:18). Paul draws particular attention to his handling of money. Rather than coveting anyone's silver, gold, or clothing (Acts 20:33; cf. 1 Sam 12:3), he has labored to support himself and others, showing that "it is necessary to help the weak" in keeping with Christ's teaching: "It is more blessed to give than to receive" (Acts 20:34–35).[61]

While on trial before the governor Felix, Paul notes that he came to Jerusalem to "bring charitable gifts [*eleēmosynas*] and offerings" to his people (Acts 24:17). This is the only reference in Acts to the collection from churches in Macedonia and Achaia that Paul carried "for the poor among the saints in Jerusalem" (Rom 15:26),[62] though earlier Paul and Barnabas bring relief to the saints in Judea in response to the famine (Acts 11:27–30). Paul speaks with Felix about faith in Christ and commends "righteousness, self-control, and the judgment to come" (Acts 24:24–25). While Felix listens to Paul's gospel testimony, his teaching about morality in light of God's future judgment proves to be "the deal-breaker."[63] Paul not only expresses generosity towards his own people (Acts 24:17), he also refuses to pay a bribe to secure his own release (Acts 24:26). His financial dealings illustrate

---

[60] On Paul's encounter with the *pneuma pythōna* in Acts 16:16, see Scott D. MacDonald, "Rejecting Syncretism: Paul and the Python," *Themelios* 47, no. 2 (2022): 280–86.

[61] Paul's letters reflect similar emphases on work, money, and generosity to the weak (e.g., 1 Thess 2:5–10; 4:11; 5:14), as discussed by Steve Walton, *Leadership and Lifestyle: The Portrait of Paul in the Miletus Speech and 1 Thessalonians*, SNTSMS 108 (Cambridge: Cambridge University Press, 2000), 167–72.

[62] Cf. 1 Cor 16:1–4; 2 Cor 8:1–9:13; F. F. Bruce, *The Book of the Acts*, rev. ed., NICNT (Grand Rapids: Eerdmans, 1988), 445; Eckhard J. Schnabel, *Acts*, ZECNT (Grand Rapids: Zondervan, 2012), 454.

[63] Walton, "What Does 'Mission' in Acts Mean," 555.

his "clean conscience toward God and man" (Acts 24:16) and the consistency of his teaching and manner of life. However, Felix, a longtime "judge" (*kritēs*) in Israel (Acts 24:10), shows partiality and seeks personal gain while delaying justice for Paul (Acts 24:26–27). Felix thus resembles the unjust judge in Jesus's parable who does not fear God or respect people (Luke 18:2).[64]

Theological Formation and Implications

This chapter surveys how justice and mercy mark Jesus's teaching and activity as the long-awaited Messiah, who proclaims good news to the poor, seeks the lost, and brings near the kingdom of God. The book of Acts shows how the outpouring of the Holy Spirit and the spread of the gospel message form a new community of believers whose unity, charity, and good works reflect the reality that Jesus reigns as Lord over all and will usher in consummate justice. I close by offering brief theological reflections and pastoral implications related to (1) the relationship of gospel preaching and good works, (2) money and possessions as a window into our hearts, and (3) living in an unjust world while awaiting consummate justice.

Gospel Preaching and Good Works

Theologians and missiologists frequently discuss the priority and relationship of gospel proclamation and deeds of justice and mercy, which directly relates to *what* the mission of the church is and *how* to pursue that mission in our world.[65] Some writers emphasize the church's core responsibility to preach the good news and make disciples of all nations, reflecting the Lord's

---

[64] Beverly R. Gaventa, *The Acts of the Apostles*, ANTC (Nashville: Abingdon, 2003), 330.

[65] This paragraph draws on material from Tabb, *After Emmaus*, 212–14.

teaching in texts such as Matt 28:19–20 and Luke 24:47.[66] Others reason that the church's "mission" is much broader, including "all that God has called the church into existence for and all that God has sent the church into the world to do."[67] In this view, evangelism and teaching are essential responsibilities of the church but do not exhaust its "mission" in the world, which also includes engaging society through justice and compassionate service and stewarding God's creation.[68] Still others argue that the socioeconomic and political thrust of the church's witness *in* society takes precedence over preaching *to* the world.[69]

The ministry of the Lord Jesus reflects both the priority of preaching and the inseparability of the gospel message and good works. He announces the fulfillment of Isa 61:1–2 (Luke 4:17–21), which emphasizes preaching good news (*euangelisasthai*) and proclaiming forgiveness (*kēryxai . . . aphesin*). He also ministers to the poor, the oppressed, and the needy with deeds of mercy that confirm his messianic identity and signal the inbreaking of God's kingdom (Luke 7:20–23; 11:20). Likewise in Acts, miraculous healings and exorcisms demonstrate the saving power of Jesus and the Holy Spirit's presence among the disciples who courageously share the gospel (Acts 3:6; 4:10, 29–31; 16:16–18).

Luke's second volume focuses on the progress of the word and the growth of the church in Jerusalem, Judea and Samaria, and to the limits

---

[66] See, for example, Jonathan Leeman, "Soteriological Mission," in *Four Views on the Church's Mission*, ed. Jason S. Sexton, Counterpoints (Grand Rapids: Zondervan, 2017), 17–45. Leeman distinguishes between the organized church's narrow mission to *make* disciples and individual believers' broader mission to *be* disciples (41).

[67] Christopher J. H. Wright, "Participatory Mission," in *Four Views on the Church's Mission*, ed. Jason S. Sexton, Counterpoints (Grand Rapids: Zondervan, 2017), 91.

[68] See Wright, "Participatory Mission," 63–91.

[69] Amos Yong, *Mission after Pentecost: The Witness of the Spirit from Genesis to Revelation*, The Mission in Global Community (Grand Rapids: Baker Academic, 2019), 278.

of the known world as an outworking of Christ's promise in Acts 1:8 (cf. Acts 6:7; 9:31; 12:24; 19:20).[70] The word's power is displayed as people "turn from darkness to light" (Acts 26:18), as disciples "produce fruit consistent with repentance" (Luke 3:8), and as they show genuine love and sacrificial generosity towards those in and beyond their community (Acts 4:34; 11:29). As they bear witness to Christ's resurrection, the missionaries in Acts speak truth to those in powerful positions, including the proconsul Sergius Paulus (Acts 13:7), the governor Felix (Acts 24:24), and King Agrippa (Acts 26:27). Presumably, Paul appeals to Caesar in hopes of testifying about Christ to him also (Acts 25:11–12). Paul does not shy away from the ethical implications of the Christian message as he reasons with the governor about righteousness, self-control, and the judgment to come (Acts 24:25).

Luke-Acts challenges readers today to teach faithfully "the whole plan of God" (Acts 20:27) and participate in the advance of the word among all nations (Acts 1:8) while seeking to help the weak (Acts 20:35) and being content and generous with the resources we have (Acts 20:33–35). As Paul says, "You know . . . how I was with you the whole time" (Acts 20:18), so we should strive for Christ-honoring conduct in private and public that reflects our confession that Jesus is Lord of all (Acts 10:36).

Possessions and Our Relationship with God

The Lord teaches that it is impossible to serve both God and money (Luke 16:13) and explains that "where your treasure is, there your heart will be also" (Luke 12:34). Thus, people's orientation towards money and possessions reveals the true state of their hearts before God. Jesus warns

---

[70] The phrase "to the ends of the earth" (*heōs eschatou tēs gēs*) in Acts 1:8 "designates the farthest regions of the earth" and so "describes the geographical scope of the missionary assignment of the disciples," according to Eckhard J. Schnabel, *Early Christian Mission* (Downers Grove, IL: IVP, 2004), 1:373, 375.

against greedily taking what belongs to others (Luke 11:39 [*harpagē*]) and insatiably desiring an abundance of possessions (Luke 12:15 [*pleonexia*]). The parable of the rich farmer illustrates the folly of amassing treasure for oneself while being stingy toward God (Luke 12:21). The rich ruler refuses to heed Jesus's challenge to give away his earthly possessions to seek heavenly treasure, illustrating how difficult it is for the wealthy to enter the kingdom of God (Luke 18:22–25). Yet the rich tax collector Zacchaeus responds favorably to Jesus. By joyfully welcoming the Lord and using his wealth to make restitution to those he wronged and generously provide for the poor (Luke 19:8), Zacchaeus shows that Jesus—not money—is his master.

The book of Acts includes positive and negative examples of how people within and outside of the church approach money and possessions. Individuals like Barnabas, Tabitha, and Cornelius are commended for their acts of charity and good works (Acts 4:36–37; 9:36; 10:4), while Simon is rebuked for trying to use money to obtain spiritual power (Acts 8:20–23). Disciples in Ephesus demonstrate their singular commitment to the Lord Jesus by burning their valuable magic books (Acts 19:18–19), while unbelievers in Philippi and Ephesus strongly oppose missionaries because their message and activity threaten their profits from unjust and idolatrous practices (Acts 16:16–21; 19:23–27). The disciples in Jerusalem express their unity of heart and soul by sharing possessions with one another such that "there was no needy person," fulfilling the hopes of Deut 15:4 (Acts 4:32, 34). The believers in Antioch send aid to the Judean church during a serious food shortage (Acts 11:29–30), showing solidarity across geographic and ethnic lines and the active involvement of the whole community—not merely wealthy benefactors, as was typical in Greco-Roman society. In contrast, Ananias and Sapphira are condemned for their false generosity that amounts to lying to the Holy Spirit (Acts 5:3–4).

Thus, Luke and Acts teach that our use of money reveals our true priorities and values. The examples of the early church and the conversion of Zacchaeus reveal that giving to the poor and needy "does not dampen joy but rather enhances it."[71] Believers today should prayerfully take to heart Jesus's teaching: "It is more blessed to give than to receive" (Acts 20:35). Even the economically poor can engage in the blessing of generosity, as was the case with the Macedonian believers (2 Cor 8:1–4). More broadly, if we extend generosity beyond financial resources, every Christian, whatever their circumstances, can join in the blessing of generosity by being generous with their time, energy, and whatever other resources God may bring them.

Current Injustice and Coming Justice

Luke-Acts reflects the Bible's wider teaching that the people of God should seek justice and love mercy now while awaiting the consummate justice that God will bring at the end of history. The parable of the persistent widow and the unjust judge in Luke 18:1–8 reassures weary believers that we should not lose heart while praying and waiting for true justice. This parable reasons from the lesser to the greater: If an unjust judge can eventually be persuaded to give justice to a determined widow, surely God the righteous Judge will all the more listen to the saints' cries for justice. As Paul explains, God "has set a day when he is going to judge the world in righteousness by the man he has appointed"—the risen Lord Jesus (Acts 17:31).

Luke records examples of unjust judgments, including the baseless condemnation of Jesus though he was truly righteous (Luke 23:47; Acts 8:33; 13:27–28), the false charges leveled against Stephen (Acts 6:13), and Paul's mistreatment and unwarranted incarcerations (Acts 16:37; 23:1–3). While experiencing consummate injustice himself, Jesus prays for his enemies' forgiveness and entrusts his spirit to God's hands (Luke 23:34, 46; cf. Ps 31:5). While awaiting resolution of his legal proceedings, Paul refuses to compromise his gospel witness by paying a bribe (Acts 24:26). Rather, he faithfully testifies to Christ Jesus and does not shrink back from explaining

[71] Schreiner, *New Testament Theology*, 764.

the uncomfortable yet urgent ethical implications of God's word related to "righteousness, self-control, and the judgment to come" (Acts 24:25).

The Scriptures consistently affirm that God is the sovereign Judge over the world he created. While the wicked seem to prosper, the righteous suffer, and injustice seems to go unchecked, a day of reckoning is coming when God will intervene and establish lasting justice. Acts clarifies that the risen Lord Jesus will execute this divine justice (Acts 17:31), and the divine retribution against deceptive disciples (Acts 5:5, 10), the wicked king Herod (Acts 12:23), and a false prophet (Acts 13:11) preview the future judgment.[72] This future hope of perfect justice motivates believers to endure in expectant prayer, to persist in courageous gospel witness, and to align their lives with the values and standards of the kingdom of God.

Questions for Further Reflection

1. How does Luke 4:16–30 summarize and preview the Gospel's overall focus on who Jesus is and what he has come to do?
2. Reflect on the parable of the persistent widow in Luke 18:1–8. What does this parable teach us about how our future hopes should motivate our present action in response to injustice and adversity?
3. Compare Luke 18:1–8 with Acts 24:22–27. In what ways does the prisoner Paul resemble the widow in Jesus's parable? How is the governor Felix similar to the unjust judge?
4. Was the early church practicing a community of goods as they "held everything in common" (Acts 4:32)? In what ways do the accounts in Acts 2:42–47 and 4:32–37 reflect the unique experience of the first Christians, and in what ways might they inform the church's contemporary practices?

---

[72] See Brian J. Tabb, *Suffering in Ancient Worldview: Luke, Seneca, and 4 Maccabees in Dialogue*, LNTS 569 (London: T&T Clark, 2017), 191–93.

5. Consider Jesus's words in Acts 20:35—"It is more blessed to give than to receive." What are several specific examples in the Gospel of Luke and Acts that illustrate this teaching?
6. How do your personal financial practices and priorities align with Christ's teaching in Luke 12:34—"For where your treasure is, there your heart will be also"? What is one way that you hope to grow in your stewardship and generosity in the coming year?

Suggested Reading

Blomberg, Craig L. *Neither Poverty nor Riches: A Biblical Theology of Material Possessions*. NSBT 7. Downers Grove, IL: InterVarsity, 1999.

Bruno, Chris. "Jesus Is Our Jubilee . . . But How? The OT Background and Lukan Fulfillment of the Ethics of Jubilee." *JETS* 53, no. 1 (2010): 81–101.

Hays, J. Daniel. "'Sell Everything You Have and Give to the Poor': The Old Testament Prophetic Theme of Justice as the Connecting Motif of Luke 18:1–19:10." *JETS* 55, no. 1 (2012): 43–63.

Tabb, Brian J. "A Light for the Nations: Salvation and Mission in Luke." In *After Emmaus: How the Church Fulfills the Mission of Christ*, 83–105. Wheaton, IL: Crossway, 2021.

Walton, Steve. "What Does 'Mission' in Acts Mean in Relation to the 'Powers that Be'?" *JETS* 55, no. 3 (2012): 537–56.

5

Justice in James

— Christopher W. Morgan —

Introduction

James instructs oppressed believers in the Dispersion and along the way offers insights related to what is called "social justice."[1] James does not fit contemporary categories. He is neither a liberation theologian nor a social gospel advocate. He also has no patience for those who profess sound theology but do not reflect it in love for others, including the marginalized. While James had no intention of setting forth a complete conception of social justice, he does teach many principles that are important elements of such a system. Such elements include at least the covenantal context of the poor, the kingdom realignment of honor, the holistic nature of holiness, the law of impartial love, the social good of true faith, the comfort of coming

[1] This essay draws from my previous works on James, which exhibit more thorough exegesis, theology, and application: Christopher W. Morgan, "Integrated Spirituality: Spirituality according to James," in *Biblical Spirituality*, Theology in Community, ed. Christopher W. Morgan (Wheaton, IL: Crossway, 2019), 137–54; Christopher W. Morgan, *A Theology of James: Wisdom for God's People,* Explorations in Biblical Theology (Phillipsburg, NJ: P&R, 2010); Christopher W. Morgan and B. Dale Ellenburg, *James: Wisdom for the Community*, Focus on the Bible (Fearn, Ross-shire, UK: Christian Focus, 2008).

justice, the church's display of future wholeness, the integration of theology and praxis, and the theological ground of social justice.[2]

The Covenantal Context of the Poor

James stands in the traditions of the Old Testament and Jesus in his understanding of social justice as covenantal. Jeff Mooney helpfully clarifies:

> Discussions concerning justice typically and appropriately address necessary actions on behalf of a marginalized community. . . . [J]ustice, though not exclusively so, primarily appears in Scripture as an ecclesiological paradigm rooted in the person of God rather than a civic paradigm rooted in common humanity or citizenship. In other words, justice texts in the Scriptures primarily apply to covenant people regarding covenantal behavior.[3]

---

[2] Work remains in researching James on this topic, including how persecution promotes Christian maturity (Jas 1:2–11); God's blessings on those who persevere (1:12); the goodness of God and how he is neither the source of sin nor temptation (1:13–18); the importance of being quick to listen and slow to speak (1:19); the danger of anger and how it does not foster justice (1:19–21); God's word and how it brings freedom even to those who seem to be powerless (1:22–25); how persecution simultaneously oppresses Christians and blasphemes Jesus's name (2:6–7); the centrality of love and how it unites the entire law (2:8–11); the Jewish traditions concerning faith and mercy in the accounts of Abraham and Rahab (2:21–26); the power paradox: how wisdom and meekness in church leaders are keys for church unity and strength amidst oppression (3:1–18); the sovereignty of God over all of life (4:13–16); and how James urges the oppressed churches to respond with joy, perseverance, prayer, boasting, listening, care for those even more marginalized, edifying words, humility, hope, patience, and repentance (5:13–20).

[3] See D. Jeffrey Mooney's important and insightful contribution concerning the covenantal context of social justice: "Holiness and Justice: Who You Are Shapes What You Do," *Biblical Justice: Theology for the Unity of the Church*, ed. Benjamin Forrest and D. A. Horton (Grand Rapids: Kregel, forthcoming).

James writes in this covenantal context. He likewise follows the traditions of the Old Testament and Jesus in his literary use of the poor, who are not righteous because of their socioeconomic standing but through faith in God. The identity of the poor also may be linked with the exiled people of God (Isa 26:6; 49:13), who hope in God's ultimate eschatological vindication (Isa 49; 51; 54; 61).[4] This was true for Israel, the Qumran community, and likely James's recipients, the Christian covenant communities of the Dispersion.

In this particular historical and Jewish context, James stresses that God cares for the poor (Deut 10:18; Ps 68:5) and that God's people ought to protect them (Deut 10:19).[5] Kamell shows how in the Old Testament, the treatment of the poor is directly tied to concepts of justice (Exod 23:6; Lev 19:15; Deut 27:19; Isa 11:4; Jer 7:8–10).[6] McCartney adds:

> The notion of the community of faith being the poor has its roots in the Old Testament (cf. Ps. 86:1 where it is the poor who are deeply aware that they are dependent on God). The Qumran community also regarded itself as the community of the poor (1QH 2:5, 1QpHab 12:3, 6, 10, 4QpPs37 2:9; 3:10). It is precisely because the community is the poor that they deserve respect (James 2:1–7) and why dishonoring them is so contrary to true faith (2:6, an echo of Prov. 14:31, which declares dishonoring the poor man to be an insult to his Maker).[7]

---

[4] Roy E. Ciampa, "The History of Redemption," in *Central Themes of Biblical Theology: Mapping Unity in Diversity*, ed. Scott J. Hafemann and Paul R. House (Grand Rapids: Baker, 2007), 292–93n94.

[5] Liberation theology overlooks this context and tends to reduce Christianity to the defense of the oppressed.

[6] Mariam Kamell, "The Economics of Humility: The Rich and the Humble in James," in *Engaging Economics: New Testament Scenarios and Early Christian Reception*, ed. Bruce W. Longenecker and Kelly D. Liebengood (Grand Rapids: Eerdmans, 2009), 163.

[7] Dan G. McCartney, "Suffering in the Teaching of the Apostles," in *Suffering and the Goodness of God*, ed. Christopher W. Morgan and Robert A. Peterson, Theology in Community (Wheaton, IL: Crossway, 2008), 104.

How frequently James follows Jesus in this is striking: blessed are the poor and woe to the rich (Jas 1:9–10; Luke 6:20–24); the poor inherit the kingdom (Jas 2:5; Matt 5:3; Luke 6:20); being rich in faith toward God (Jas 2:5; Luke 12:21); the merciful receive mercy (Jas 2:13; Matt 5:7; 18:21–35); giving food and clothes to God's people as proofs of salvation (Jas 2:14–17; Matt 25:34–46); impending judgment of the rich/wicked (Jas 5:1–6; Luke 6:24–25); and accumulated possessions decayed by moths and corrosion (Jas 5:2–4; Matt 6:19–20).

In general, James refers to two groups of the poor. First are the severely poor, destitute of decent clothes and lacking daily food (Jas 2:14–17). Second are the working people of the land (akin to contemporary day laborers) who had very little but evidently enough to be responsible to help the severely poor. The people of the land comprised the majority in these churches, as well as the vast majority of the regional population.

James discloses the identity of the poor in several passages. In Jas 1:9–11, the poor are the oppressed covenant people of God who will find ultimate vindication in a future reversal. In 1:26–27, the widows and orphans are the especially vulnerable and marginalized in society. They include the covenant people of God and outsiders. James's reference to the widows and orphans reflects the Old Testament, particularly Exodus 22, Leviticus 19, Deuteronomy 10, Psalm 146, and Zechariah 7. Note that each of these passages also includes concern for aliens/sojourners (Exod 22:21–22; Lev 19:9–10; Deut 10:18–19; Ps 146:9; Zech 7:9–14). In Jas 2:1–7, the poor are the righteous people of God, who are destitute but chosen by God to be rich in faith, heirs of the kingdom, and recipients of the covenant promise extended to those who love God. In Jas 2:14–26, the poor are described as "brothers" and are obviously Christians. In Jas 5:1–6, the poor are described as the exploited day laborers, "righteous," and, in language reminiscent of God's people in Egypt (Exod 3:7), as those who will be avenged by God.

James also reveals the identity of the poor through his contrasts of these believers with the rich. The rich are not simply those with financial abundance but are characterized as proud (Jas 1:9–11) and meriting eschatological humiliation (Jas 1:9–11). The rich are the oppressors, defrauders, and persecutors of believers (Jas 2:5–7; 5:1–6), even blasphemers of Christ (Jas 2:7). The rich in James are wicked, and they will be severely punished by the just God (Jas 5:1–6).[8]

James primarily stresses God's concern for his oppressed covenant people and how the church is to embody that same concern. While James's teachings about social justice focus primarily on God's people, Jas 1:26–27 shows that love, mercy, and justice should extend to all. God's people are to reflect God's love for all. God's people are to "work for the good of all, especially for those who belong to the household of faith" (Gal 6:10). As they do, they display God's goodness and showcase God's kingdom: "The church is the community that anticipates the eschatological reversal by caring for and respecting the poor . . . [P]artiality belies the eschatological nature of the community, which ought to display in advance God's exaltation of the poor."[9] When the church does so, it participates in kingdom work.

The Kingdom Realignment of Honor

James 1:9–11 teaches poverty-stricken believers that being righteous and exploited is far better than being the wicked exploiters. James here echoes a reversal theme often taught by Jesus (cf. Luke 6:20–26). But notice that this reversal is not merely eschatological. On first glance, many read the passage as saying that the poor, humble believer will one day be exalted and that the proud, rich oppressor will one day be humbled. While no doubt true theologically, James claims more than this. Notice that the "brother of humble circumstances" should "boast in his exaltation" (Jas 1:9). The lowly brother sits at the bottom of the pecking order. He is undistinguished in position, power, and esteem. Or so it seems! But James redefines honor. He

[8] Duane Warden, "The Rich and Poor in James: Implications for Institutionalized Partiality," *JETS* 43, no. 2 (2000): 247–57.

[9] McCartney, "Suffering in the Teaching of the Apostles," 107.

radically asserts that the humble brother is really exalted—exalted in Christ. The oppressed Christian has reason for boasting! He can celebrate not only his future exaltation, but also his present honor in Christ. The poor man already has kingdom honor.

In contrast, the rich should boast in their humiliation (Jas 1:10). The rich (not just the riches) pass away like dried up wildflowers on a scorching, windy day. Indeed, the rich will "wither away while pursuing his activities" (Jas 1:11). Humiliation is both appropriate now and coming soon.

Honor is not about power, class, or money. Honor is about knowing God and walking with God. Those dishonoring others do not possess true honor but shame. Those being dishonored for Christ are not marked by shame but true honor. For the people of God experiencing injustice, this kingdom honor is reason for boasting. In addition, kingdom honor is linked to holiness, as James shows.

The Holistic Nature of Holiness

James 1:26–27 follows the argument in vv. 19–25 where James teaches that biblical faith is more than hearing the Word but actually living it. This means self-control over words (Jas 1:26), loving the marginalized and vulnerable (Jas 1:27), and living in holiness (Jas 1:27). Such faith is "pure and undefiled," and it is acceptable to God. James contrasts this with the pseudo-spirituality of some, whose so-called worship is unclean, defiled, and utterly unacceptable to the holy God. By referring to true religion as keeping oneself "unstained from the world" (Jas 1:27), he critiques their ceremonial cleanness that lacks the more central ethical cleanness. He debunks their worship as "useless," in part since it does not bless others in need.

So James brings them back to the Old Testament and shows how holiness and love for others are inextricably interwoven. He frequently alludes to Leviticus 19, taking his audience back to study the very law they claim to be defending.[10] Leviticus 19:2 declares, "Be holy, because I, the LORD your God, am holy." In what ways was Israel to be holy? Christopher Wright comments:

> We are inclined to think of "holiness" as a matter of personal piety or, in Old Testament terms, of ritual cleanness, proper sacrifices, clean and unclean foods, and the like. Certainly, the rest of Leviticus 19 includes some of these dimensions of Israel's religious life. But the bulk of the chapter shows us that the kind of holiness that reflects God's own holiness is thoroughly practical. It includes generosity to the poor at harvest time, justice for workers, integrity in judicial processes, considerate behaviour to other people (especially the disabled), equality before the law for immigrants, honest trading and other very "earthy" social matters. And all throughout the chapters runs the refrain "I am the LORD," as if to say, "*Your* quality of life must reflect the very heart of *my* character. This is what I require of *you* because this is what reflects *me*."[11]

James likewise underlines how holiness is necessarily covenantal, holistic, and practical. He further exhorts the churches "to look after orphans and widows in their distress" (Jas 1:27), applying the principles of holiness and love in Leviticus 19 as well as other key holiness texts:

> "You must not mistreat any widow or fatherless child." (Exod 22:22)

> "Learn to do what is good. Pursue justice. Correct the oppressor. Defend the rights of the fatherless. Plead the widow's cause." (Isa 1:17)

---

[10] Luke Timothy Johnson, "The Use of Leviticus 19 in the Letter of James," *JBL* 101, no. 3 (1982): 391–402.

[11] Christopher J. H. Wright, *Old Testament Ethics for the People of God* (Downers Grove, IL: IVP Academic, 2004), 39. Italics original.

Together widows and orphans represent those without protection or provision. Ben Witherington III observes, "Our discourse is about a God who is impartial, faithful, righteous, just, merciful—and who requires of his followers the same sort of behavior."[12] Only such holistic holiness is acceptable religion and worship (cf. Deut 10:16–19; Ps 69:32–33; Isa 1:10–17; Zech 7:9–14; Rom 12:1–2). Further, this holiness follows the law of impartial love.

The Law of Impartial Love

James 2:1–13 highlights how God chose "the poor in this world to be rich in faith and heirs of the kingdom that he has promised to those who love him" (Jas 2:5). God's election is gracious and leads to an abundance of blessings. The world rejects them, but God has chosen them. They live on daily wages, but they are rich in faith. They lack material possessions, but they are heirs in Christ. They are marginalized by the oppressors, but they love God and have his covenantal promise. Just like we saw in Jas 1:9–11, they have kingdom honor!

Yet these believers are not living according to these kingdom values. They are not showing this honor to the extremely poor (Jas 2:6). Ridiculously, they are showing partiality to the rich who are exploiting them. James exposes their hypocrisy through an anecdote of two guests coming to church. The first guest is rich, "wearing a gold ring and dressed in fine clothes" (2:2). The second guest is poor, "dressed in filthy clothes" (2:2). Who gets better treatment? The rich person receives the red-carpet treatment, and is even invited to sit in a place of honor (cf. Matt 23:6). The poor person is marginalized and told, "Stand over there," or "Sit here on

---

[12] Ben Witherington III, *Letters and Homilies for Jewish Christians: A Socio-Rhetorical Commentary on Hebrews, James and Jude* (Downers Grove, IL: IVP Academic, 2007), 436.

the floor by my footstool" (v. 3). The rich person is honored, and the poor person is devalued as a social disgrace.

James accuses these believers of prejudice, judging, and making distinctions (Jas 2:4). He then charges them: "you have dishonored the poor" (Jas 2:6). Instead of honoring their spiritual sibling whom God has chosen, they shamed him. James then rhetorically shows the absurdity of the prejudice. They honored the rich, but the rich exploited them and dragged them into court (Jas 2:6). Even worse, these rich were wicked, blaspheming the name of Jesus.[13] The honor must go toward the poor, as Dan McCartney clarifies:

> The church is the community that anticipates the eschatological reversal by caring for and respecting the poor. Therefore James has little tolerance for those who show favoritism to the rich. This kind of favoritism is offensive first because it violates the law of love and misrepresents the character of God, who cares about the poor. Note that the context of the law of love in Leviticus 19 specifically condemns partiality (Lev 19:15). Second, partiality belies the eschatological nature of the community, which ought to display in advance God's exaltation of the poor. James 2:1–17 thus teaches us that faithful living does not just pity the poor, it *respects* the poor. This is a difficult concept for most of us who are not poor, especially because suffering, poverty and destitution can make a person appear repulsive, which in turn has the effect of increasing that person's suffering.[14]

Verses 8–13 expand on the importance of impartiality, linking it directly with love: "Love your neighbor as yourself" (Jas 2:8; cf. Lev 19:18).

---

[13] Andrew Chester and Ralph P. Martin, *The Theology of the Letters of James, Peter, and Jude*, New Testament Theology (New York: Cambridge University Press, 1994), 33.

[14] McCartney, "Suffering in the Teaching of the Apostles," 107, emphasis original.

Leviticus 19 calls for love for the poor, oppressed, deaf, blind, sojourner, servants, women, and elderly. Prejudice against the poor is contrary to the royal law of love and is sin (Jas 2:9). James reminds listeners that whoever fastidiously "keeps the entire law, and yet stumbles at one point, is guilty of breaking it all" (Jas 2:10). The law is a unity, and the royal law of love is central to it. Love fulfills the law, esteems others, and exposes the hypocrisy of partiality. Such love springs from authentic faith.

The Social Good of True Faith

The classic passage Jas 2:14–26 begins by asking: "What good is it, my brothers and sisters, if someone claims to have faith but does not have works? Can such faith save him?" (Jas 2:14). James probes, "What good is it?" He raises the question here and in v. 16 to show how such so-called faith is "useless" (Jas 2:20). A faith without love is good for nothing. It will not justify the sinner and never gets around to helping the needy.

James explains this in Jas 2:15–16 by telling another story. He pictures fellow believers in desperate need, lacking the basics of life in food and clothes.[15] Instead of receiving practical help from their fellow believers, they are offered a blessing, "Go in peace, stay warm, and be well fed" (Jas 2:16). "Go in peace" is a common Jewish farewell—*shalom* (cf. Judg 18:6; 1 Sam 1:17; 20:42; 2 Sam 15:9). Today it would be like saying, "Good-bye and God bless you." Instead of food and clothes, they only get religious clichés. Words of peace are given, but practical needs of life are left unmet. How can they go in peace when in reality they will go hungry and cold?[16]

---

[15] Kamell helpfully observes that James relates similar themes and the same two illustrations as Deut 10:17–18: "For the Lord your God is the God of the gods and Lord of lords, the great, mighty, and awe-inspiring God, showing no partiality and taking no bribe. He executes justice for the fatherless and the widow, and loves the resident alien, giving him food and clothing." See Kamell, "The Economics of Humility," 165.

[16] I owe these questions to Dale Ellenburg.

How can these supposed believers think they are following Christ when they prize their possessions more than they value their impoverished fellow believers?

James then sets forth his assertion, "In the same way faith, if it does not have works, is dead by itself" (Jas 2:17). He then raises a potential objection, "But someone will say, 'You have faith, and I have works'" (Jas 2:18). He answers, "Show me your faith without works, and I will show you faith by my works" (Jas 2:18). James spotlights how they love to quote the beginning of the *Shema* ("God is one" in Jas 2:19; cf. Deut 6:4) but fail to carry out its inherent requirement: "Love the Lord your God with all your heart, with all your soul, and with all your strength" (Deut 6:5). James taunts: "Good! Even the demons believe—and they shudder!" (Jas 2:19). How ridiculous to claim the faith taught in Deut 6:4 without displaying the corollary of love commanded in v. 5! Such faith is a sham. Real faith in God shines in tangible love for others.

As examples of real faith and love, James points to Abraham and Rahab—a Jew and a Gentile, a patriarch and a prostitute.[17] In his example of Abraham, James shows that faith is displayed by works (Jas 2:21), is "active together with his works" (Jas 2:22), is completed by works (Jas 2:22), and results in his being credited as righteous (Jas 2:23). John Calvin observed, "Faith alone justifies, but faith that justifies is never alone."[18] In the example of Rahab, James establishes the same assertion (Jas 2:25). Regardless of her previous role as a prostitute, Rahab became a heroine of faith in Jewish tradition after she protected Jewish spies (cf. Josh 2:11; Heb 11:31). Rahab's works of mercy demonstrated her true faith.[19]

---

[17] Mark Proctor, "Faith, Works, and the Christian Religion in James 2:14–26," *EQ* 69, no. 4 (1997): 322–31.

[18] John Calvin, *Commentaries on the Catholic Epistles*, trans. John Owen, Calvin's Commentaries (repr., Grand Rapids: Baker, 1979), 309.

[19] This section is especially informed by my previous coauthor Dale Ellenburg as well as by Richard Bauckham, *James: Wisdom of James, Disciple of Jesus the Sage* (London: Routledge, 1999).

In Jas 2:26, James wraps up his argument, "For just as the body without the spirit is dead, so also faith without works is dead." The old maxim claims that Christians are so heavenly minded they are no earthly good. James would probably agree that this is true for pseudo-Christians. He, however, argues the contrary about true Christians. True faith in Christ leads to much social good because faith works, faith loves, faith shows mercy. Genuine faith also looks to the future and the coming of God's justice that brings comfort now.

The Comfort of Coming Justice

According to Jas 5:1–6, while justice is often intermingled with injustice now, ultimately justice will prevail. With the passion and directness of an Old Testament prophet, James scolds the rich who are subjugating God's people. The exploiters should presently "weep and wail over the miseries that are coming on" them (Jas 5:1). The "corrosion" of their gold and silver will testify against them at the judgment. The pay that they "withheld from the workers" is crying out. The wicked landowners have more than enough money to pay the workers, but all that wealth just sits corroding. This form of greed, fraud, corruption, and exploitation was all too common, and many passages denounce it (Lev 19:13; Deut 24:14–15; Jer 22:13; Mal 3:5).[20]

James vividly depicts the withheld wages crying out. He then portrays the "outcry of the harvesters" (Jas 5:4). Who hears these cries? The cries are not heard by the evil landowners who are preoccupied with living "luxuriously" in self-indulgence (Jas 5:5). The cries are not heard by the crooked political and judicial leaders whom the rich control (Jas 5:6; cf. 2:1–7).[21]

---

[20] Alec Motyer, *The Message of James,* Bible Speaks Today (Downers Grove, IL: InterVarsity, 1985), 177. James's teaching again reflects Leviticus 19.

[21] Douglas J. Moo, *The Letter of James,* PNTC (Grand Rapids: Eerdmans, 2000), 54.

Is anyone with power to help listening? Does anyone hear their cries? James replies that cries have reached the ears of God himself, "the Lord of Armies" (Jas 5:4).[22]

The portrayal of God as "the Lord of Armies" (or "Lord of hosts") pictures God as a warrior leading an army of warriors to triumph over evil and promote justice. Douglas J. Moo observes, "Sometimes this army is an earthly one. . . . More often it is the heavenly host that God is pictured as leading."[23] It stresses that God has infinite power, far more power than anyone who is mistreating his people. So the covenant Lord (Jas 5:11) is also the God of unlimited power, and he presently hears the cries of his oppressed people.

In due time, the Lord will come, punishing the oppressors and vindicating his people. Injustice is all too real and painful now. But injustice has an expiration date. James explains that "the Lord's coming is near" (Jas 5:8), and when he comes, evil loses, God wins, and justice prevails. These realities are comforting to God's oppressed people. Ben Skaug helpfully explains: "In response to God's promise to bring vindication, the righteous poor can take comfort in knowing that God will carry out his justice. They can be encouraged that their God has not allowed the wicked to live without punishment for their crimes."[24] God will judge the evildoers; the certainty of his coming judgment leads believers to combine faith and practice.

---

[22] Luke Timothy Johnson, *The Letter of James: A New Translation with Introduction and Commentary*, Anchor Bible 37A (New York: Doubleday, 1995), 302: "Here James definitely evokes the experience of Israel in Egypt. At the burning bush Yahweh says to Moses, 'I have seen the affliction of my people in Egypt and I have heard their shouts (Exod. 3:7).'"

[23] Moo, *The Letter of James*, 216–17.

[24] Benjamin Michael Skaug, "The Doctrine of Hell as It Functions as a Means of Comfort for the Persecuted People of God in the New Testament" (PhD diss., Gateway Seminary, 2020), 123.

The Church's Display of Future Wholeness

Obviously, the church is not yet all that God intended it to be. It still struggles with inconsistency, division, sin, pride, and even hypocrisy. James would not have needed to write his letter if otherwise. Yet the church is massively important.

> The church is the eschatological covenant community that exists in the already and not yet and displays even if imperfectly the arrival of the kingdom through its relationships to God, with one another, and to society. Longing for the final arrival of the kingdom, the church, as the people of Jesus, together pursues and fosters wholeness. The church is an eschatological, covenantal, worshipping community of believers, created and shaped by the word, where the truth is taught, church leaders exemplify shalom, love for one another is genuine, mercy to the poor is displayed, mutuality and accountability are evident, and the restoration of wanderers is sought. It is God's new creation, exemplifying the arrival of the kingdom as the firstfruits of the way things should and will be (1:18). As the church displays the way of the kingdom, it pleases God as acceptable and pure (1:26–27), and it shines as a light to the world, as a blessing to the nations.[25]

The church lives in the already and not yet of God's grace. Therefore, it partially displays love, shalom, and justice.

The Integration of Theology and Praxis

James views truth holistically, as David Scaer astutely observes: "James's theological and literary genius and uniqueness lie in his ability to blend

---

[25] Morgan, *Theology of James*, 189. See also xiii–xviii, 7–10, 14–18, 40–43, 99–109, 160–64.

theology into the immediate application. He does not first have to lay down theological principles from which he draws applications."[26]

James's integrated holistic approach does not neatly fit into contemporary polarizations. In fact, James's integrated approach corrects such false dichotomies. Many evangelicals today have a tendency to separate such things as love for God and love for others, faith and works, evangelism and social ministry, and theology and practice. In contrast, James sees these truths as united. Love for God is most clearly demonstrated in love for others. Faith in Christ is made visible through works of mercy. A real burden for someone's salvation inescapably also desires their overall good—spiritually, physically, emotionally, and materially. Such integrated thinking characterizes James. Tim Keller captures the importance of this for today's church:

> Jesus calls Christians to be "witnesses," to evangelize others, but also to be deeply concerned for the poor. He calls his disciples *both* to "gospel-messaging" (urging everyone to believe the gospel) *and* to "gospel-neighboring" (sacrificially meeting the needs of those around them, whether they believe or not!). The two absolutely go together. (1) They go together theologically. The resurrection shows us that God not only *created both* body and spirit but will also *redeem* both body and spirit. The salvation Jesus will eventually bring in its fullness will include liberation from *all* the effects of sin—not only spiritual but physical and material as well. Jesus came both preaching the Word and healing and feeding. (2) They go together practically. We must be ever wary of collapsing evangelism into deed ministry as the social gospel did, but loving deeds are an irreplaceable witness to the power and nature of God's grace, an irreplaceable testimony to the truth of the gospel.[27]

---

[26] David P. Scaer, *James: The Apostle of Faith: A Primary Christological Epistle for the Persecuted Church* (St. Louis: Concordia, 1994), 60.

[27] Tim Keller, "The Gospel and the Poor," *Themelios* 33, no. 3 (2008): 18. Emphasis original.

The church unites theology and praxis in the present and longs for wholeness in the future at Christ's second advent.

The Theological Ground of Social Justice

For James, social justice is firmly grounded in the doctrine of God. James bases many of his ethical exhortations on his theology proper.[28] In doing so, he reflects the Old Testament. Wright notes:

> What shape, then, should Israel's response take? What was to be the substance and quality of their ethical behavior? Here again, the answer is thoroughly theological: nothing less than the reflection of the character of God. . . . That is why *knowing God* is such an important theme in the Old Testament. It means more than just what God has done (the stories), or knowing what God has said (the teachings). It means knowing the LORD in person, as a living character; knowing what his values, concerns and priorities are; knowing what brings him joy or makes him angry. And that in turn will mean living in the light of such knowledge.[29]

In Jas 1:26–27, James states that pure and undefiled religion that God accepts looks after orphans and widows in their distress. On what basis does James call for this? God himself, who "in his holy dwelling is a father of the fatherless and a champion of widows" (Ps 68:5). Just as God defends and

---

[28] Many other Old Testament texts to which James alludes, besides Leviticus 19, ground commands in the doctrine of God. James 1:26–27, like Ps 68:5, Exod 22:22, and Isa 1:10–17, point to God's concern for and the necessity of Israel's concern for the widow and orphan. James 2:1–13 and texts like Leviticus 19 urge the loving treatment of others, especially the poor and marginalized, because of the nature of God. James 5:1–11 again reflects Leviticus 19 as it warns against withholding wages from day laborers because of God's concern for the oppressed. James 5:11 quotes Exod 34:6 to promote perseverance in the midst of adversity by reminding of the covenant faithfulness of God.

[29] Wright, *Old Testament Ethics for the People of God*, 36. Emphasis original.

cares for the widows and fatherless, so must his people. The powerless must not be subjected to abuse but protected.[30] Daniel Doriani notes: "Kindness to the needy is God-like. *We* sustain aliens, widows, and orphans because *he* sustains aliens, widows, and orphans (Ps. 146:9)."[31]

In Jas 2:1–7, James urges believers not to show favoritism toward the rich and against the poor. It rebukes those who give the red-carpet treatment to the rich but disregard the poor. While James sets forth multiple reasons for not showing partiality, a primary one is that God chose the poor to be rich in faith and inherit the kingdom. God chose the poor, so why would God's people neglect or reject them? Moo explains: "God, the NT suggests, delights especially to shower his grace on those whom the world has discarded and on those most keenly aware of their own inadequacy. James calls on the church to embody a similar ethic of special concern for the poor and the helpless."[32]

In Jas 5:1–11, James points to the divine judgment coming upon wicked landowners. He then encourages God's people to be patient and stand firm. On what basis does he make this appeal? On the nature of God, who both hears the cries of his people and will do battle against evil with unstoppable power.[33] James then warns them not to grumble against each other. Why? Because "the judge stands at the door!" (Jas 5:9). He then urges them to persevere in the midst of their suffering. Why? Because "the Lord is compassionate and merciful" (Jas 5:11). Here James recalls Exod 34:6: "The Lord—the Lord is a compassionate and gracious God, slow to anger and abounding in faithful love and truth." So in Jas 5:1–11, he urges the people to persevere because of who God is and what God does: The Lord is near; he

---

[30] Robert W. Wall, *Community of the Wise: The Letter of James*, New Testament in Context (Valley Forge, PA: Trinity Press International, 1997), 99.

[31] Daniel M. Doriani, *James*, Reformed Expository Commentary (Phillipsburg, NJ: P&R, 2007), 59. Emphasis original.

[32] Moo, *The Letter of James*, 108. Cf. Chester and Martin, *The Theology of the Letters of James, Peter, and Jude*, 33–34.

[33] Wall, *Community of the Wise*, 231–32.

knows the plight of his people; he is a mighty warrior who punishes evil; he is coming soon to deliver his people and to judge the world; and he abounds in love and is faithfully committed to his covenant people.[34]

Conclusion

Although not intending to construct an overall approach to social justice, James contributes significant elements. James's approach is characterized by the covenantal context of the poor, the kingdom realignment of honor, the holistic nature of holiness, the law of impartial love, the social good of true faith, the comfort of coming justice, the church's display of future wholeness, the integration of theology and praxis, and the theological ground of social justice. A faithful Christian theology and praxis of social justice will necessarily incorporate James's guidance.

Questions for Further Reflection

1. Who are the poor in James's letter?
2. How does James redefine honor, and how does that give us hope?
3. According to Jas 2:1–13, what is the relationship between love and justice?
4. How does James's teaching on final judgment comfort believers?
5. Since the church displays future wholeness, what are tangible ways we can portray love and justice today?

Suggested Reading

Johnson, Luke Timothy. "The Use of Leviticus 19 in the Letter of James." *JBL* 101 no. 3 (1982): 391–402.

[34] Wall, *Community of the Wise*, 184.

Moo, Douglas J. *The Letter of James*. PNTC. Grand Rapids: Eerdmans, 2000.

Mooney, D. Jeffrey. "Holiness and Justice: Who You Are Shapes What You Do." In *Biblical Justice: Theology for the Unity of the Church*, edited by Benjamin Forrest and D. A. Horton. Grand Rapids: Kregel, forthcoming.

Morgan, Christopher W. "Integrated Spirituality: Spirituality according to James." In *Biblical Spirituality*. Theology in Community, edited by Christopher W. Morgan, 137–54. Wheaton, IL: Crossway, 2019.

———. *The Theology of James: Wisdom for God's People*. Explorations in Biblical Theology. Phillipsburg, NJ: P&R, 2010.

Morgan, Christopher W. and B. Dale Ellenburg. *James: Wisdom for the Community*. Focus on the Bible. Fearn, Ross-shire, UK: Christian Focus, 2008.

6

Justice in the New Covenant

— Joshua M. Greever —

Introduction

This chapter contends that Christ fulfills the scriptural mandate for justice and righteousness through his inauguration of the new covenant, and that therefore the church as the new covenant community is and should be the place where biblical justice and righteousness appear. In light of the fact that the new covenant is not yet consummated, the church must be vigilant against propagating injustice and should continue to pray for Christ's return, who will on that day usher in ultimate justice and righteousness. Thus, in the biblical metanarrative the restoration of lasting justice among humanity comes to fruition with the first and second advents of Christ.

In order to demonstrate this thesis, this chapter will analyze texts in both the Old Testament and New Testament, with a view to interpreting biblical texts from across the canon in light of progressive revelation and the biblical metanarrative. As a result, the analysis of individual texts is necessarily brief, for the focus is drawing from a wide breadth of texts that shed light on the biblical framework for the problem of injustice and its proper solution in the arrival of the Messiah. The chapter will conclude with a section on theological formulation and implications drawn from this study for the notion of justice, its relationship to the gospel, and the mission of the church.

Biblical Texts and Exegesis

This section will explore the twofold Old Testament problem of injustice, how the Old Testament presents the new covenant as answering this twofold problem, and how the New Testament identifies Jesus as the fulfillment of the Old Testament hope.

The Twofold Problem of Injustice in the Old Testament

According to the Old Testament, injustice is present and rampant within humanity for two reasons. First, the root of injustice lies deep within the human heart and is pervasive and has its way in human behavior. Second, in the Old Testament, there was no one—whether from Israel or the nations—who was able to overcome the problem of sin and deliver humanity from their injustices.

Sin Deep and Pervasive in the Human Heart

When God created Adam and Eve in the garden of Eden, he made them in his image, and they were to treat one another and God's creation in right ways—that is, with justice and righteousness. But when they rebelled against God, they and all humanity with them exchanged God's justice and righteousness for human injustice. The problem was not outside of themselves but within, for they lost both the ability to perceive genuine justice and the desire to carry it out. Immediately after the fall in Genesis 3, we see the injustice of fratricide (Gen 4:8) and the injustice of a violent and domineering husband, Lamech, who misperceived and misapplied divine retributive justice (Gen 4:23–24; cf. 4:15).[1] Such injustice found full expression in the flood generation when we see "that human wickedness was widespread on the earth and that every inclination of the human mind was nothing but evil all the time" (Gen 6:5). After the flood Ham, Noah's son, committed injustice towards his parents (Gen 9:22), showing that the new start with Noah and his family was not going to suffice for the return of Edenic justice and righteousness.

The pervasiveness and universality of humanity's problem of injustice is well-attested throughout the Old Testament. For example, Ecclesiastes says "don't be astonished at the situation" when there appears a "perversion of justice and righteousness" at every level of leadership, even up to the king himself (Eccl 5:8–9 [MT 5:7–8]).[2] Even in places where one would expect the righteous administration of justice, "there is wickedness" (Eccl 3:16), an indicator of the hopelessness of finding divine justice anywhere on earth (cf. Eccl 7:20).[3]

Indeed, throughout the Old Testament the nations consistently misperceive divine justice and commit injustice. For instance, when Israel wanted a king like the nations, God warned Israel that the kings of the nations have "customary rights" (*mišpāṭ*, 1 Sam 8:9). The king's *mišpāṭ*—his self-determined standard of kingly conduct, over and against Yahweh's *mišpāṭ*—would include the enforcement of servitude from the people and the exactment from them of the best of their possessions (1 Sam 8:10–17). Similarly, when Israel was sent into exile by Assyria,

---

[1] The term Lamech uses for "avenge" (*nqm*) also occurs in Yahweh's promise of retributive justice in Gen 4:15. It shares a semantic domain with other justice terminology and can be used positively to refer to the enactment of retributive justice (e.g., Exod 21:20; Deut 32:43; Nah 1:2).

[2] Franz Delitzsch, *Commentary on the Song of Songs and Ecclesiastes*, trans. M. G. Easton (repr., Grand Rapids: Eerdmans, 1975), 291–93.

[3] Tremper Longman III, *The Book of Ecclesiastes*, NICOT (Grand Rapids: Eerdmans, 1998), 126–27.

Assyria repopulated the land with people from the nations who did not know "the requirements [*mišpāṭ*] of the god of the land" (2 Kgs 17:26). Instead, they acted "according to the practice [*mišpāṭ*] of the nations" (2 Kgs 17:33), which included the evil of idolatry and child sacrifice (2 Kgs 17:29–31). In the time of Habakkuk, the Chaldeans were no different in their injustices, for they were "fierce and terrifying" since "their views of justice [*mišpāṭ*] and sovereignty stem from themselves" (Hab 1:7). So-called Chaldean justice was culturally determined, originating from themselves, and thus did not at all approximate true divine justice.[4] Finally, in a penetrating critique at the time of Judah's exile, God chides Jerusalem for failing to uphold not only Yahweh's "ordinances" (*mišpāṭîm*) but even the "ordinances" (*mišpāṭîm*) of the nations (Ezek 5:7). The Old Testament consistently presents the nations as places of injustice, with injustice occurring at every level of society. Because of the deep-rootedness of sin in the human heart, its manifestation in injustices is pervasive and widespread.

Israel's experience with injustice should have been different from the nations, for unlike the nations Israel received greater revelation of divine justice through the giving of the law at Sinai. Indeed, the just and righteous character of the Sinai legislation is clear. It is often called *mishpatîm*—commonly rendered as "ordinances" (CSB, NASB), "rules" (ESV), "laws" (NIV), or "judgments" (KJV)[5]—and refers to the divine judicial standards or regulations by which Israel should live.[6] Along with the label "statutes" (*chûqqîm*), the term *mišpāṭîm* appears at various section divisions within the legislation to highlight the justice of the specific stipulations of the covenant (e.g., Exod 21:1; Lev 19:37; Deut 4:1; 12:1). Moreover, various legislative

---

[4] Michael B. Shepherd, *A Commentary on the Book of the Twelve: The Minor Prophets*, Kregel Exegetical Library (Grand Rapids: Kregel Academic, 2018), 318.

[5] Cf. Exod 21:1; 24:3; Lev 18:4–5; 26:15; Num 36:13; Deut 4:1; 12:1.

[6] According to BDB, the term can refer to an "ordinance promulgated by *šōpēṭ* [judge]" and a "decision of the *šōpēṭ* [judge] in a case of law."

texts in the Sinai covenant call for justice within Israel. Broadly, this meant that each Israelite was called to a right treatment of another person based on a right discernment of what that person deserved or was owed. Narrowly, in the law court this meant that Israel's judges needed to mete out verdicts based on a right perception or discernment of legal cases. Judicial impartiality was based on truthful speech and behavior throughout the entire legal process, so judges were warned against receiving bribes and false accusations (Exod 23:1–9; Deut 16:18–20).[7] Similarly, in the marketplace business dealings needed to be done with honesty and fairness by utilizing equal weights and measures so as not to defraud and cheat one another (Lev 19:35–36; Deut 25:13–16). Hence, the Sinai legislation clarified both the divine standard of justice and the necessary means by which it must be enacted. It was meant to correct any misperception of justice and to warn against its miscarriage by calling for a commitment to truthfulness and faithfulness to one another in a covenant framework.

Nevertheless, despite Israel's reception of the law, their experience highlights the depth and pervasiveness of sin, for Israel still rejected knowledge of God's just ways and consistently promulgated injustice. Instead of rejecting bribes, Israel's judges "turned toward dishonest profit, took bribes, and perverted justice" (1 Sam 8:3), as did Israel's prophets and priests (Jer 6:13; 8:10; Mic 3:11). Those in the marketplace used unjust weights and measures because of their intent to deal dishonestly (Amos 8:5–6; Mic 6:11–12). Even more, the problem of injustice was not committed only by the rich and powerful within Israel but by everyone in the covenant community. "No one makes claims justly [*tsedeq*]" (Isa 59:4), and "there is no justice [*mišpāṭ*] in their ways" (Isa 59:8). Instead, "justice [*mišpāṭ*] is far from us" (Isa 59:9; see 59:11, 14). Jeremiah notes, "For from the least to the greatest of them,

---

[7] Israel's judges were to give special attention to justice for the poor, for the poor were the most vulnerable to the use of bribes against them (Exod 23:6, 8). At the same time, the judge was not to grant preferential treatment to the poor simply because of their poverty (Exod 23:3; cf. Lev 19:15).

everyone is making profit dishonestly" (Jer 6:13; cf. 8:10).[8] The phrase "from the least to the greatest of them" refers not simply to Israel's leadership but to every kind of Israelite in the community, including children, young men, husbands, wives, and the elderly (see Jer 6:11).[9] Accordingly, God's judgment will fall on all those who, "from the least to the greatest," rejected God's warning through Jeremiah not to flee to Egypt for safety and protection (Jer 44:12; cf. 42:1, 8). Israel should have been different from the nations, for they knew the justice of God, having been redeemed from Egypt and given the Sinai legislation. But their experience matched that of the nations, for they failed to internalize the law and obey it from the heart. Their sin of injustice was rooted in a failure to know and love God and his ways from the heart. And Israel lacked a commitment to be faithful and act truthfully towards their fellow Israelites. Therefore, the solution for Israel's injustice—and that of the nations—was a right and true knowledge of God, from which would flow a right treatment of one another.

The Absence of a Just King

The other problem leading to humanity's promulgation of injustice was the lack of a righteous and just king. This point is related to the previous one, for the king was to lead God's people to a right knowledge of God and his ways. According to Deut 17:18–19, the responsibility of Israel's king was Torah-centered: he was to copy the Torah, carry it with him, and read it. On the one hand, such obedience showed that the king did not rule apart from the sovereign kingship of Yahweh. On the other hand, the king's obedience to the Torah ensured that he would rule with God's justice over God's

[8] The phrase translated as "making profit dishonestly"—it is the verb *bts'* with its cognate noun *betsa'*—refers to gain or profit obtained through either violence or, more broadly, injustice. See BDB.

[9] The phrase occurs, with minor variations, six times in Jeremiah: 6:13; 8:10; 31:34; 42:1, 8; 44:12; cf. 16:6. Similarly, in the parallel passage in Jer 8:10, it is "these people" and "my people" who are in view (see Jer 8:5–7).

people, since the Torah contained the divine standard of justice. Hence, King David was measured as a successful king inasmuch as he was faithful to God's rules and statutes (2 Sam 22:23).

That having a just king is crucial for the enactment of justice is evident from the fact that justice terminology proliferates in the descriptions of the kingships of David and Solomon. Immediately after the Davidic covenant, we are given a commendable summary of David's reign: "So David reigned over all Israel, administering justice and righteousness for all his people" (2 Sam 8:15; cf. 1 Chr 18:14). At the end of his reign, David issued final instructions to Solomon, which included the charge to heed the Sinai covenant's legislation (1 Kgs 2:2–3). After his death, David is similarly commended as having reigned "in faithfulness, righteousness, and integrity" (1 Kgs 3:6). When Solomon became king, he asked God for "a receptive heart to judge [*shaphat*] your people," which God interpreted as a request to "administer justice [*mišpāṭ*]" (1 Kgs 3:9, 11). The following narrative underscores this point, in which Solomon arbitrates between a motherly dispute. As a result, "All Israel heard about the judgment [*mišpāṭ*] the king had given, and they stood in awe of the king because they saw that God's wisdom was in him to carry out justice [*mišpāṭ*]" (1 Kgs 3:28). In recognition of his duty to administer justice for the people, Solomon made a "Hall of Judgment" as part of his palace complex (1 Kgs 7:7). Finally, when the Queen of Sheba visited Solomon, she recognized that the purpose of his reign was "to carry out justice and righteousness" (1 Kgs 10:9; cf. 2 Chr 9:8). These depictions of David and Solomon's reign, far from whitewashing the unjust elements of their reign, show the crucial link between justice and God's anointed king. As the king goes, so go the people. The hope of justice within Israel and the nations rested on the arrival of a righteous and just king.

Nevertheless, Israel's kings often exacerbated the problem of injustice and did not lead the people to love and obey God. When Solomon turned aside from God, he lost sight of justice and attempted to murder Jeroboam since the latter was deemed a threat to the kingdom (1 Kgs 11:40). A common indictment against Israel's kings is that they led Israel into sin (e.g.,

1 Kgs 15:26, 34; 16:26; 2 Kgs 10:31). Ahab's wife Jezebel concocted false accusations against Naboth that led to his unjust execution in order to take possession of Naboth's inheritance (1 Kgs 21:1–16). Ahaz even committed the injustice of child sacrifice (2 Kgs 16:3; cf. 2 Kgs 3:27), and Manasseh "shed so much innocent blood that he filled Jerusalem with it from one end to another" (2 Kgs 21:16). According to Jeremiah 21–22, many kings in the house of David failed to reign justly, including Zedekiah, Shallum, Jehoiakim, and Coniah. The house of David was to "administer justice every morning" (Jer 21:12; cf. Jer 22:3). In the case of Jehoiakim, his reign was unlike his father Josiah's because Josiah did "justice and righteousness" (Jer 22:15), whereas Jehoiakim had "eyes and a heart for nothing except your own dishonest profit" (Jer 22:17). As Jeremiah 23 indicates, the failure on the part of the Davidic kings to do justice and righteousness did not nullify the promises of God to David but showed the need for a better Davidic king who would reign consistently with the justice and righteousness of Yahweh. While Israel's leaders were collectively culpable for failing to uphold the justice of the Torah (see Mic 3:1; Zeph 3:1–4), it was the king who was chiefly responsible to set a standard of justice and righteousness for the people.

Summary

The Old Testament locates the sin of injustice in the twin problems of humanity's deep, pervasive sin and the absence of a just king. As even a casual reading of the Old Testament will show, Israel did not experience the restoration of Edenic justice. While God's covenants with Abraham, Israel, and David confirmed God's intent to restore Edenic justice and clarified how God planned to restore it, they did not in themselves make all things new. The power and effects of sin were so pervasive that they permeated the family of Abraham and the house of David. The problem was internal, and so the external gift of the law at Sinai, which clarified the standard of divine justice, did little to overcome the problem of sin.

The Twofold Solution to Injustice in the Old Testament

Since the Old Testament problematizes injustice along the lines of sin's pervasiveness and the absence of a just king, the Old Testament frames the hope for justice along similar lines. God would restore Edenic justice only through a new covenant, in which he would give his people new hearts so that they would know and love God and his just ways. Corresponding to this new covenant would be the arrival of a just Davidic king who would rule God's people with perfect justice and righteousness. The inauguration of the new covenant and the arrival of a just king comprise the twofold Old Testament solution to injustice.

Justice as the Result of the Transformation of the Heart

Given the depth and pervasiveness of sin, it is not surprising that the Old Testament stresses the need for God to transform the hearts of his people so that they would be able to apprehend God's standards for justice and carry it out appropriately. The hope for such heart transformation appears as early as Deuteronomy, but it becomes especially prominent in prophets like Jeremiah, Hosea, and Zechariah.[10]

The link between heart transformation and justice appears in Deut 10:16, in which Moses called Israel to "circumcise your hearts and don't be stiff-necked any longer" (cf. Deut 30:6). Circumcision of the heart refers to being devoted to God, his ways, and his purposes.[11] In the context of Deuteronomy 10, God's ways and purposes are characterized by justice and

---

[10] The following analysis is not exhaustive but representative of biblical texts. For instance, nothing is said of Ezekiel's description of the new covenant, which includes the promise that God would put his Spirit within his people, such that they obey God's commands from the heart (see Ezek 11:18–20; 36:26–27). As in the Sinai covenant, the just character of these commands is often in view, as seen from their common label "ordinances" (*mishpatîm*; e.g., Ezek 11:20; 36:27).

[11] John D. Meade, "Circumcision of Flesh to Circumcision of Heart: The Typology of the Sign of the Abrahamic Covenant," in *Progressive Covenantalism:*

righteousness. He shows "no partiality" and takes "no bribe" (Deut 10:17). "He executes justice for the fatherless and the widow, and loves the resident alien, giving him food and clothing" (Deut 10:18). Hence, Israel's heart circumcision would result in their imitation of God in doing justice and righteousness. Moses knew that Israel did not yet have circumcised hearts (Deut 29:4 [MT 29:3]), but he prophesied that God would one day transform his people's hearts, resulting in their obedience to God's just commands (Deut 30:6–8).

Jeremiah also ties transformation of the heart to justice and righteousness. Jeremiah 4:4 calls Judah to "circumcise yourselves to the LORD" and "remove the foreskin of your hearts." Verses 1–4 are a literary unit with two sections (vv. 1–2, 3–4).[12] Verses 3–4 restate the command in v. 1 to return to God and put away idolatry. Verse 2 is distinct in that it forms the apodosis of v. 1, depicting the necessary result of repentance. Verse 2 envisions an Israelite swearing allegiance to God, and doing so not with disingenuousness and deceit but "in truth, justice, and righteousness." In other words, their oath of allegiance would be accompanied by a heart of sincerity and a lifestyle characterized by right treatment of one another. Such sincerity and justice were the necessary result of heart circumcision. Similarly, Jer 31:33–34 promised a new covenant with God's people, in which God would internalize his instruction and inculcate a community-wide knowledge of God: "I will put my teaching within them and write it on their hearts. . . . No longer will one teach his neighbor or his brother, saying, 'Know the LORD,' for they will all know me, from the least to the greatest of them" (Jer 31:33–34). The "teaching" (*tôrah*) written on the heart refers to the new covenant's legislation, which evokes the just and righteous

---

Charting a Course Between Dispensational and Covenant Theologies, ed. Stephen J. Wellum and Brent E. Parker (Nashville: B&H Academic, 2016), 127–57.

[12] Even though McKane suggests that originally vv. 1–2 and vv. 3–4 were distinct oracles, the MT links them with *kî* ("for") such that even McKane recognizes that the verses share "the same theme." See William McKane, *Jeremiah 1–25*, ICC (Edinburgh: T&T Clark, 1986), 87.

character of the Sinai covenant's legislation. Also, the promised community-wide knowledge of God refers to an internal disposition of the heart to fear, serve, and love God, and to imitate him in "showing faithful love, justice, and righteousness on the earth" (Jer 9:24 [MT 9:23]; cf. Jer 32:40). Such an internal knowledge of God and his ways was necessary for an outworking of justice and righteousness.

Hosea also indicates that the new covenant will bring about heart transformation within God's people, resulting in justice and righteousness. To stress the need for such transformation, Hosea utilizes the metaphor of marriage between God and his people. In the old covenant, Israel had been unfaithful to God like an adulteress, having sought refuge and joy in idols. However, God promised to marry his people once again in a new covenant relationship (Hos 2:14–23 [MT 2:16–25]). But this marital union would be better than the Sinai covenant, for God promises, "I will take you to be my wife forever. I will take you to be my wife in righteousness, justice, love, and compassion. I will take you to be my wife in faithfulness, and you will know the Lord" (Hos 2:19–20 [MT 2:21–22]). This new covenant is better than the Sinai covenant in that it is inviolable—note the word "forever" in 2:19—and transforms God's people. While it is possible that the terms "righteousness" and "justice" in 2:19 refer only to God's actions on behalf of his people, it is more likely that they also include righteous and just actions among God's people due to his transformative work in their hearts.[13] In the old covenant God was righteous and just, but Israel was not; the labor of Hosea 1–2 is to show the reversal of Israel's infidelity. Commenting on this text, Calvin captures the transformative element well: "We now then see what the Prophet means by righteousness and judgment, even this, that God would cause the marriage vow to be kept on both sides; for the

---

[13] Derek Kidner, *The Message of Hosea: Love to the Loveless*, The Bible Speaks Today (Downers Grove, IL: InterVarsity, 1981), 35–36; Bo H. Lim and Daniel Castelo, *Hosea*, Two Horizons Old Testament Commentary (Grand Rapids: Eerdmans, 2015), 77.

people, restored from exile, would no more violate their pledged faith nor act unfaithfully."[14]

Finally, Zechariah portrays the new covenant people of God doing justice and righteousness from the heart. According to Zechariah 7, Israel's failure in the old covenant to uphold justice was one reason they were sent into exile (Zech 7:8–14). Accordingly, in Zechariah 8 God promised to make a new covenant with his people (Zech 8:8), and the new covenant community should be characterized by truth and justice: "These are the things you must do: Speak truth to one another; make true and sound decisions within your city gates. Do not plot evil in your hearts against your neighbor, and do not love perjury, for I hate all this" (Zech 8:16–17). The phrase the CSB renders as "make true and sound decisions" can be rendered as "judge with truth and with the judgment of peace," a phrase that refers to a commitment to do business with one another faithfully and with the goal of the other's well-being. The focus is not simply on external behavior but also on the motives of the heart, for it includes an injunction against deception and against attempts to pervert justice. Life in the new covenant community is borne out of heart transformation.

Justice as the Result of the Just Davidic King

The new covenant would also coincide with the arrival of a righteous and just Davidic king. This is particularly evident from the prophecies of Isaiah, Jeremiah, and Ezekiel. Isaiah 11 depicts the arrival of a shoot "from the stump of Jesse," who is endowed fully with the Spirit of the Lord (Isa 11:1–2). Unlike the kings of Israel, he will administer justice with "the fear of the Lord," and his verdicts will be based not on external appearances but on the heart (Isa 11:3). Indeed, "he will judge the poor righteously and execute

---

[14] John Calvin, *Hosea*, vol. 1 of *Commentaries on the Twelve Minor Prophets*, trans. John Owen, Calvin's Commentaries (Edinburgh: Calvin Translation Society, 1846; repr., Grand Rapids: Baker, 2003), 113.

justice for the oppressed of the land" (Isa 11:4), which indicates his aversion to bribery and the perversion of justice. Righteousness and faithfulness are metaphorized as his "belt" (Isa 11:5), indicating the foundational place of these qualities in his reign.[15] Since justice in the Old Testament is based not only on a right discernment of motives and behavior but also a resolve to act with faithfulness towards one another, it is not surprising that the king's reign is founded on both righteousness and faithfulness. Moreover, the king's reign would coincide with the arrival of the new covenant era. In Isa 55:3, God ratifies "a permanent covenant with you on the basis of the faithful kindnesses of David." The "permanent covenant" refers to the inviolability of the new covenant, and the covenant ratification is based on the faithfulness and loyal love of the future Davidic king.[16]

Jeremiah also stresses that the new covenant would coincide with the arrival of a just Davidic king. In contrast with the unjust kings from the house of David in Jeremiah 21–22, Jeremiah 23 promises a future righteous Davidic king. God would "raise up a Righteous Branch for David," who would "reign wisely as king and administer justice and righteousness in the land" (Jer 23:5). Later in in the book, when God promises to restore his people through a new covenant (Jer 30–33; esp. 31:27–34), the promise of a future righteous Davidic king is restated (Jer 33:15; cf. 30:9).[17] Further, the use of the phrase "in those days" in Jer 33:15 locates the time of the future king's arrival as coinciding with the time of the fulfillment of "the good

---

[15] Peter J. Gentry and Stephen J. Wellum, *Kingdom through Covenant: A Biblical-Theological Understanding of the Covenants* (Wheaton, IL: Crossway, 2012), 581.

[16] For a full treatment of the Hebrew syntax of Isa 55:3, see Peter J. Gentry, "Rethinking the 'Sure Mercies of David' in Isaiah 55:3," *WTJ* 69, no. 2 (2007): 279–304. Both Isa 11:5 and 55:3 use the same Hebrew root (*ʾmn*) to depict the future Davidic king as "faithful."

[17] That the entire Book of Consolation (Jer 30–33) focuses on a new covenant relationship between God and his people is evident from the appearance of the covenant formula (with minor variation) throughout the section (Jer 30:22; 31:1, 33; 32:38).

promise that I have spoken concerning the house of Israel and the house of Judah" (Jer 33:14). While the "good promise" probably refers to the promise of a future Davidic king since it restates the promises of Jer 23:5–6,[18] it also evokes the promise of the new covenant since the new covenant passage (Jer 31:27–34) is the only other place in the Book of Consolation (Jer 30–33) where the phrase "the house of Israel and the house of Judah" appears (Jer 31:27, 31).

Ezekiel also links the coming of a just and righteous Davidic king with the arrival of the new covenant. In Ezekiel 34, Israel's self-serving leaders are contrasted with the future Davidic king. Unlike the "shepherds" who eat and mistreat the sheep, God will rescue the sheep and "establish over them one shepherd, my servant David, and he will shepherd them" (Ezek 34:23; cf. 37:24–25). God promises to "shepherd them with justice" (Ezek 34:16), which refers to a right distinguishing between the flock so that each receives proper care (Ezek 34:17–22). Since God appoints the future David as the better shepherd-king, he too will shepherd God's people with justice. Moreover, each time the name "David" appears in Ezekiel (Ezek 34:23–24; 37:24–25), it is immediately followed by mention of a "covenant of peace," which is the new covenant described with a view to its effect (Ezek 34:25; 37:26). Hence, in Ezekiel, the arrival of a just shepherd-king coincides with the ratification of the new covenant that brings peace for God's people.

Summary

The Old Testament thus stresses the need for the arrival of the new covenant, in which God would transform the hearts of his people to treat one another in right ways, with hearts full of faithful and loyal love for God and one another. Without such heart transformation, injustice would remain. Additionally, coinciding with the arrival of the new covenant would be the

---

[18] Gerald L. Keown, Pamela J. Scalise, and Thomas G. Smothers, *Jeremiah 26–52*, WBC 27 (Dallas: Word, 1995), 173.

righteous and just Davidic king, who would shepherd God's people with justice and righteousness and lead them to do likewise.

Jesus as the Fulfillment of the Old Testament Hope for Justice

In keeping with the Old Testament hope for justice, the New Testament highlights Jesus as the fulfillment of that hope since Jesus solves the twofold Old Testament problem of injustice. As the just Davidic king, Jesus inaugurates the new covenant with its concomitant heart transformation.

Jesus as the Just Davidic King

The New Testament explicitly identifies Jesus as the rightful Davidic king. His Davidic lineage is consistently affirmed (Matt 1:1–17; Rom 1:3; 2 Tim 2:8; Rev 22:16), and throughout the Gospels he is given the messianic title "Son of David" (e.g., Matt 1:1; 15:22; Mark 10:47–48; Luke 18:38–39). He is greater than the historical David, for he is not only David's son but also David's Lord (Matt 22:41–46; cf. Ps 110:1).

As the promised Davidic king, Jesus exhibited a true knowledge of God and a commitment to justice and righteousness. He is called "the Righteous One" (*ho dikaios*) as a statement of his righteous character in the sight of God (Acts 7:52; 22:14; cf. 1 Pet 3:18; 1 John 2:29; 3:7). Hebrews 1:9 quotes Ps 45:7 (Ps 44:7, LXX) that Jesus as the Davidic king "loved righteousness and hated lawlessness." Even from a young age his wisdom and commitment to know God amazed his teachers (Luke 2:40–52).[19] Indeed, in keeping with the expectations for Israel's king in Deut 17:18–20, Jesus knew the law and exhibited faithfulness to God in the face of temptation

---

[19] That Jesus's interaction with the religious leaders brings about astonishment from the audience shows the depth of Jesus's wisdom. Darrell L. Bock, *Luke 1:1–9:50*, BECNT (Grand Rapids: Baker, 1994), 267–68.

(Matt 4:1–11; cf. Deut 6:13, 16; 8:3; 1 Pet 2:22).[20] Later in his ministry, his interactions with Israel's leaders again demonstrated his knowledge of the law and wisdom in its application to Israel's life (Matt 22:15–40). Unlike Israel's leaders, Jesus was committed to "the more important matters of the law—justice, mercy, and faithfulness" (Matt 23:23; cf. Luke 11:42). He was Ezekiel's Davidic shepherd-king who lays down his life for the sheep (John 10:11–18). Being similar to but greater than Solomon, he has surpassing wisdom to administer justice and righteousness (Matt 12:42; Luke 11:31). In the passion narrative he is portrayed as innocent, a fact noticed by even Pilate's wife and a Roman centurion (Matt 27:19; Luke 23:47). God himself testified to Jesus's righteousness by raising him from the dead (Acts 2:25–36; 17:31; Rom 4:25).

Moreover, Jesus exhibited the authority and ability to give right judgment, for he accurately discerned human intentions. The Gospel of John especially emphasizes this point through a proliferation of "judgment" terms (i.e., the **krin* root).[21] Jesus has "all judgment" given him by the Father (John 5:22), and he has this authority "because he is the Son of Man" (John 5:27). Such judgment, which includes eternal condemnation of evildoers (John 5:29), is "just" because it ultimately comes from what he hears from the Father (John 5:30; cf. 8:26). Unlike the Jews who rendered judgments "by human standards," Jesus's judgment is "true" because it is in agreement with the Father (John 8:15–16). When Jesus was condemned by the Jews for healing a man on the Sabbath, he called the Jews to judge not "according to outward appearances," but to judge "according to righteous judgment" (John 7:24). In contrast to the Jews, whose standards of justice were awry

---

[20] Joshua W. Jipp rightly suggests that according to Hellenistic literature and the Old Testament, the "ideal king" would be a "living law," an ideal that Christ fulfills. *Christ Is King: Paul's Royal Ideology* (Minneapolis: Fortress, 2015), 43–76.

[21] The verb *krinō* ("to judge") and its nominal derivatives *krima* and *krisis* ("judgment") often have to do with the law court, whether the act of judging or the verdict rendered. But it can also refer in nonjudicial contexts to the act of making a decision (e.g., Acts 20:16; Rom 14:5).

(John 7:24; 8:15), Jesus exhibited the authority and ability to judge with divine discernment and in accordance with divine justice.

Two texts in Matthew (4:13–16; 12:16–21) highlight that Jesus as the Davidic king fulfills the prophetic hope for justice. First, according to Matt 4:13–16, Jesus fulfilled Isa 9:1–2 (MT 8:23–9:1) by beginning his public ministry at the Sea of Galilee. Isaiah 9:1–2 prophesied the dawning of light and joy for God's people, for the son of David wins the victory against God's enemies and establishes the kingdom of David "with justice and righteousness from now on and forever" (Isa 9:7 [MT 9:6]). Matthew's citation of Isaiah 9 at the outset of Jesus's public ministry shows that Jesus is the prophesied Davidic king who brings his people, both Jews and Gentiles, the light and joy of salvation on the basis of his inaugurated kingdom that shatters oppression and is characterized by justice and righteousness. Second, according to Matt 12:16–21, Jesus fulfilled Isa 42:1–4, the first of Isaiah's Servant Songs. The Servant of the Lord is the delight of God and is empowered by God's Spirit, which suggests he is identical to the Spirit-endowed king of Isa 11:1–5. The focus of the text is on the task the Servant is empowered to complete, which centers around the proclamation and enactment of justice for the Gentiles. Indeed, justice for the nations is the central task of the Servant, with *mišpāṭ* ("justice") appearing three times in the passage (Isa 42:1, 3–4). J. Alec Motyer suggests a threefold referent for *mišpāṭ* in the text: (1) God's "judgment at law" that declares to the nations "that there is only one God" (see Isa 41:21–29), (2) the revelation of "the truth of God to the world," and (3) "the righting of wrongs, the establishment of a just order."[22] Particularly the last referent finds fruitful application in Jesus's ministry, for the justice and righteousness Jesus proclaimed and enacted aimed at restoring the Edenic standard, since it far surpassed the righteousness of Israel's religious leaders (Matt 5:20), corresponded to God's own righteous character (Matt 5:48), and was borne from an internal disposition to accomplish it

[22] J. Alec Motyer, *The Prophecy of Isaiah: An Introduction and Commentary* (Downers Grove, IL: IVP Academic, 1993), 319.

(Matt 6:1–18).[23] Interpreting Jesus's proclamation and enactment of justice along these lines fits with his basic proclamation of the redemptive reign of God to both Jews and Gentiles.

Finally, the New Testament identifies Jesus as the eschatological judge of humanity. As such, he will rightly distinguish between the wheat and the chaff (Matt 3:12) and the weeds and the wheat (Matt 13:37–43). According to Matt 25:31–46, Jesus is the shepherd-king and judge who rightly discerns the righteousness of the sheep, even when the sheep are uncertain about their righteousness (Matt 25:37–40). The appointed day of judgment is the time when God will "judge the world in righteousness by the man he has appointed" (Acts 17:31; cf. Rev 19:11). On that day, Jesus will enact consummate justice for and with his people (Matt 19:28). As "the righteous Judge," Jesus will award his people the crown of life (2 Tim 4:8) and enact retributive justice on God's enemies (2 Thess 1:8). While Jesus's role as humanity's judge transcends his identity as the just Davidic king—he also judges as the eternal Son of the Father and as the Son of Man (John 5:22, 27)—the descriptions of Jesus as judge cohere with the Old Testament depiction of the Davidic king as humanity's just ruler. As Davidic king, Jesus's just reign is already inaugurated but not yet consummated. Inasmuch as Jesus is the Davidic king now, he reigns with justice and righteousness on the earth among his people. But his just reign is not yet consummated, for it awaits his return when he will mete out righteous judgment on behalf of his people and eradicate all injustice.

---

[23] Similarly, John Nolland considers the "justice" of Matt 12:18 to refer to "the establishment of a just order under God in place of the manifest injustices of the present life." *The Gospel of Matthew*, NIGTC (Grand Rapids: Eerdmans, 2005), 493. While Matt 12:17–21 fits aptly in its present context of illustrating why Jesus withdrew from the Pharisees, commentators often recognize that the quotation—the longest of Matthew's Old Testament citations—captures more broadly Matthew's presentation of Jesus as Isaiah's Servant. See W. D. Davies and Dale C. Allison Jr., *Commentary on Matthew VIII–XVIII*, vol. 2 of *A Critical and Exegetical Commentary on the Gospel According to Saint Matthew*, ICC (London: T&T Clark, 1991), 324; Nolland, *Gospel of Matthew*, 492.

Jesus and Hearts Transformed for Justice

Not only is Jesus the just Davidic king, but he also inaugurated the new covenant through his sacrificial death. The new covenant promise Jesus highlighted at the Last Supper was definitive forgiveness of sins, the foundational promise of the new covenant (Matt 26:28; Luke 22:20; cf. Jer 31:34). Still, since his death brought into effect the new covenant arrangement, all its promises are already inaugurated, including the promises of heart transformation and community-wide knowledge of God. As a result, the new covenant community possesses transformed hearts and should therefore act with justice and righteousness towards one another.

Throughout the letters of the New Testament, Christians are depicted as having experienced the new covenant's promises of heart transformation and community-wide knowledge of God. Romans 2:29 defines a true Jew as one who has a circumcised heart, which is synonymous with heart transformation. Paul's label of Christians as "the circumcision" (Phil 3:3) affirms both that Christians are the true people of God and that they are the recipients of the new covenant's promise of heart circumcision. At Corinth the Christians had experienced not Moses's ministry of death with "tablets of stone" but Paul's new covenant ministry of the life-giving Spirit who had written on "tablets of human hearts" (2 Cor 3:3). Christians have no need for anyone to teach them since they are already taught by God himself (1 Thess 4:9; 1 John 2:20, 27; cf. Isa 54:13; John 6:45), which indicates a true and saving knowledge of God through the Spirit's regenerative work in the heart. Indeed, Paul often highlights the Spirit's indwelling presence, which is qualitatively different than the experience of the Spirit among God's people in the old covenant era (cf. Rom 8:9–11; 1 Cor 3:16; 6:19; Gal 4:6; 2 Tim 1:14).[24] Christians obey God from the heart and love one another genuinely because of Christ's redemption from sin (Rom 6:17; 1 Pet 1:22–23). Such

---

[24] See James M. Hamilton Jr., *God's Indwelling Presence: The Holy Spirit in the Old and New Testaments*, NAC Studies in Bible and Theology (Nashville: B&H, 2006).

texts indicate that Christians have experienced the reality of the new covenant's promises of heart transformation and community-wide knowledge of God. Christians experience these promises in an already inaugurated but not yet consummated way, for Christians still face temptations to sin, and local churches must beware of those who are Christians in name only but not in substance. Still, the new covenant's promises are inaugurated for all those in Christ, for all God's promises have their "yes" in him (2 Cor 1:20).

Given the inauguration of the new covenant's promises of heart transformation and community-wide knowledge of God, the New Testament calls God's people to live in just and right ways towards one another, and in a manner consistent with truth, faithfulness, and right discernment. Christians should imitate the impartial God in showing no favoritism (1 Tim 5:21; Jas 2:1, 9).[25] Masters should treat their servants "justly and fairly, since you know that you too have a Master in heaven" (Col 4:1).

Two texts that draw out the new covenant's implications for justice, right discernment, and truth are 1 Corinthians 6 and Ephesians 4–6. According to 1 Corinthians 6, since Christians will be partially responsible to enact consummate justice, they are equipped now to enact justice within the inaugurated new covenant community. Christians will be responsible for enacting eschatological justice, for "the saints will judge the world" and "will judge angels" (1 Cor 6:2–3; cf. Matt 19:28; Luke 22:30). Whatever the precise details included in such an eschatological promise, Christians will play some role in the final judgment.[26] Such a role will require an impartial application of God's righteous standards to individual humans and angels. Paul's argument runs from the greater to the lesser: If Christians are going to have a role in enacting eschatological justice in matters both eternal and universal in scope, they should be competent to enact justice in the church in "matters of

[25] For texts depicting God as impartial, see Acts 10:34; Rom 2:11; Gal 2:6; Eph 6:9; Col 3:25.

[26] See David E. Garland, *1 Corinthians*, BECNT (Grand Rapids: Baker Academic, 2003), 202–3; Gordon D. Fee, *The First Epistle to the Corinthians*, NICNT, rev. ed. (Grand Rapids: Eerdmans, 2014), 256–57.

this life" (1 Cor 6:3).[27] Paul's indictment that there was "not one wise person among you who is able to arbitrate between fellow believers" was a "shame" to the Corinthian Christians (1 Cor 6:5). The logic of Paul's argument hangs on the assumption that in the inaugurated new covenant era, Christians are endowed with the wisdom necessary for right discernment that leads to just action. Injustice among the pagan law courts was to be expected due to preferential treatment given to the social elites of Corinth, who could often obtain unjust verdicts through the use of bribes.[28] But the church has been given wisdom from God in Christ, and this wisdom comes from the Spirit, who endows the "spiritual person" with divine wisdom for accurate discernment and judgment of all things (1 Cor 2:12–16). Elsewhere in the letter Paul contends that each individual Christian has the Spirit residing within them (1 Cor 6:19) who enables the Christian confession of Jesus as Lord and gives each Christian gifts for the upbuilding of the church (1 Cor 12:3–12). Thus, in 1 Corinthians 6 Paul urges the Corinthians to live in discerning and just ways towards one another in light of the new covenant reality of heart transformation effected by the indwelling Spirit.[29]

---

[27] Garland, *1 Corinthians*, 203; Roy E. Ciampa and Brian S. Rosner, *The First Letter to the Corinthians*, PNTC (Grand Rapids: Eerdmans, 2010), 234.

[28] For evidence of bribery in the Greco-Roman court system, see the primary texts listed in Garland, *1 Corinthians*, 197. See also Bruce W. Winter, "Civil Litigation in Secular Corinth and the Church: The Forensic Background to 1 Corinthians 6:1–8," *NTS* 37, no. 4 (1991): 559–72.

[29] Regarding the importance and pursuit of justice, Paul has two different concerns. On the one hand, Paul is concerned that Christians who have been mistreated should refrain from the pursuit of justice from pagan law courts, because to do so demeans the name of Christ and destroys the public witness of the church (1 Cor 6:7; see Ciampa and Rosner, *The First Letter to the Corinthians*, 235). On the other hand, Paul issues a dire warning to those Christians engaging in injustice (*adikeite*, 1 Cor 6:8): the "unjust" (*adikoi*) will not inherit God's kingdom (1 Cor 6:9–10). Campbell interprets 1 Cor 6:1–11 through the lens of power: "Paul challenges the elites to resist the systemic injustice of the court system and to seek an alternative kind of arbitration within the church." But this reads too much into the text, for the passage says nothing of "systemic injustice" or oppression of the poor.

Ephesians 4–6 also draws out the implications of the new covenant's heart transformation for justice and righteousness. In three texts, Paul stresses the need to live with "righteousness" (*dikaiosynē*) and "truth" (*alētheia*), which correspond to the prophetic call to live in righteous and just ways towards one another based on a commitment to faithfulness and truth (Eph 4:24; 5:9; 6:14).[30] At conversion Christians "put on the new self, the one created according to God's likeness in righteousness and purity of the truth" (Eph 4:24). The "new self" depicts the new covenant reality of a heart transformed by God so that it is aligned with God's own character ("according to God's likeness") and is committed to faithfulness ("of the truth"). This interpretation of *alētheia* as "faithfulness" is substantiated by Paul's quote of Zech 8:16 in the next verse (Eph 4:25), a text analyzed above in which *alētheia* corresponds to the Hebrew *'emet* and refers to truthfulness and faithfulness towards one another in the new covenant community. Similarly, in Eph 5:9 Paul links righteousness with truth and interprets both virtues as "the fruit of the light." The "light" refers to God's regenerative act, promised in the new covenant, by which the Spirit enlightens the minds and hearts of individuals so that they possess godly desires (cf. Eph 1:18; 2:1–10). Since righteousness and truth are the "fruit" of the light, they are the effect of that heart transformation. Finally, in Eph 6:14 the two pieces of armor are righteousness and truth. In the analysis above, we saw that both "righteousness" and "faithfulness" are the Messiah's garments (Isa 11:5; cf. Isa 59:14–17). These correspond precisely to the terms Paul uses for the Christian's armor in Eph 6:14.[31] Thus, through union with the just Davidic king, Christians are now clothed with the justice, righteousness, and

---

See Charles L. Campbell, *1 Corinthians*, Belief: A Theological Commentary on the Bible (Louisville: Westminster John Knox, 2018), 102–6, esp. 104.

[30] In Ephesians *dikaiosynē* only occurs in these three texts. The noun *alētheia* occurs six times (1:13; 4:21, 24–25; 5:9; 6:14), with *alētheuō* ("to be truthful") occurring once (4:15).

[31] Clinton E. Arnold, *Ephesians*, ZECNT (Grand Rapids: Zondervan, 2010), 451–52.

faithfulness that characterize his reign. True justice cannot be separated from a commitment to truth, honesty, and faithfulness, and such is borne from the new covenant's promise of a transformed heart.

Summary

The New Testament identifies Jesus as the solution for the Old Testament hope for the restoration of Edenic justice. He is the just Davidic king who inaugurated the new covenant's promises of heart transformation and community-wide knowledge of God. He possesses unique authority and the ability to enact justice based on right discernment and a commitment to the truth. Unlike human rulers and kingdoms, Jesus's reign is characterized by justice and righteousness. Moreover, since Jesus inaugurated the new covenant by his death, his just reign is exhibited in the present time through his people, whose hearts have been transformed by the promised Spirit. Due to this new inward reality, they are now able to apprehend God's standards for justice and the goodness of those standards, and in the strength of that right apprehension, they are committed and empowered to treat one another in right and just ways.

Theological Formulation

Our expectations for justice in the world are grounded in the way in which the Bible frames the problem of and solution for injustice. On the one hand, the pervasiveness of sin in the human heart should temper our optimism for solving injustice in the broader society. On the other hand, the reality of the gospel creates and sustains an appropriate optimism for justice around us.

First, our expectations for justice in the world must reckon with the pervasive problem of sin. By God's common grace, non-Christians can sense that the world is broken, and they can play a role in alleviating some of sin's effects. For instance, we can think of World War II when the Allies, some of whom were undoubtedly non-Christians, fought against the injustice of the Nazi regime. Similarly, non-Christian civic leaders can promote just policies and laws. As Christians, we can be grateful that God's common grace prevents societies from being as unjust as they can possibly be (albeit to varying degrees).

At the same time, Christians should not be surprised if a non-Christian or the broader society misperceives the nature of justice or fails to solve injustice. Like Lamech in Genesis 4 and the Chaldeans in Habakkuk 1, non-Christians continue to be under the noetic effects of sin and can easily misperceive notions of justice. Again, this does not mean that non-Christians possess no sense of justice, but only that we should not be surprised if that sense is skewed. Similarly, while some in society may locate the solution for injustice in better education or government policies,[32] the Christian recognizes that these things in themselves cannot solve the root problem of injustice. As we saw in this chapter, the story of Old Testament Israel makes us acutely aware that even with the best curriculum and government policies, Israel was not significantly more just than the unjust societies around them. While it is good and right for Christians to promote justice, Israel's story warns against an overly optimistic expectation that apart from Christ our society will be an idyllic place where justice reigns.

Second, the victory of Christ over sin and death creates an appropriate optimism that the church will be a place of justice, even though that justice is not yet consummated. As members of the new covenant, Christians have God's standard of justice written on their hearts, such that we treat others around us with truth, honesty, and fairness. As Christ's

[32] For one example of this at the popular level, see Phyllis Lockett, "Nine Ways We Can Address Racial Injustice in Our Schools, Today," *Forbes*, September 18, 2020, accessed April 19, 2024, https://www.forbes.com/sites/phyllislockett/2020/09/18/nine-ways-we-can-address-racial-injustice-in-our-schools-today/?sh=2843b40b362f.

visible new covenant community on earth, the local church is and should be the place where justice is most clearly visible within a communal setting. Those who comprise that community, from the least to the greatest, have the Spirit of God indwelling them, producing the fruit of justice and righteousness. Of course, Christ has not yet returned and consummated for his people the new covenant's blessings, so Christians and local churches still commit sins of injustice. Sadly, the history of Christianity is littered with such sins, and when this occurs, Christians should neither justify nor condone the injustice but quickly condemn it. We all long for the return of Christ when he will finish making all things new. At the same time, since Christ has already inaugurated the new covenant's blessings for us, his victory over our own sin creates and sustains our optimism that in the inaugurated era we as Christians will be characterized by justice and righteousness.

Implications

This chapter offers several implications for the individual Christian, the local church, and local church pastors.

First, individual Christians should care about justice. Because God is a God of justice and we are called to imitate him, Christians should promote the right treatment of others in society. Because through the gospel we have been empowered to do justice and righteousness, we must not be silent in the face of injustice around us, whatever form that injustice might take (e.g., abortion, ethnic partiality). Of course, how to speak against injustice requires discernment as to the source and effects of the injustice, for injustice may take vastly different forms depending on the community. We may sense the reality of injustice without being exactly sure where the source of injustice lies or what precise measures we should take to assist those in need. Still, the implication of this chapter is that Christians must not be silent about injustice, but rather speak and work against it with appropriate wisdom and biblical fidelity.

Second, the Bible's commitment to justice should lead individual Christians to boast in Christ to those around them. Since Christ has come and inaugurated the new covenant, we as Christians must make Christ known. Practically, if we care about justice, we will want to see our families and neighbors taste and see the justice and righteousness the new covenant brings by faith in Christ our just King. Of course, the gospel is not a magic pill that automatically creates perfectly sinless justice and righteousness in our hearts, our homes, or our workplaces. We still must mortify our sin and fight against our sinful passions and desires (Rom 8:13; Gal 5:16–17; 1 Pet 2:11–12). Nevertheless, this chapter has labored to show that the only hope for lasting justice in the world is through the victorious reign of Christ in the human heart, which overcomes our sin. Evangelism is thus a necessary implication for Christians who care about justice, for it is foundational for lasting justice in society.

Third, the mission of the local church is to preach the gospel and to make disciples. In the local church's disciple-making mission, the church baptizes new disciples and instructs them so that they can obey Christ's teachings as they live in the world as his disciples (Matt 28:19). In its teaching ministry, the local church indirectly promotes justice in society in the sense that it teaches, exhorts, and encourages its members to obey Jesus's teachings in the world. But this influence is only indirect, for it happens as the church prioritizes its mission to make disciples through the ministry of the word and sacraments.[33] As Jonathan Leeman has recently

[33] For examples of those who see justice as an integral part of the church's mission, see Christopher J. H. Wright, *The Mission of God's People: A Biblical Theology of the Church's Mission*, Biblical Theology for Life (Grand Rapids: Zondervan, 2010), 273–82; Michael Barram, *Missional Economics: Biblical Justice and Christian Formation* (Grand Rapids: Eerdmans, 2018), 238. For a better approach, see Chapter 9 of this volume by John Wind, as well as Jonathan Leeman, "Soteriological Mission: Focusing in on the Mission of Redemption," in *Four Views on the Church's Mission*, ed. Jason S. Sexton (Grand Rapids: Zondervan, 2017), 17–45.

put it, there's a difference between *making disciples* and *being disciples*.[34] The church does the former, whereas individual Christians do the latter. Practically, it is thus right and appropriate for our church services and sermons—the weekly rhythm of church life—to be centered around the gospel and its necessary effects in the Christian life, including the necessity of doing justice and righteousness.

Questions for Further Reflection

1. How does the way the Old Testament frames the problem of injustice differ from the way the problem of injustice is typically framed today?
2. How does the new covenant's solution for injustice in the transformation of the heart shape our methods and aims for justice?
3. How does the new covenant as inaugurated but not yet consummated both excite and temper our expectations for justice in the world around us?
4. How does the Bible's Christocentric solution to injustice propel the Christian pursuit of justice today?
5. How does the gospel relate to justice and righteousness in the Christian life?

Suggested Reading

DeYoung, Kevin and Greg Gilbert. *What Is the Mission of the Church? Making Sense of Social Justice, Shalom, and the Great Commission*. Wheaton, IL: Crossway, 2011.

Gentry, Peter J. and Stephen J. Wellum. *Kingdom through Covenant: A Biblical-Theological Understanding of the Covenants*. 2nd ed. Wheaton, IL: Crossway, 2018.

[34] Jonathan Leeman, *What Is the Church's Mission?* Church Questions (Wheaton, IL: Crossway, 2022).

Schreiner, Thomas R. *Covenant and God's Purpose for the World.* Short Studies in Biblical Theology. Wheaton, IL: Crossway, 2017.

Shenvi, Neil and Pat Sawyer. *Critical Dilemma: The Rise of Critical Theories and Social Justice Ideology—Implications for the Church and Society.* Eugene, OR: Harvest House, 2023.

Williams, Thaddeus J. *Confronting Injustice Without Compromising Truth: 12 Questions Christians Should Ask About Social Justice.* Grand Rapids: Zondervan Academic, 2020.

7

Justice and the Character of God

— Justin McLendon —

Introduction

Our concern in this chapter will be to unfold a theological rationale for Christian engagement within the important conversations related to social justice. To be sure, there is no shortage of societal interest in the ongoing dialogue pertaining to matters that broadly address social justice concerns. Indeed, persistent interest in these matters seems appropriate, for all image-bearers inherently discern the brokenness of this east-of-Eden life. Further, we cannot unsee the images nor silence the cries contained within the twenty-four-hour news cycle. For our purposes, it seems prudent to acknowledge that Christian participation in these topics will no doubt vary and presumably fall within the familiar corridors of those Christian communities whose advocacy on these matters remains consistent and expected. Still, many other Christians will engage these issues for different purposes and with varying levels of activity, often due to their proximity to localized events or regional disputes that require thoughtful Christian listening and dialogue. Christians are never far from social justice concerns, and our nearness to these issues provides an entry point to speak and act in ways that are commensurate with the gospel. From every vantage point, our pluralistic society cries for justice, but few seem to provide a clear understanding of what this entails.

This essay will briefly delve into the multifaceted concepts of God's moral attributes within Christian theology, exploring their theological foundation and the responsibility Christians possess to view all of life *coram Deo*, especially as we shape a theological framework from which to view and engage social justice concerns. In what follows, our task is not to construct a guide of practical steps for Christians and/or churches to employ as we assess how to engage conversations, and/or how we should implement strategic changes. Other contributors will explore critical issues of practical theology and ministry. While I am at ease with the reality that Christian cultural engagement will have a diversity of practical expressions, I am jealous that we think and respond Christianly by anchoring our concern and advocacy through the theological lens of the God who is there (to borrow a term from Francis Schaeffer), thus instilling in believers a methodological scrutiny against the floodwaters of relativism. Stated simply, the burden of this chapter is to urge Christians to view all matters pertaining to social justice through the lens of the doctrine of God. God is good, holy, and just, and Christian image-bearers are tasked with embodying these traits in every facet of our daily lives. At the very least, this involves the intellectual patience to think carefully about how the brokenness of our world is to be confronted in both word and deed. Pastors and church leaders bear the responsibility to provide their congregations with a theological framework to live under the lordship of Christ in all things (Ps 103:19; Col 1:15–17). In what follows, we will structure a theological framework for pastors and church leaders to guide Christians in their social justice advocacy.

God and Derivatives

As Christians observe and engage social justice discussions, my concern is twofold: first, and to no one's surprise, the evolution of secular worldviews has produced no shortage of substitutes from which we may ground the legitimacy of social justice protests. Regardless of how they differ in content or workability, these secular substitutes uniformly avoid the inclusion of a transcendent creator whose claims of sovereignty have been unambiguously revealed: "The earth and everything in it, the world and its inhabitants, belong to the LORD; for he laid its foundation on the seas and established it on the rivers" (Ps 24:1–2). Or perhaps it would be helpful to remember with Job that we, mere creatures, were not present when God laid the earth's foundations, nor can we bind the chains of the Pleiades, and we are even less likely to possess the wisdom to number the clouds (Job 38). Thus, any responsible *Christian* talk of social justice (or "biblical justice") is inseparable from responsible Christian talk of God. One cannot propose a genuinely Christian advocacy if God is derivative of their concerns and protest.

Despite differences on matters of cultural engagement within the Christian tradition, we must affirm the objective, transcendent standard by which we judge all things. When Christian responses ignore this starting point, we inevitably become acolytes armed with clickbait slogans and superficial resolutions, ultimately failing to provide a counter to secular proposals, or even worse, we inevitably promote a hollowed-out version of Christianity that obscures the inherent hope of the gospel once for all delivered to the saints. Herman Bavinck reminds us that the gospel, understood in its fullest sense, addresses the aims we seek when we look through the lens of the gospel upon the sin-ravaged landscape of our world: "The Gospel is a joyful tiding, not only for the individual person but also for humanity, for the family, for society, for the state, for art and science, for the entire cosmos, for the whole groaning creation."[1] This vision foregrounds man's separation from God, and the outworking of God's redemptive work extends "as far as the curse is found."

A second concern relates to how Christian social engagement is tethered to Scripture. "Christian theology is biblical reasoning," argues theologian

---

[1] Herman Bavinck, "The Catholicity of Christianity and the Church," *Calvin Theological Journal* 27, no. 2 (1992): 224.

John Webster. As such, biblical reasoning "is an activity of the created intellect, judged, reconciled, redeemed and sanctified through the works of the Son and the Spirit."[2] Regardless of topic, theological inquiry requires the steadfast work of biblical reasoning, for through an encounter with divine revelation, our intellectual architecture is shaped by and conformed to Scripture. Further, because this subject generates no shortage of cultural commentators, it is not uncommon to hear advocacy that employs biblical imagery or expressions, even if the appeal to biblical texts or principles is borne from ignorance. "The truth will set you free" can be shouted by anyone and for any cause, and this proclamation will no doubt stir a crowd to action, but on its own, this declaration may not stir anyone's heart toward its true author. Biblical reasoning, therefore, must follow our submission to the God who *is*, forming for believers a decidedly different epistemological framework among the contested worldviews of our day.

Thaddeus Williams rightly notes that "social justice is one of the most epic and age-defining controversies facing the twenty-first-century church."[3] Few will challenge this observation, but Christians cannot rightly address a topic of such importance without a biblical framework inclusive of the true story of God's character, humanity's purpose, sin's treachery, Jesus's mission to save sinners and renew the cosmos, and the Spirit's sanctifying work in and through the church (in both its local and global expressions). Biblical reasoning, therefore, frames our witness to comport with divine revelation. We are all too aware of how often biblical reasoning is jettisoned or maligned in favor of procuring ready-made responses, often void of theological precision, to accommodate the Bible (or God) according to modern sensibilities.

---

[2] John Webster, *The Domain of the Word: Scripture and Theological Reason* (London: Bloomsbury T&T Clark, 2014), 115.

[3] Thaddeus Williams, *Confronting Injustice without Compromising Truth: 12 Questions Christians Should Ask About Social Justice* (Grand Rapids: Zondervan Academic, 2020), 1.

A classic example of this can be found in John Steinbeck's 1939 novel, *The Grapes of Wrath*. This classic tells the story of the Joads, a dispossessed Oklahoma farming family forced to migrate to California during the Great Depression. Tom Joad is the story's protagonist, serving as a mediatorial figure between his parents (Pa and Ma Joad) and his much younger siblings (Ruthie and Winfield). Tom also serves as an authority figure with the older Joad children (Al, Noah, and Rose of Sharon), especially as their Oklahoma exodus confounds their moral reasoning. The story begins as Tom is paroled from prison after incarceration for manslaughter, having been released on good behavior, and his release is just in time to join his family in their arduous westward journey to the promise of California's abundance and security. In the Joad family's wanderings, Steinbeck carefully recounts the challenges many American families encountered during this era, especially as economic hardships often gave way to discrimination and exploitation. Steinbeck painstakingly portrays the voracious greed of the rich and powerful, while frequently displaying the moral self-justification the powerful employ to oppress the impoverished. For our purposes, throughout the novel, Tom Joad assesses these social challenges with the aid of an influential religious interlocutor.

Shortly upon his prison release, Tom finds Jim Casy, a well-known preacher with a reputation for holding revival meetings and baptisms in the irrigation ditch. Initially, Casy was a conventional minister whose interests centered upon salvation and morality, but when we meet him in the opening pages of the novel, he is mentally processing the suffering and exploitation of the indigent workers during the Dust Bowl era. Casy's evaluation of social injustice creates a disillusionment with and a subtle rejection of his belief that organized religion could adequately address the plight of the sufferer. Casy's spiritual evolution unmoors him from traditional or orthodox theological convictions to embrace what can only be described as secular humanism.

We are alerted to Casy's shifting theological commitments on the occasions when he is called upon to pray, and whenever this occurs, he acknowledges his doubts about the adequacy of prayer in the face of suffering. In these instances, Casy alerts anyone who will listen of his threadbare faith and his resolute conviction that he is no longer a preacher and has no interest in playing the part. But we also detect Casy's theological shift when he is questioned about sin, which happens at several intervals in the story's plot. In one of his early replies, Casy declares, "There ain't no sin and there ain't no virtue. There's just stuff people do."[4] His growing antipathy of traditional Christianity foments in the face of societal hardship and injustice, ultimately affecting the Joad family's worldview. Steinbeck uses these characters to adjudicate the moral responsibility of aligning religious dogma to the blight of social injustices. As Rachel McCoppin observes, for Steinbeck, "Christ must be recast in modern terms in order to meet contemporary needs, and, for this reason, Casy's Christ-likeness must downplay its spiritual dimension and privilege its moral responsibility toward his fellow humans instead."[5] Though Steinbeck's story is fictional, our real-world experiences provide ample opportunity to overturn or rearrange our first-order theological commitments, refashioning our perception of God under the rubrics of our protestations. When preachers like the Reverend Casy fail to account for the presence of a good and transcendent God in the face of evil and injustice, we can only expect the continual erosion of biblical reasoning to those under clerical influence.

Preacher Casy's theological unraveling recalls one of C. S. Lewis's observations about a modern shift in man's appropriation of God. Lewis observes that ancient man approached God with a sense of reverential awe, as if they

---

[4] John Steinbeck, *The Grapes of Wrath*, with an introduction by Robert DeMott (New York: Penguin, 1992), 32.

[5] Rachel McCoppin, "The Many Faces of Jesus in Steinbeck's *The Grapes of Wrath*," *Studies in the Literary Imagination* 46, no. 2 (2013): 42. There are reams of literary criticism focused upon Steinbeck's entanglement of religion in his literary corpus, especially in *The Grapes of Wrath*. As such, Preacher Jim Casy is often viewed as a prominent Christ figure throughout Steinbeck's masterpiece. See, for example, Tamara Rombold, "Biblical Inversion in The Grapes of Wrath" *College Literature* 14, no. 2 (1987): 146–66; Charles T. Dougherty, "The Christ-Figure in The Grapes of Wrath," *College English* 24, no. 3 (1962): 224–26.

were accused persons accountable to and appearing before a sovereign judge. In contrast, modern man has circumvented his status before God, reversing the roles of authority and submission. Thus, modern man becomes the judge and "God is in the dock." As Lewis describes, "He [man] is quite a kindly judge: if God should have a reasonable defence for being the god who permits war, poverty and disease, he is ready to listen to it. The trial may even end in God's acquittal. But the important thing is that Man is on the Bench and God in the Dock."[6] Perhaps it is here that we must wrestle our minds out of any theological slumber by admitting that when God is derivative of creatures, and when creatures prosecute their creator, we have abandoned our moral compass and marginalized and domesticated the transcendence of God.[7] If we fail to think theologically, we will resort to joining the world's epistemological framework when judging all that ails our world.

Thankfully, when we return to biblical reasoning, we can recall as we must that Paul envisions worship as a giving of ourselves *in toto*, for it is holy and pleasing to God when we offer ourselves as living sacrifices (Rom 12:1). What follows, of course, is Paul's prohibition of conforming ourselves to this age and his insistence upon reordering our lives to God's will through the Spirit's renovation of our hearts and minds. "Do not be conformed to this age," Paul commands, "but be transformed by the renewing of your mind, so that you may discern what is the good, pleasing, and perfect will of God" (Rom 12:2). As Thomas R. Schreiner aptly summarizes, "Give yourselves wholly to God; do not be shaped by the old world order, but let new thought patterns transform your life."[8] John Calvin connects consecration of self as the genesis of how we fashion our actions before the living God: "To know ourselves to be consecrated to God is the beginning of a proper

---

[6] C. S. Lewis, *God in the Dock: Essays on Theology and Ethics* (Grand Rapids: Eerdmans, 1970), 264.

[7] I am borrowing this phrase from William C. Placher, *The Domestication of Transcendence: How Modern Thinking about God Went Wrong* (Louisville: Westminster John Knox, 1996).

[8] Thomas R. Schreiner, *Romans*, BECNT (Grand Rapids: Baker, 2018), 609.

course of life for attaining good works, since it hence follows, that we cease to live to ourselves, with the intention of devoting all the actions of our lives to God."[9] Because sin, evil, and dehumanization are a global pollution, we can expect Christians to respond in various ways through their local churches, parachurch ministries, and their own individual efforts. We must take great care in resisting a one-size-fits-all response to all that ails this fallen world, while also acknowledging that which distinguishes a theologically informed perspective over and against all other responses.

To be sure, we should inquire of the good in any proposal, regardless of its author. We should affirm with Calvin that

> "all truth is from God; and consequently, if wicked men have said anything that is true and just, we ought not to reject it; for it has come from God. Besides, all things are of God; and, therefore, why should it not be lawful to dedicate to his glory everything that can properly be employed for such a purpose?"[10]

Thus, we have a responsibility to listen and learn from everyone, seeking truth wherever it may be found. From a Christian worldview, however, God's goodness, holiness, and justice must inform our appraisal and our advocacy.

---

[9] John Calvin, *Commentary on Romans*, ed. Timothy George (Nashville: B&H Academic, 2022), 364.

[10] John Calvin, *Commentaries on the Epistles to Timothy, Titus, and Philemon* (Grand Rapids: Baker, 2005), 300–301. In the *Institutes,* Calvin argues, "Whenever we come upon these matters in secular writers, let that admirable light of truth shining in them teach us that the mind of man, though fallen and perverted from its wholeness, is nevertheless clothed and ornamented with God's excellent gifts. If we regard the Spirit of God as the sole fountain of truth, we shall neither reject the truth itself, nor despise it wherever it shall appear, unless we wish to dishonor the Spirit of God." See John Calvin, *Institutes of the Christian Religion*, ed. John T. McNeill, trans. Ford Lewis Battles (Louisville: Westminster John Knox, 1960), 1:323–24. As such, we should not be surprised to find biblically faithful concerns or solutions from "secular" audiences.

God's Attributes

Calvin famously begins his *Institutes* by acknowledging that man's wisdom comprises knowledge of self and God.[11] True wisdom begins with self-knowledge, he argues, which involves recognizing our creaturely limitations, our inherent sinfulness, and our utter dependency upon God. This self-awareness leads to a broader and deeper appraisal of the human condition, especially humanity's moral bankruptcy and the universal need for redemption. Calvin believes mere knowledge of self is incomplete without knowledge of God; however, if we are to understand ourselves truly, we must also have a proper understanding of God. In other words, we must grapple with the Creator-creature distinction in our assessment of God and all things derivative of his majesty and works.

Yet in our quest to know God, we quickly and inevitably contemplate the sheer reality of God's incomprehensibility. Of course, when we speak of God's incomprehensibility, we are not claiming an absolute inability to know God. Rather, we are acknowledging that we cannot grasp God exhaustively. So, Aquinas attests, "It is impossible for any created intellect to comprehend God."[12] Human experience proves that we exist within finite boundaries, and we knowingly and frustratingly operate within finite perspectives. Our sphere of existence, confined within finite realms, contrasts with God's existence, which transcends human perceptibility (Ps 145:3).

God's incomprehensibility acts as a boundary, cautioning any presumption we may have of mastering the entirety of God's essence. We can recall Isaiah's admission, knowing that he speaks for all of us: "For my thoughts are not your thoughts, and your ways are not my ways," and what is the heavenly response? "This is the LORD's declaration. 'For as heaven is higher than earth, so my ways are higher than your ways, and my thoughts than

---

[11] Calvin, *Institutes*, 1:92.

[12] Thomas Aquinas, *Summa Theologica* 1.12.4 (Notre Dame: Christian Classics, 1948).

your thoughts'" (Is 55:8–9). How can this gulf be resolved, and how can we speak with any certainty that we have knowledge of God and his ways? Bavinck's response is worth quoting in full. He answers,

> The distance between God and us is the gulf between the Infinite and the finite, between eternity and time, between being and becoming, between the All and the nothing. However little we know of God, even the faintest notion implies that he is a being who is infinitely exalted above every creature. While Holy Scripture affirms this truth in the strongest terms, it nevertheless sets forth a doctrine of God that fully upholds his knowability. Scripture, one must remember, never makes any attempt to prove the existence of God, but simply presupposes it. Moreover, in this connection it consistently assumes that human beings have an ineradicable sense of that existence and a certain knowledge of God's being. This knowledge does not arise from their own investigation and reflection, but is due to the fact that God on his part revealed himself to us in nature and history, in prophecy and miracle, by ordinary and by extraordinary means. In Scripture, therefore, the knowability of God is never in doubt even for a moment. . . . The purpose of God's revelation, according to Scripture, is precisely that human beings may know God and so receive eternal life (John 17:3; 20:31).[13]

While human finitude restrains our comprehension of God, Christians affirm that true knowledge of God leads to adoration, consecration, worship, and an informed life of walking by faith.

At this point, we must note critical errors that may arise when we acknowledge this mystery.[14] One error is to conclude that since God is

---

[13] Herman Bavinck, *Reformed Dogmatics: God and Creation*, ed. John Bolt, trans. John Vriend (Grand Rapids: Baker, 2004), 2:30.

[14] For a helpful description of common errors, see Matthew Barrett, *None Greater: The Undomesticated Attributes of God* (Grand Rapids: Baker, 2019), 28–29.

incomprehensible, our attempts to articulate his essence become nonsensical, rendering all discourse about God meaningless. In response, we can affirm the rationality of God while acknowledging his incomprehensibility. Though our understanding of God remains limited, God's initiative in revealing himself to us must be seen as intelligible communication, not irrational babble or meaningless expressions, so we must claim that the incomprehensible God has genuinely revealed himself and has willed that we know him. Again, Aquinas clarifies, "God is called incomprehensible not because anything of Him is not seen; but because He is not seen as perfectly as He is capable of being seen."[15] In fact, we can affirm that God, being personal and possessing distinct attributes, has chosen to reveal himself intimately, allowing for a true and personal understanding of his nature.

The recognition that God is incomprehensible underscores that we have not attained exhaustive knowledge of God but possess a functional understanding crucial for our lives. It requires us to question how we can meaningfully articulate concepts regarding the incomprehensible God, especially as we seek to live in conformity to his will. For our purposes, we must recall the differences between univocal, equivocal, and analogical speech when we speak of God. In sum, univocal language suggests that the words and concepts used to describe God have the exact same meaning and understanding when applied to God as they do when applied to human beings. But we know this approach fails, because "God is wise" and "man is wise" cannot have the exact same meaning. Equivocal language refers to the use of words or concepts that have completely different meanings. For example, we know the difference between a "dog's bark" and "tree bark." When we discuss God's perfections and human image-bearers, we understand that the communicable attributes do not have completely different meanings. For these reasons, we recognize that we speak of God analogically, which means we use the same word to convey two meanings. In doing so, we recognize that human language and concepts are limited in their ability to fully

[15] Aquinas, *Summa Theologica* 1.12.7.

and directly describe or comprehend God, who is transcendent and beyond humanity's comprehensive understanding.[16] So, "God is good" and "man is good" is best understood analogously. Created in God's image, we know something of human goodness because we know that God *is* good, for his goodness is quantitatively and qualitatively different from any creaturely goodness. Michael Horton claims that the doctrine of analogy "is the hinge on which a Christian affirmation of God's transcendence and immanence turns. A univocal view threatens God's transcendence, while an equivocal view threatens God's immanence. The former leads to rationalism, while the latter engenders skepticism."[17]

From these considerations, we can recall that theologians frequently distinguish God's attributes between incommunicable and communicable, especially as this distinction serves as a conceptual framework to comprehend the nature and characteristics of God and creation.[18] This differentiation serves our efforts to categorize the attributes of God into two distinct groups based on their relation to human beings and the extent to which they can be shared or mirrored in humanity. God's incommunicable attributes are often expressed by way of negation, clarifying ways in which God is *not* like creatures (e.g., God is *not* limited in knowledge, wisdom, power, etc.). Scripture overwhelmingly attests to qualities of God that are wholly unique to his divine nature and cannot be replicated or shared with humanity. These attributes underscore God's transcendence and uniqueness, his self-existence, omnipotence, omniscience, and omnipresence. Thus, incommunicable attributes distinguish the inherent differences between God and humanity, emphasizing God's unparalleled and transcendent nature beyond all creaturely limitations.

---

[16] See Francis Turretin, *Institutes of Elenctic Theology*, ed. James T. Dennison Jr., trans. George Musgrave Giger (Phillipsburg, NJ: P&R, 1992), 1:190–91.

[17] Michael Horton, *The Christian Faith: A Systematic Theology for Pilgrims on the Way* (Grand Rapids: Zondervan, 2011), 55.

[18] See Horton, *The Christian Faith*, 225–72.

Conversely, the communicable attributes of God denote those aspects of God's character that can be shared or communicated to humanity in some capacity. These attributes highlight the aspects of God's nature that can be reflected in *all* image-bearers and sanctified among God's people. Examples include love, goodness, justice, mercy, and holiness. While we cannot fully exhibit these attributes to the same extent as God, we can reflect them to a limited degree in our lives, vocations, relationships, and interactions with others. Furthermore, within the communicable attributes, theologians speak of God's moral attributes. Bavinck, for example, follows this approach, listing goodness, holiness, and justice as communicable, moral attributes.[19] Goodness, holiness, and justice are seen as communicable because they are qualities that can be imitated or reflected in the lives of human beings, and they serve as a rubric for how we ascertain that which is true, good, and beautiful.

Before we briefly explore God's moral attributes, it is worth remembering that God is simple; he is not divided into parts because he is not a composite or compounded being.[20] As Petrus Van Mastricht notes, "All the attributes together in God are nothing but one certain most simple and most pure act, his very essence, and his infinite perfection."[21] We may say that an automobile is an accumulation of parts and taking a look under the hood gives us a sense of how each part connects to the whole, but we think this way because we know that automobiles are the result of accumulating and connecting various parts. Unlike an automobile, God cannot be divided into separate parts. Rather than viewing God's attributes as parts of a whole, we confess that God *is* his attributes, so all that is in God *is* God. His divine nature is singular and simple, which means that his attributes exist in perfect

---

[19] Bavinck, *Reformed Dogmatics*, 2:210–28.

[20] For more on divine simplicity, see Steven Duby, *Divine Simplicity: A Dogmatic Account* (London: Bloomsbury T&T Clark, 2016).

[21] Petrus Van Mastricht, *Theoretical-Practical Theology: Faith in the Triune God*, trans. Todd M. Rester; ed. Joel R. Beeke (Grand Rapids: Reformation Heritage, 2019), 2:117.

harmony with who he is. In essence, God's attributes are not abstract qualities that exist independently from him; rather, they are inseparable from his entire being and perfection as the one true God. John Webster explains the significance,

> To inquire into the attributes of God is thus not to ask about supposed attributes of deity in general, about what a god must be. It is to ask about the particular perfection in which God is himself, inquiring into the characteristic and wholly unique depth of the divine being in which God confirms himself in all his abundance and grace.[22]

We can now ask about the particular perfections of God's moral attributes, especially as we seek to form a theological vision for engaging matters of social justice. Detailed treatments of goodness, holiness, and justice can be found in various systematic theologies, but for our purposes brief summaries suffice.

Goodness

Scripture overwhelmingly testifies that God is good in his character and his actions: "You are good, and you do what is good; teach me your statutes" (Ps 119:68). As Maximus the Confessor explains, "For just as it is the property of light to shine, just so it is the property of God to do good."[23] God's goodness is plentiful (Exod 34:6; Ps 31:19) and remains constantly present in our lives (Ps 23:6). All that is good originates from God (Jas 1:17), and our weary souls can only find genuine satisfaction through his benevolent goodness (Ps 107:8–9). God is inherently good, performs acts of goodness,

---

[22] John Webster, *Confessing God: Essays in Christian Dogmatics II* (London: Bloomsbury T&T Clark, 2014), 112.

[23] Maximus the Confessor, *Two Hundred Chapters on Theology*, trans. Luis Joshua Salés (New York: St. Vladimir's Seminary Press, 2015), 63.

and bestows good gifts upon his children (Ps 119:68; Luke 11:13). Not to be left out in the Bible's consistent proclamation of God's goodness, Jesus affirms that "No one is good except God alone" (Mark 10:18). God's goodness exists by necessity, for as the texts above demonstrate, God's goodness is something he *is* and something he *does.* Thus, Bavinck summarizes God's goodness in terms of perfection, "All virtues are present in him in an absolute sense. . . . He does not have to become anything, but is what he is eternally."[24] Ivor Davidson agrees, claiming that divine goodness is "all that he is at once and essentially."[25] Katherine Sonderegger similarly expresses, "It is not simply that God is good, though to be sure that is true; it is rather that God is Infinite Goodness, the Good of every kind and degree and instance, infinitely His own."[26]

We can press further, though. God's goodness is not dependent on anything or anyone else. He is inherently good, and all other goodness comes from him. Creatures exist, become good, and remain good because of God's love for them. God is perfectly good, with no possibility of becoming better or worse.[27] So, Charnock claims, when we speak of God's goodness, we are speaking of "a boundless goodness that knows no limits, a goodness as infinite as his essence, not only good, but best; not only good, but goodness itself, the supreme inconceivable goodness."[28]

For our purposes, we must also consider that divine goodness is communicative, but what does this mean? In sum, this means that God not only possesses goodness within his nature but actively wills, communicates,

---

[24] Bavinck, *Reformed Dogmatics*, 2:211.

[25] Ivor J. Davidson, "Divine Sufficiency: Theology in the Presence of God," in *Theological Theology: Essays in Honour of John Webster*, ed. R. David Nelson, Darren Sarisky, and Justin Stratis (London: Bloomsbury T&T Clark, 2015), 67.

[26] Katherine Sonderegger, *Systematic Theology: The Doctrine of God* (Minneapolis: Fortress, 2015), 1:129.

[27] Thomas Joseph White, *The Trinity: On the Nature and Mystery of the One God* (Washington, DC: The Catholic University of America Press, 2022), 275.

[28] Stephen Charnock, *Discourses Upon the Existence and Attributes of God* (Grand Rapids: Baker, 1979), 2:211.

and extends that goodness to his creation. God's goodness is demonstrated through various means, such as his acts of love, mercy, compassion, and provision. Bavinck speaks to the communicative expression, noting that "God's goodness is much more glorious when it is shown to those who only deserve evil."[29] It is evident in his care for creation, his willingness to forgive and restore, and his desire for the well-being and flourishing of all that he has made. In this sense, then, this communicative aspect of God's goodness highlights God's desire to be in relationship with creatures and to make his goodness known. Christopher Holmes explains,

> Divine goodness, because it is divine, is not a participated goodness, that is, had in relation to another. Goodness and God are one and the same, even if there were no world. The marvel of marvels is that God communicates his profound goodness to us in creation and in Christ (and the Spirit) to make us perfect, and not to make himself perfect.[30]

Thus, it is through this communication of God's goodness that we can experience and participate in the blessings and benefits that flow from God's nature. Divine goodness as communicative also implies that God invites humanity to participate in his goodness and reflect it in their own lives. As recipients of God's goodness, we are called to emulate and extend it to others, becoming channels through which God's goodness is communicated to the world.

Holiness

The whole sweep of redemptive history is a presentation and magnification of God's holiness. We recall the Song of Moses: "Lord, who is like you

---

[29] Bavinck, *Reformed Dogmatics*, 2:214.

[30] Christopher R. J. Holmes, *The Lord is Good: Seeking the God of the Psalter* (Downers Grove, IL: IVP Academic, 2018), 29.

among the gods? Who is like you, glorious in holiness, revered with praises, performing wonders?" (Exod 15:11). We remember that Moses is commanded to tell the Israelites: "Be holy because I, the Lord your God, am holy" (Lev 19:2). And few preachers can resist expounding Isaiah's encounter with and vision of the exalted Lord, surrounded by angelic beings who proclaim, "Holy, holy, holy is the Lord of Armies; his glory fills the whole earth" (Isa 6:3). When we gaze upon absolute holiness, we join Isaiah's declaration that we have unclean lips and dwell among those who have unclean lips (Isa 6:5). Moreover, we are reminded of the Bible's proclamation that God is "the Holy One" (Isa 40:25; Ezek 39:7; Hab 1:12), and he is the "Holy One of Israel" (2 Kgs 19:22; Isa 1:4; 43:3; Jer 50:29; 51:5). From this we can conclude that Israel's call to holiness is rooted in the essential nature of God's holy being, and that these attributes are eternal and unchanging.

To speak of God's holiness is to speak of God's moral perfection, purity, and separation from sin. Sometimes theologians speak of holiness as encompassing God's unique and transcendent nature, righteousness, and unapproachable greatness. So, John Goldingay claims, "In Christian parlance 'holy' is a moral category; it points to the absolute integrity, uprightness, goodness and righteousness of God, to be reflected by those who claim to belong to God."[31] While this is helpful, we should also consider holiness as consecration or devotion, especially in the realm of God's holy love.[32] Thus, Millard Erickson claims, "One's holiness is fully and correctly assessed only when measured by the standard of perfect holiness, that of

---

[31] John Goldingay, *Old Testament Theology: Israel's Faith* (Downers Grove, IL: IVP, 2006), 23.

[32] It is worth noting that Peter Gentry challenges what he considers to be a common error among systematic theologians as it relates to the biblical definition of holiness. Instead of moral purity or transcendence, Gentry claims the term means consecrated or devoted. See Peter Gentry, "The Meaning of 'Holy' in the Old Testament," *BibSac* 170 (2013): 400–417.

God."[33] Yet God's holiness also serves as the means by which he governs the world. As Stephen Wellum argues, God's holiness is "the objective moral standard of goodness, justice, and righteousness so that all that stand in opposition to God's will and nature is sin."[34]

As a holy God, he cannot overlook or tolerate sin because it is fundamentally contrary to his nature and character. Sin is an offense against his holiness and violates his perfect standard of righteousness. Being holy, God "will not leave the guilty unpunished" (Exod 34:7). Bavinck claims that God's holiness is "the principle of punishment and chastisement" brought by God against sin: "When Israel breaks covenant, desecrates his name, and violates his laws, it is precisely God's holiness that incites him to mete out punishment."[35]

As believers, we are called to imitate God and reflect his character in our thoughts, attitudes, and actions (1 Pet 1:16). God's holiness sets the standard for our own holiness, and we are called to pursue righteousness and purity. This prompts us to pursue personal sanctification, allowing the Holy Spirit to work in our lives, transforming us into the likeness of Christ. Recognizing God's holiness compels us to worship, acknowledging his worthiness and majesty (Ps 96:9). God's holiness also influences our relationships with others. We are called to love others as God has loved us, showing compassion, forgiveness, and grace. Our interactions with others should reflect God's holiness and demonstrate his love. Finally, a holy life involves actively participating in God's mission to bring redemption, justice, and reconciliation to the world. We are called to share the good news of salvation while caring for the widow and orphan (Jas 1:27).

---

[33] Millard Erickson, *Christian Theology*, 2nd ed. (Grand Rapids: Baker Academic, 1998), 326.

[34] Stephen Wellum, "Thinking Biblically and Theologically about Justice," *Christ Over All* (July 7, 2023), https://christoverall.com/article/longform/thinking-biblically-and-theologically-about-justice/.

[35] Bavinck, *Reformed Dogmatics*, 2:220.

Justice

Both Old and New Testaments provide countless references to God's justice, emphasizing his righteousness, fairness, and impartiality. Psalm 89:14 proclaims, "Righteousness and justice are the foundation of your throne; faithful love and truth go before you." God's justice is consistently upheld as an essential facet of his character. Psalm 33:5 declares, "He loves righteousness and justice; the earth is full of the LORD's unfailing love." Christopher Wright argues that for Israel, "Justice was no abstract concept or philosophical definition. Justice was essentially theological. It was rooted in the character of the LORD, their God . . . Justice on earth flows from justice in heaven."[36]

When we acknowledge that God is infinitely, eternally, and unchangeably just, we affirm that he never turns a blind eye to wrongdoing. He does not disregard sin or make excuses for wickedness: "The Rock—his work is perfect; all his ways are just. A faithful God, without bias, he is righteous and true" (Deut 32:4). Thus, God's justice is an essential aspect of his character and is inseparable from his unchanging and inherently righteous nature, ensuring that he always acts in accordance with what is right and good. The biblical concept of justice demonstrates that God's justice is both retributive and reparative.[37] As Brakel claims, "God, by virtue of His perfect, holy, and righteous character is inclined as the only wise God to punish sin at a time and in a manner suitable to Him."[38]

Retributive justice means that wrongdoing should be met with appropriate punishment or consequences. Because of his just character, God will not spare the wicked (Ezek 7:4), he will not take a bribe (Deut 10:17), he hates

---

[36] Christopher J. H. Wright, *Old Testament Ethics for the People of God* (Downers Grove, IL: IVP Academic, 2004), 254.

[37] See Bavinck, *Reformed Dogmatics*, 2:221–28.

[38] Wilhelmus à Brakel, *The Christian's Reasonable Service: God, Man, and Christ*, trans. Bartel Elshout, ed. Joel R. Beeke (Grand Rapids: Reformation Heritage, 1992), 128.

unjust scales (Prov 11:1), and his judgment is impartial (Rom 2:12–16). As the ultimate Judge of all the earth, Paul acknowledges that we must keep in view that God will judge all evil: "Friends, do not avenge yourselves; instead, leave room for God's wrath, because it is written, 'Vengeance belongs to me; I will repay,' says the Lord" (Rom 12:19). This aspect of God's justice has been hijacked, however. As Tim Keller rightly notes, "Identity politics grounded claims for justice not in an objective moral order but in their own group's unique perceptions and experience."[39]

Biblical justice is also remunerative or reparative. While retributive justice focuses on punishment and consequences, reparative justice accounts for the possibility of redemption, reconciliation, and restoration. The ultimate expression of God's reparative justice is seen in the work of redemption through Jesus Christ. Through his sacrificial death and resurrection, Jesus offers forgiveness, reconciliation, and the restoration of relationship with God. This act of divine justice provides the means for humanity to be reconciled with God and experience true healing and restoration. As Wellum summarizes, "These attributes remind us that God is not only the absolute standard of objective moral norms but also the one who upholds his own glory in the redemption of his people and in his judgment of all sin and evil."[40]

Applications for Pastors and Ministry Leaders

How does this brief survey inform Christian engagement in social justice concerns? The question itself is far more difficult to answer than we might immediately realize. After all, take a moment and consider the vast differences in social justice concerns for Christians in the West compared to the

---

[39] Tim Keller, "The Decline and Renewal of the American Church," *Gospel in Life* (2022), 28. https://quarterly.gospelinlife.com/decline-and-renewal-of-the-american-church-extended/.

[40] Wellum, "Thinking Biblically."

everyday experiences of religious repression in China.[41] We could go on, for international examples abound, especially in the aftermath of the bloody twentieth century and the growing pockets of war near and far. Closer to home, we cannot forget that urban and rural citizens confront similar but also decidedly different challenges, yet in both cases, the universality of sin's curse and devastation remains the same and must be confronted. To refashion Kuyper's famous "every square inch" quote, while it is true that Christ's lordship extends to every square inch of creation, it is equally true that every square inch is contested real estate.[42] We rightly affirm the Bible's storyline of God's covenant of redemption from creation to re-creation, yet we also know that "our ancient foe doth seek to work us woe."[43] For these reasons, there is no shortage of thoughtful resources that provide specific answers to Christian engagement in these matters, but these resources are only as good as the methodological structure that supports them. Until Christ returns, we bear the responsibility to construct a theological vision whose methodology accounts for a decidedly biblical vision of God and creatures.

For starters, as we explored above, a Christian's theological vision is in direct contrast to all rival visions, all of which uniformly operate from a diverse array of worldview constructions. Because of the Spirit's sanctifying work of renewal, we walk in newness of life (Rom 6:4), putting to death our old way of thinking and our selfish methodologies, and are by God's grace having our thoughts, affections, and actions reordered to our transcendent

---

[41] For a concise summary of China's recent religious repression, see Sam Brownback and Erica Lizza, "China's Proxy War Against Faith," *The Hill* (April 23, 2023), https://thehill.com/opinion/congress-blog/3965263-chinas-proxy-war-against-faith/. For a recent account of the house church movement, see Wang Yi, *Faithful Disobedience: Writings on Church and State from a Chinese House Church Movement*, ed. Hannah Nation and J. D. Tseng (Downers Grove, IL: IVP Academic, 2022).

[42] From Abraham Kuyper's 1880 inaugural address at the founding of the Free University of Amsterdam: "There's not a square inch in the whole domain of human existence over which Christ, who is Lord over all, does not exclaim, 'Mine!'"

[43] From the hymn "A Mighty Fortress Is Our God."

God. Thus, a theological vision must possess the same goal as Christian theology, which according to Webster,

> "is a work of regenerate intelligence, awakened and illuminated by divine instruction to consider a twofold object. This object is, first, God in himself in the unsurpassable perfection of his inner being and work as Father, Son and Spirit and in his outer operations, and, second and by derivation, all other things relative to him."[44]

What do we have to offer our world in our joint concern over social justice issues? We have a regenerate intelligence that helps us proclaim light into the darkness, compassion to the downtrodden, and rebuke to evil imbalances of power that marginalize and victimize image-bearers.

As we consider this, we can find help from John M. Perkins, a civil rights leader, Christian minister, and community developer. Throughout his life and ministry, he experienced racism and discrimination firsthand, and these experiences led to his involvement in the Civil Rights Movement in the 1960s. He was a leader in the Freedom Rides and the March on Washington. He also founded the Christian Community Development Association (CCDA), a network of Christian organizations that work to address poverty and injustice. Perkins's tireless advocacy for the poor and marginalized spans decades, and his commitment to this work was borne out of his belief that Christians bear a responsibility to spread truth and justice against all its opponents.[45] As for methodology, Perkins argues,

> "First, *start with God!* God is bigger than we can imagine. We have to align ourselves with his purpose, his will, his mission to let justice roll down, and bring forgiveness and love to everyone on earth.

[44] John Webster, *God Without Measure: Working Papers in Christian Theology, Volume I: God and the Works of God* (London: T&T Clark, 2016), 3.

[45] See John Perkins, *With Justice for All: A Strategy for Community Development* (repr., Grand Rapids: Baker, 2014); John Perkins, *Let Justice Roll Down* (repr., Grand Rapids: Baker, 2012).

The problem of injustice is a God-sized problem. If we don't start with him first, whatever we're seeking, it ain't justice."[46]

All Christians should heed this counsel, and pastors and ministry leaders must lead Christians to operate from this doxological and transcendent starting point. God's moral attributes serve as the ultimate rubric by which we can evaluate and discern the presence of sin and evil in our world.

Second, a theological vision prioritizes God's redemptive work through the cross. So long as creation persists in its groaning (Romans 8), our fallen world beckons our attention as we anticipate its renewal. Mariam Kamell rightly notes that "we need to repeat the story—as Israel was instructed to do—about God's character and mighty works on our behalf, particularly the story of the cross, lest we, like Israel, become comfortable and forget this calling, acting instead to protect our own interests primarily."[47] The proclamation of the gospel remains the church's primary weapon, knowing that "our struggle is not against flesh and blood, but against the rulers, against the authorities, against the cosmic powers of this darkness, against evil, spiritual forces in the heavens" (Eph 6:12). The gospel is not only what we offer the world, it is the lens through which we are to follow the example of Jesus, who came not to be served but to serve (Mark 10:45). While the language of "this is a gospel issue" can be confusing and sometimes unhelpful, we can envision ways in which we seek to approach all of life under Christ's lordship, seeking to articulate the gospel in diverse settings and addressing issues that gospel people should care about (abortion, human rights, racism, etc.). Again, as Kamell claims, we must resist an isolationist posture that is only concerned with our self-interests, ultimately sequestering the gospel and its implications from the fallen world. To be sure, we must recall texts that summon action, such as: "Speak up for those who have no voice, for the justice of all who are dispossessed. Speak

---

[46] John Perkins, "Foreword," in Thaddeus J. Williams, *Confronting Injustice*, xv.

[47] Mariam J. Kamell, "How Does God's Love Inspire Social Justice?" in *The Love of God*, ed. Christopher W. Morgan (Wheaton, IL: Crossway, 2016), 215.

up, judge righteously, and defend the cause of the oppressed and needy" (Prov 31:8–9).

As we seek to prioritize God's redemptive work through the cross, we can make use of Thaddeus Williams's taxonomy of "Social Justice A" and "Social Justice B" issues.[48] "Social Justice A" refers to the incorporation of biblical principles to society's laws, as exemplified in the lives of William Wilberforce, Frederick Douglass, Harriet Tubman, and Sophie Scholl. From these examples (and we could think of others), Williams highlights those whose biblically informed work sought to "abolish human trafficking, work with the inner-city poor, invest in microloans to help the destitute in the developing world, build hospitals and orphanages, upend racism, and protect the unborn."[49] This approach is in contrast with "Social Justice B," which Williams describes as a social justice advocacy that operates from the "oppressor vs. oppressed" narrative, which is so pervasive in modern discourse. With this taxonomy in place, Christian pastors and ministry leaders can shape a theological vision that prioritizes the gospel while also providing a category for practical application (Social Justice A).

This clarifying taxonomy creates a theological vision of eschatological discipleship as we help Christians engage a fallen world with the good news of the biblical story (creation, fall, redemption, consummation). Keith Johnson explains, "The act of learning how to think and speak rightly about God is an act of faith and obedience that involves our participation in the mind of Christ and our partnership with Christ by the power of his Spirit. In this sense, the practice of theology takes place as an act of discipleship to Christ."[50] Moreover, Michael Allen understands theological discipleship as a way "to mortify and vivify the intellectual commitments

---

[48] Williams, *Confronting Injustice*, 4–5. But see his whole introduction.

[49] Williams, 4.

[50] Keith L. Johnson, *Theology as Discipleship* (Downers Grove, IL: IVP Academic, 2015), 37.

of the theologian."[51] We are shaped by our experiences, formed as we are by our ongoing engagement with the existential challenges consistent in the personal, familial, vocational, and societal realms of our lives. As such, the redeemed Christian imagination must initiate protective measures to protect the formation of our intellectual commitments and practical engagement with social justice concerns. We seek to mortify unbiblical worldviews while also vivifying our redeemed intellect to view the brokenness of our world through the lens of God's character.

Conclusion

This chapter has sought to articulate a theological rationale for Christian engagement in social justice conversations. The brokenness of our world, evident to all image-bearers, requires a careful and theologically robust Christian response. Christians are intimately connected to social justice concerns because we live and move and have our being across various contexts where opportunities arise to speak and act in alignment with the gospel. Flannery O'Connor was right: "if you believe in the divinity of Christ, you have to cherish the world at the same time that you struggle to endure it."[52] In the face of a broken world, Christians endure the world as we are called to be vessels of light, reflecting God's goodness, holiness, and justice in every corner of our lives. This requires a redeemed mind, open to the Holy Spirit's transformative power and committed to seeking wisdom in the face of complexity. At the very least, this entails pastors and ministry leaders working to help instill in Christ's church the intellectual patience to carefully consider how to address the brokenness of our world through word and deed.

---

[51] Michael Allen, *The Fear of the Lord: Essays on Theological Method* (London: T&T Clark, 2022), vii.

[52] Quoted in George A. Kilcourse Jr., *Flannery O'Connor's Religious Imagination: A World with Everything Off Balance* (New York: Paulist, 2001), 91.

Questions for Further Discussion

1. Discuss the balance between acknowledging the incomprehensibility of God and the call to pursue justice. How can Christians navigate the tension between recognizing the limitations of understanding God fully and the imperative to pursue justice as a reflection of God's character?
2. How does understanding the character of God, particularly his moral attributes of goodness, holiness, and justice, shape your responsibility towards social justice in your current church and vocational setting?
3. When speaking to non-Christians, how would you explain and defend God's moral attributes in the presence of evil and injustice?
4. In your current ministry setting, how might a theological framework for social justice issues provide an opportunity to promote the gospel?

Suggested Reading

Barrett, Matthew. *None Greater: The Undomesticated Attributes of God.* Grand Rapids: Baker, 2019.

Holmes, Christopher R. J. *The Lord is Good: Seeking the God of the Psalter.* Downers Grove, IL: IVP Academic, 2018.

Kilner, John F. *Dignity and Destiny: Humanity in the Image of God.* Grand Rapids: Eerdmans, 2015.

Webster, John. *The Domain of the Word: Scripture and Theological Reason.* London: Bloomsbury T&T Clark, 2014.

———. *God Without Measure: Working Papers in Christian Theology, Volume I: God and the Works of God.* London: Bloomsbury T&T Clark, 2016.

Williams, Thaddeus. *Confronting Injustice without Compromising Truth: 12 Questions Christians Should Ask About Social Justice.* Grand Rapids: Zondervan Academic, 2020.

8

Justice and Redemption

— Kenneth J. Reid —

Introduction

What has redemption to do with social justice? Does God's work of redemption intersect at all with social justice? The term redemption articulates a profound idea that describes God's work in the lives of Christians. It is a term that points to the work of the cross and to the salvation that God has offered in Jesus Christ. For some, it may be difficult to see how God's redemption has any connection with social justice.

This chapter will discuss God's work of redemption and its relevance to social justice. The thesis of this chapter is that God's work of redemption is holistic. In an already/not-yet fashion, he redeems individuals and the created order based on Jesus's death and resurrection. Social justice, properly understood, is grounded in God's holistic redemption plan. This introductory section will discuss working definitions of redemption and social justice. Next, I will examine the exegetical foundation for redemption and social justice. The next section will describe the theological foundations regarding redemption and social justice. The last section will discuss some implications.

Definition of Redemption

Broadly, the biblical portrait of redemption "involves deliverance from slavery by the payment of a price."[1] To redeem is to render a payment to purchase (Rom 6:23). One may redeem family property or other family members from slavery (Lev 25:23–55). In Scripture, redemption also describes God's saving work (Col 1:13–14). Everett Harrison notes: "Though closely allied to salvation, redemption is more specific, for it denotes the means by which salvation is achieved, namely, payment of a ransom. In salvation's case, redemption may denote temporal, physical deliverance."[2] Scripture also describes those who have been delivered by God or experience his salvation as the redeemed (cf. Ps 107:2; Eph 1:7).[3]

Definition of Social Justice

Debates about social justice often obscure the realities of people who are affected. The very term social justice brings about ideas of political activism or a particular approach to government policy. While there can be a political dimension in the discussion about social justice, the focus for our purposes is a biblical-theological emphasis. Social justice must be discussed because injustices affect real people. When injustice occurs, opportunities to fulfill one's vocation and earn economic stability are thwarted and undermined. When injustice occurs in the form of poor immigration policy or

---

[1] Robert Letham, *Systematic Theology* (Wheaton, IL: Crossway, 2019), 557.

[2] Everett F. Harrison, "Redeemer, Redemption," in *Evangelical Dictionary of Theology*, 3rd ed., ed. Daniel J. Treier and Walter A. Elwell (Grand Rapids: Baker Academic, 2017), 727.

[3] The term *gaal* means to redeem, deliver, or ransom. See Robert L. Hubbard Jr., "*gaal*," *NIDOTTE* 1:789. The term *pdh*, while having legal overtones, is broader than *gaal*. See Robert L. Hubbard Jr., "*pdh*," *NIDOTTE* 3:578–82. The Greek family of terms under *luō* (specifically *lytron*, *apolytrōsis*) generally combine the two Hebrew terms above. For more discussion regarding the use of these terms, see Fredrich Büchsel, "*luō*," *TDNT* 4:335–56.

mass incarceration, families are split. When injustice occurs resulting in the death of someone, lives are forever changed. Injustice is not just about politics; it is about real people who are made in the image of God. All image-bearers are valuable before God and have a God-given right to live, to engage their vocations, to worship, and to pursue a life that glorifies God and produces human flourishing for them, their families, their community, and society. Injustice robs people of this, so visions of social justice seek to remedy this reality.

The idea of justice is that state of affairs in life that is right in God's sight. In *Generous Justice: How God's Grace Makes Us Just*, Tim Keller states that doing justice occurs "when we give all human beings their due as creations of God. Doing justice includes not only the righting of wrongs, but generosity and social concern, especially toward the poor and the vulnerable. This kind of life reflects the character of God."[4] Kevin DeYoung and Greg Gilbert summarize that doing justice, after examining the biblical evidence, "means treating people equitably."[5] Social justice, in a biblical framework, is the idea that everyone should be treated fairly. This is particularly true for those who are marginalized in a majority society. For this study, Kevin DeYoung's definition of social justice is our definition: "treating people equitably, working for systems and structures that are fair, and looking out for the weak and the vulnerable."[6]

---

[4] Timothy Keller, *Generous Justice: How God's Grace Makes Us Just* (New York: Dutton, 2010), 18.

[5] Kevin DeYoung and Greg Gilbert, *What Is the Mission of the Church? Making Sense of Social Justice, Shalom, and the Great Commission* (Wheaton, IL: Crossway, 2011), 183n12. A detailed examination of the biblical evidence for justice is beyond the scope of this paper. See John R. Donahue, *Seek Justice That You May Live: Reflections and Resources on the Bible and Social Justice* (New York: Paulist, 2014). See also Jessica Nicholas, *God Loves Justice: A User-Friendly Guide to Biblical Justice and Righteousness* (Los Angeles: S&E Educational Press, 2017).

[6] Kevin DeYoung, "Is Social Justice a Gospel Issue?," *The Gospel Coalition* (blog), September 11, 2018, https://www.thegospelcoalition.org/blogs/kevin-deyoung/social-justice-gospel-issue/.

Injustice may occur at two levels. The first level is personal. Our personal sins may lead to oppression or taking advantage of others. One biblical example is the delay or refusal to pay a worker his/her wage (Lev 19:13). If a person does not pay a worker his/her wage, that person is not honoring the worker's vocation and is stealing their time and labor and acting in a dishonest way by not rendering to the worker what is due. Even the delay in paying a worker his/her wage causes stress and hardship for that worker. Another personal example today is the use of racial slurs or misogynistic comments, which often convey that a person is devalued because of his/her race or gender. These descriptions rob image-bearers of honor and dignity, even conveying that they are not worthy of love and respect. We should deal with one another fairly, honoring one another in our interpersonal relationships and avoiding these common, personal attacks.

Social justice is not limited to the personal sphere. Beyond the personal, there is a second level that encompasses the structural or systemic dimension (also referred to as institutional injustice). A system or structure may be an organization with its rules, policies, and procedures. When the policies and procedures are followed, the result of these procedures may create injustice regardless of the intent of the individuals who follow the procedures. Social injustices are a result of social sin. Robert Pyne presents a helpful description of sin at the structural or social level:

> The values of a community are often expressed in particular social structures. On a national level our retail and healthcare industries demonstrate our collective commitment to consumerism and vitality, while our educational and political systems reveal our desire for training and order. Such social structures reflect our collective interests, sometimes even enforcing those interests against other nations or groups. That observation raises the possibility that the structures themselves express the collective sin of our community. Many theologians have described this pattern as "structural sin"

> implying that the prejudices of a particular group live on in the social systems they have created.[7]

This type of sin breeds systemic injustice. Duke Kwon and Gregory Thompson describe institutional injustice, saying that "the same prejudices and estrangement that mark our individual and relational lives are encoded—often invisibly—in the institutions that shape our common life."[8]

A prime example of systemic injustice in Scripture is Egyptian slavery. While Pharaoh gave orders, the citizens of Egypt eagerly participated. Egyptian rulers established laws and policies that enslaved the Israelites. This enslavement reflected Egyptian fears of national security and their prejudices against the Israelites (Exod 1:8–22). The Egyptians denied the Israelites an equal status by oppressing them, making them labor without pay and forbidding them from worshiping God.

Several practices in the United States contributed to systemic racism. One example is the denial of voting rights to African Americans historically. Despite the passage of the 15th Amendment to the US Constitution, voting rights were systemically denied to African Americans, especially in the southern states. Citizens were denied these rights through poll taxes, unfair quizzes, and intimidation of violence and lynching. These practices clearly denied fair treatment and affected citizens financially, culturally, and psychologically.

Social justice advocates for fair treatment. This treatment should be done both at the individual and social level. In places where systems and structures are unjust, Christians should work to change the conditions so that every person is treated equitably.

---

[7] Robert Pyne, *Humanity and Sin: The Creation, Fall, and Redemption of Humanity* (Nashville: Thomas Nelson, 1999), 223.

[8] Duke L. Kwon and Gregory Thompson, *Reparations: A Christian Call for Repentance and Repair* (Grand Rapids: Brazos, 2021), 38.

Biblical Texts and Exegesis

The biblical exegesis portion of this study will focus on the various ways in which redemption is portrayed in Scripture. This section will first examine the variety of ways that redemption is spoken of in the Old Testament. It will then discuss redemption in the New Testament.

Redemption in the Old Testament

God's act of deliverance from slavery is the prime act of redemption in the Old Testament. God made a covenant with Abraham to make him a great nation and to bless all the people of the earth (Gen 12:1–3; 15:1–6). The Lord disclosed that his descendants would be enslaved in a foreign land, but that he would deliver them (Gen 15:13–16).

The exodus narrative begins with the description of Abraham's family in Egypt. Years after Joseph's death, a Pharaoh rose to power who did not know Joseph and chose to enslave the Israelites out of a motivation to secure the nation by population control (Exod 1:8–22). After Yahweh called Moses as the deliverer of Israel, and after Pharoah imposed the requirement to make bricks without straw, Yahweh declared his intention to deliver Israel. In Exod 6:6, the Lord reflects that he will bring Israel out from slavery and will redeem them with mighty acts. The phrasing in this text indicates that the act of redemption is identical to his deliverance of Israel from Egyptian slavery. Hamilton notes that "the basic idea in 'redeem, redemption,' then, is to restore something to its original condition. In the case of oppressed Israel, he will restore the people to their earlier condition of liberty."[9] T. Desmond Alexander describes God's act of redemption as a sign of his relationship with Israel:

> In most OT contexts the verb 'redeem' is associated with a member of a family assisting other relatives in a time of trouble. Since

[9] Victor P. Hamilton, *Exodus: An Exegetical Commentary* (Grand Rapids: Baker Academic, 2011), 102–3.

> God has already spoken of Israel as his son (4:22), the liberation of the Israelites may be viewed appropriately as a family affair. Furthermore, by introducing the concept of redemption at this point, a strong connection is forged between the Israelites' rescue from slavery and the special relationship mentioned and v. 7, which is later fulfilled when the covenant is established at Mount Sinai.[10]

The act of liberation from slavery is God's intimate and personal expression of love.[11]

The Lord proclaims that he has redeemed Israel in Isa 43:1. According to the context of the passage, this redemption is the Lord's prophecy to the future Israelite generations and exile. To reassure Israel in exile, Yahweh described this special status of the nation. The Lord created, formed, and redeemed Israel. He also called him by name. That he created and formed Israel points to his gathering of Israel during the time of the patriarchs and building them as a great nation. The redemption of Israel from Egyptian slavery, his calling them by name, as well as forming them and creating them expresses his ownership of Israel.[12] Gary Smith notes that the special status of Israel would encourage them as they faced exile:

> The present circumstances of the nation were quite difficult (42:18–25), but these factors did not nullify God's committed covenant relationship to his special people. These creative, redemptive, and ownership words conveyed to the audience God's special commitment, protection, and kinship relationship to the members of his own family. What are the implications of these claims? God's past deeds and present relationship with Israel should motivate the

---

[10] T. Desmond Alexander, *Exodus* (London: Apollos, 2017), 126–27.

[11] God provides a similar declaration in Deut 7:8: by his own sovereign grace and out of his love he redeemed Israel from slavery.

[12] John D. W. Watts, *Isaiah 34–66: Revised Edition*, WBC (Nashville: Thomas Nelson, 2005), 132.

prophet's audience to have no fear about the future, for God is fully committed to them. In times of trouble God's message to Abram (Gen 15:1), Isaac (Gen 26:24), and the Israelites (Exod 14:10, 13) was to "fear not," for God would intervene on behalf of his people. If he faithfully did this in the past, is he not able to do it now and in the future?[13]

God also redeemed Israel from Babylonian exile, communicating with his people through Jeremiah's prophecies to the southern kingdom of Judah as they faced the exile. Within the the book of consolation portion of Jeremiah, which focuses on God's promised restoration of Israel, the Lord proclaims that he will gather scattered Israel to himself and will watch over them; he says he will redeem them from the land of the ones who are stronger than them (Jer 31:10–11). This redemption refers to Israel's liberation in exile.[14] Walter Kaiser Jr. notes that the Hebrew terms coincide with the language that was used for Egyptian liberation:

> More reasons are given why the nations should pay close attention to Yahweh's deliverance of Jacob: Yahweh will "ransom" (*padah*) his people, and he will "redeem (*gaal*) them from the hand of those stronger than he [Jacob]." These two verbs often describe the work of God in the past when Israel was delivered from Egypt (Exod 6:5; 15:13; Deut 7:8; 9:26). This setting of the people free will be the exclusive work of God and his intervention with power and might.[15]

---

[13] Gary V. Smith, *Isaiah 40–66*, vol. 15B, NAC (Nashville: B&H, 2009), 193. Edward Young argues that the meaning of redemption, which pointed back to Egypt, has broader connotations. It not only may refer to deliverance from exile but also to the redemption that Jesus paid at the cross. See Edward J Young, *The Book of Isaiah: Volume III* (Grand Rapids: Eerdmans, 1972), 140.

[14] J. A. Thompson, *The Book of Jeremiah*, 2nd rev. ed., NICOT (Grand Rapids: Eerdmans, 1995), 571.

[15] Walter C. Kaiser Jr. and Tiberius Rata, *Walking the Ancient Paths: A Commentary on Jeremiah* (Bellingham, WA: Lexham, 2019), 357.

In Jer 50:33–34, the Lord is portrayed as their Redeemer; he will defend their cause and, by defending their cause, he will judge Babylon. Just as the Lord delivered Israel from the Egyptians, he is powerful enough to deliver them from Babylon.[16] Being brought back into their land means deliverance from exile. Furthermore, there will be unrest to those who live in Babylon. The Lord's deliverance from exile is an act of redemption followed by his judgment of Babylon.

God's redemption of Israel is also a future reality. The extended section from Isaiah 28–35 deals with God's judgment on Jerusalem and the nations for their acts of oppression; the prophecies also discuss the redemption of the righteous.[17] It is likely that these prophecies occurred during Assyria's invasion of Judah.[18] Chapter 34 discusses the judgment of the wicked nations while chapter 35 describes the future joy of those who are redeemed. The language of beauty, blooming, and the awesome nature of the Lord's presence point to a reality beyond post-exilic Israel. Smith notes that "the plan of God will be accomplished when the transformational power of God's holy presence redeems the earth and mankind."[19] The desert will bloom and rejoice, as those redeemed will see the glory of the Lord (Isa 35:1–2). God encourages his people, and he will bring about the transformation of the blind and weak, as well as the desert (Isa 35:3–8). The result will be peace with nature for those who are redeemed because of the Lord's work. He will bring them everlasting joy (Isa 35:9–10). The term *redeemed* refers to someone who is delivered from an obligation (35:9d), while the act of the Lord's ransom emphasizes the payment to release one from a debt (35:10a).[20] The language of this oracle points to God's eschatological deliverance. Smith states:

---

[16] Thompson, *The Book of Jeremiah*, 744.

[17] Gary Smith, *Isaiah 1–39*, vol. 15A, NAC (Nashville: B&H, 2007), 468.

[18] Smith, 468.

[19] Smith, 578.

[20] Smith, 581.

> Both terms emphasize that the people's status as the redeemed or ransomed is based on an act of divine grace to free them from the bondage of an earlier obligation. This indebtedness is broader than the bondage to a personal sin; it includes all the effects of sin on the world. These acts of God will remove the curse on man and the world and inaugurate the holy kingdom of God. Those who "will return" . . . to God will experience "everlasting joy", . . . they will be overtaken with gladness, and all sorrow will end (cf. 25:8; 65:19).[21]

The theological importance of this text is that it portrays the redeemed people of the Old Testament as having future eschatological blessings.

Redemption and Justice in the Old Testament

The combination of Yahweh's redemption and social justice appears also in Isaiah 1:16–28, which is quoted at length below.

> Wash yourselves. Cleanse yourselves. Remove your evil deeds from my sight. Stop doing evil. Learn to do what is good. Pursue justice. Correct the oppressor. Defend the rights of the fatherless. Plead the widow's cause. "Come, let's settle this," says the LORD. "Though your sins are scarlet, they will be as white as snow; though they are crimson red, they will be like wool. If you are willing and obedient, you will eat the good things of the land. But if you refuse and rebel, you will be devoured by the sword." For the mouth of the LORD has spoken.
>
> The faithful town—what an adulteress she has become! She was once full of justice. Righteousness once dwelt in her, but now, murderers! Your silver has become dross to be discarded, your beer is diluted with water. Your rulers are rebels, friends of thieves. They all love graft and chase after bribes. They do not defend the rights

[21] Smith, 581.

> of the fatherless, and the widow's case never comes before them. Therefore the Lord God of Armies, the Mighty One of Israel, declares: "Ah, I will get even with my foes; I will take revenge against my enemies. I will turn my hand against you and will burn away your dross completely; I will remove all your impurities. I will restore your judges to what they were at first, and your advisers to what they were at the start. Afterward you will be called the Righteous City, a Faithful Town."
>
> Zion will be redeemed by justice, those who repent, by righteousness. At the same time both rebels and sinners will be broken, and those who abandon the Lord will perish.

The text reveals God's call for justice in Judah and their practices of injustice. They were to seek justice by defending the cause of the fatherless and the widow (Isa 1:17). Earlier in the passage, Yahweh expressed that their worship has no value because of their violence to one another. In v. 16, they are not told merely to reform their worship and cultic practices but to practice justice. Smith elaborates:

> The implications of a changed life are not limited to following proper practices at worship. Acceptable behavior extends to all areas of life and particularly how leaders treat the weak and vulnerable in society (1:17). Such behavior requires that everyone in a position of authority should learn the principles of justice from the laws of God (Exod 20–23) and learn how to put those principles into practice. Shedding the innocent blood of the weak is unacceptable (1:15; 2 Kings 21:16). Instead, God is pleased when rulers act justly and defend the widow and orphan from the unscrupulous ways of their oppressors (Deut 10:18; 24:17). In 66:3–4 the prophet makes the same point; proper worship and judicial ethics go hand in hand for those who desire to please God.[22]

---

[22] Smith, 109.

He describes the city, portraying the rulers as rebels who bribe and pursue gifts (Isa 1:23). They are unjust to the orphan and the widow (Isa 1:23). Yet the Lord promises restoration (Isa 1:26). A key verse is v. 27, in which the Lord promises to deliver Zion with justice.[23] This deliverance is again an act of redemption. Yet this deliverance will happen with justice and righteousness. The concrete expression of this justice is that the fatherless and the widow will be defended, and the leaders will act with justice. Social justice will prevail through Yahweh's redemptive work in Zion. The call for justice also reflects his original intent as he delivered Israel from Egyptian slavery. His law reflects his holy standard regarding how Israel should relate to him and to one another.

Redemption in the New Testament

God's work of redemption is accomplished at the cross. Mark 10:45 is a critical verse found in a passage within the literary context of a larger transitional section (Mark 8:22–10:52) which is bracketed by Jesus's healing of the blind—the blind man at Bethsaida (Mark 8:22–26) and blind Bartimaeus (Mark 10:46–52). Jesus predicts his passion three times (8:31; 9:31; 10:33–34) followed by the disciples' failure to understand. Among some transitions in this section, the narrative shifts from Galilee to Jerusalem, the teaching focuses less on the crowd and more on the disciples, and there is a more explicit revelation of Jesus's identity.[24] In the immediate context, Jesus's declaration in Mark 10:45 follows James and John's request for exaltation at Jesus's left and right in glory. Jesus reveals that true greatness is to become a servant. This statement reflects Jesus's life as a servant and as one who will give his life. He models what he requires of his disciples.

---

[23] For an extensive analysis of the relationship of Isa 1:27 to the work of Isaiah's suffering servant, see Chapter 2 by Peter Gentry.

[24] This transition section summarizes M. Eugene Boring, *Mark: A Commentary* (Louisville: Westminster John Knox, 2006), 231–32.

Jesus states that the son of man did not come to be served but to serve and give his life a ransom for many (Mark 10:45). The word for ransom is *lytron*, which means "the price for release."[25] Strauss expounds on the significance of this word in relation to Christ's act.

> The verb form, "redeem" (*lutroō*), could mean to free by paying a ransom, but was also used in the more general sense, "to liberate from an oppressive situation, set free, rescue, redeem." It is commonly used in the LXX of God's deliverance of the nation Israel from slavery in Egypt (Exod 6:6; 15:13; Deut 7:8; 9:26; 13:6, etc.). Though the noun ransom (*lutron*) appears in the NT only here and in the Matthean parallel (29:28), the verb (*lutroō*) and its cognate nouns (*apolutrōsis*, "redemption"; *antilutron*, "ransom") are common in the NT to describe the redemption accomplished through the sacrificial death of Christ.[26]

This ransom is given "for many." Robert Stein notes that "the preposition 'for' (*anti*) can mean 'instead of' (i.e., as a substitute for) or 'for the sake of.'"[27] That "ransom" carries the idea of a replacement, especially in the context of setting slaves free, better conveys the substitutionary element.[28] Jesus's gift of his life as a ransom points to his death on the cross. This idea of ransom for someone is an act of redemption. Jesus gave his life as payment in order to benefit others. Edwards summarizes the significance of Jesus's death on the cross.

> The initiative of his atoning work lies within himself as the Son of Man [in contrast to Isaiah's servant], who, in stark contrast to the

---

[25] Mark L. Strauss, *Mark*, ECNT (Grand Rapids: Zondervan Academic, 2014), 458.

[26] Strauss, 458–59.

[27] Robert H. Stein, *Mark*, BECNT (Grand Rapids: Baker Academic, 2008), 488.

[28] Stein, 488–89.

> power-mongers of v. 42, freely offers his life as the ransom price for all (John 10:11; Rom 8:2–4). As God's own delegate, and through his suffering, death, and resurrection, Jesus freely and obediently offers his life as a substitute *in behalf of* humanity. Jesus is supremely conscious of offering a payment to God that can be offered by no one else. The ransom Jesus offers in his life is not contingent on something outside himself. Origen (third century A.D.) would later develop the theory that the ransom of Jesus was necessitated by and paid to Satan. Satan, however, is not mentioned in v. 45, not even in Mark's passion account. Satan was last mentioned in 8:33, and there he attempts to *avert* Jesus from suffering and death! The death of the Son of Man on behalf of 'the many' is a sacrifice of obedience to God's will, a full expression of his love, and a full satisfaction of God's justice.[29]

Jesus's death is the ransom that set believers free.[30]

The author of Hebrews addresses the importance of redemption and ransom in the context of the new covenant. The author is writing to a community of likely Jewish Christians who may return to their cultic rituals in the face of persecution.[31] The letter warns them not to abandon their commitment to Christ because his salvation is greater. In the context of this passage, Christ is a better high priest, a better mediator of a better covenant than the sacrifices and the priesthood under the old covenant. Thus, Christ entered the greater tabernacle through his blood rather than the blood of goats and calves (Heb 9:11–12). The blood of goats and calves ceremonially cleansed the recipients (Heb 9:13). If the imperfect sacrifices under the old covenant could provide some cleansing, how much more would the blood of Christ,

---

[29] James R. Edwards, *The Gospel According to Mark*, PNTC (Grand Rapids: Eerdmans, 2001), 327–28.

[30] See also Rom 3:24; Gal 3:13.

[31] F. F. Bruce, *The Epistle to the Hebrews*, rev. ed., NICNT (Grand Rapids: Eerdmans, 1990), 9.

offered by the eternal Spirit, cleanse our consciences (Heb 9:14)? Yet this passage states that by entering the most holy place by his own blood, Christ obtained eternal redemption (Heb 9:12). Redemption "signifies the paying of a price in order to obtain freedom from bondage for those redeemed."[32] The redemption that Christ's blood provides is much more than what was provided in the exodus. This redemption deals with the liberation from sin that alienates us from fellowship with God.[33] This sin will result in judgment. Bruce observes that

> "that first redemption was temporal in both the benefits it provided and their duration. This second is 'eternal' in its effectiveness, benefits, and duration. The price of 'eternal redemption' was costly beyond measure, for it could be procured by nothing less than the 'once-for-all' self-offering of the eternal Son of God."[34]

The redemption is holistically greater than anything that was experienced under the old covenant.

In Heb 9:15, Jesus is the mediator of a new covenant because he died as a ransom. The new covenant is the covenant that God inaugurated that provides for the forgiveness of sins (Jer 31:34). This death points back to the covenant sacrifice that ratified the old covenant in Exodus 24. As the covenant sacrifice, Jesus's death concluded the old covenant and inaugurated the new covenant. Lane notes that "as the priestly mediator of a new covenant, he is able to administer the eschatological blessings that specify the newness of the *diathēkēs kainēs*, 'new covenant.'"[35] Jesus's death as a ransom ratified the new covenant and set believers free from sins that were committed under the Mosaic and new covenants. Thus, Jesus's death was a work of redemption.

---

[32] Bruce, 395.

[33] Bruce, 395.

[34] Bruce, 395.

[35] William L. Lane, *Hebrews 9–13*, vol. 47B, WBC (Dallas: Word, 1991), 242.

Paul focuses on redemption in Eph 1:7. This verse occurs in the prologue of the letter as Eph 1:3–14, but it is one Greek sentence. It may function as a doxology or an introductory eulogy of praise.[36] He describes the blessings "through the Spirit to all who are connected to Jesus Christ in a dynamic, personal relationship."[37] In v, 7 Paul says, "In him we have redemption through his blood, the forgiveness of our trespasses, according to the riches of God's grace." In him—signifying union with Christ—God has graciously given us redemption. Redemption means to release from bondage due to the payment of a ransom. Just like God's work in Exodus, redemption is God's work of reclaiming people to himself (1 Pet 2:4–5, 9). Salvation is the consequence of this redemption. Constantine Campbell notes:

> In Paul's world, redemption often referred to the retrieval of kidnapped people or the liberation of slaves through the payment of a ransom. Redemption also has a strong biblical background with the exodus as its most powerful example (Exod 6:6; 15:13; Deut 7:8; 2 Sam 7:23; Mic 6:4). When Yahweh freed the Israelites from their Egyptian captivity, he did so in such a way as to claim them as his possession—though they were already his. This is a key element of redemption, as it views salvation in terms of *belonging*. God's redeeming of Israel was a reclaiming of a people who rightly belonged to him in the first place. Their salvation freed them from captivity and restored them to a rightful posture as God's people. In Eph 1:7,

---

[36] Constantine R. Campbell, *The Letter to the Ephesians*, PNTC (Grand Rapids: Eerdmans, 2023), 41. Clinton E. Arnold, *Ephesians*, ZECNT (Grand Rapids: Zondervan Academic, 2010), 72. Arnold continues, "Paul's blessing of God is unusually long—one sentence containing 202 words. He does this by using 32 prepositional phrases, 21 genitive expressions (not counting genitives connected to a preposition), 6 relative clauses, and 5 adverbial participle clauses. Paul weaves this together into a beautiful, artistic, and smooth-flowing declaration of praise to God for his indescribable work on our behalf. It is expressed with emotion and is designed to profoundly move all who hear it."

[37] Arnold, 73.

> redemption likewise ought to be understood as a reclaiming of a people to belong to God. Though they may not have been his special people previously (i.e., the gentiles), in Christ all are redeemed since they rightly belong to God their Creator. He has made them and given them life. Now in Christ, whether Jew or gentile, they are restored to a right posture toward God (cf. 2:13, 16).[38]

This redemption is accomplished through his blood, which points to Jesus's sacrificial death at the cross.[39] The phrase "the forgiveness of sins" shows the result of redemption. Christ's death is the payment, redemption is the result of the payment, but "redemption is the cause and forgiveness is the effect."[40] Another aspect to consider is that the present tense of "we have" (*echomen*) points to our current status as redeemed and forgiven people.[41] Arnold observes that "this enables Paul to stress the present experience of redemption and forgiveness that believers enjoy through their dynamic relationship to the exalted Lord."[42] Thus, an important aspect of our present salvation is that we are redeemed and forgiven people.

The term redemption also focuses on God's cosmic plan to bring in the new creation. In Rom 8:18–25, Paul discusses the renewal of creation:

---

[38] Campbell, *The Letter to the Ephesians*, 50–51.

[39] Campbell also notes that it may refer to the deliverance of Israel through the blood of the Passover lamb. See Campbell, 51.

[40] Harold W. Hoehner, *Ephesians: An Exegetical Commentary* (Grand Rapids: Baker Academic, 2002), 208. He states, "However, this verse shows that as a result of redemption in Christ through his blood, God has canceled or forgiven sins and the necessary punishment that goes with them. Redemption is the cause and forgiveness is the effect. God is not lenient with sin because sin had to be paid in order for the sinner to be set free. The effect of this payment is the cancellation of or release from all the obligations caused by sin. Christ in his sacrificial death has taken the punishment for us. The supreme sacrifice of Christ clearly shows that God does not take sin lightly."

[41] Arnold, *Ephesians*, 85.

[42] Arnold, 85.

> I consider that our present sufferings are not worth comparing with the glory that will be revealed in us. For the creation waits in eager expectation for the children of God to be revealed. For the creation was subjected to frustration, not by its own choice, but by the will of the one who subjected it, in hope that the creation itself will be liberated from its bondage to decay and brought into the freedom and glory of the children of God. We know that the whole creation has been groaning as in the pains of childbirth right up to the present time. Not only so, but we ourselves, who have the firstfruits of the Spirit, groan inwardly as we wait eagerly for our adoption to sonship, the redemption of our bodies. For in this hope we were saved. But hope that is seen is no hope at all. Who hopes for what they already have? But if we hope for what we do not yet have, we wait for it patiently.

In Rom 8:1–17, Paul discusses life in the Spirit as grounded in the believer's justification and reconciliation. The focus of Rom 8:18–25 is the hope that believers have in this present time of suffering. We have hope because we know that creation and our bodies will be renewed. This renewal of creation occurs or coincides with the resurrection of humanity. In v. 23, Christians who have the first fruits of the Spirit await their adoption. This completed adoption is the redemption of our bodies. The redemption of our bodies refers to the future bodily resurrection. The hope of the Christian is for the resurrected body to appear when the Lord returns. This resurrection of the body is the final adoption or the final sign of adoption. Thus, there is an eschatological dimension to our adoption. Douglas Moo notes:

> "Redemption" shares with "adoption" and many other terms in Paul the "already-not-yet" tension that pervades his theology, for the redemption can be pictured both as past and as future. As Paul has hinted in v. 10, it is not until the body has been transformed that redemption can be said to be complete; in this life, our bodies share in that "frustration" which characterizes this world as a whole

> (see v. 20). At the same time, resurrection is closely tied to the overall theme of the paragraph, the hope of glory."[43]

The Spirit is the sign of our adoption (Rom 8:16) and is the first fruit of the coming eschatological blessings.

And this final adoption of the resurrection is the event that creation itself awaits. Verse 20 says creation is subjected to frustration by God's will, a condition that occurred because of God's curse on creation in Gen 3:17–19; however, this created order will ultimately be liberated from its bondage and decay once the children of God enter into their glory. The liberation of creation coincides with the final redemption of God's adopted children at the resurrection. As Tom Schreiner attests, "The redemption they await is so stupendous that it will involve the entire created order. Just as creation fell when Adam sinned, so too it will be transformed when the children of God experience the completion of their redemption."[44] When creation itself is liberated, the emergence of the new creation is its redemption. God's work of redemption includes the entire created order, which leads to new creation.[45]

Redemption in the New Testament is portrayed in three ways. The first is through the act of Jesus's death on the cross. This death is portrayed as the redeeming action of God in Christ. The second is as a descriptor of God's work of salvation. The third is as the consummation of God's cosmic restoration purposes. Redemptive history describes God's plan to redeem creation. It is God's work of dealing with sin that occurred in the garden of Eden and of transforming not only individuals but the entire created order so that the result would be the new heavens and the new earth—peace in all the earth with God ruling and present with his people in the new creation.

---

[43] Douglas J. Moo, *The Letter to the Romans*, 2nd ed. NICNT (Grand Rapids: Eerdmans, 2018), 543.

[44] Thomas R. Schreiner, *Romans*, BECNT (Grand Rapids: Baker Academic, 1998), 438.

[45] Ephesians 1:14 and 4:30 refer to the day or time of redemption, which is the future consummation of God's blessings for believers and creation.

Redemption and Justice in the New Testament

Paul expresses one purpose for redemption in Titus 2:14. Paul instructs Titus to rebuke those who live ungodly in the latter portion of chapter 1. He provides instruction to various members in Titus's church community (Titus 2:1–10). Paul then states:

> For the grace of God has appeared that offers salvation to all people. It teaches us to say "No" to ungodliness and worldly passions, and to live self-controlled, upright and godly lives in this present age, while we wait for the blessed hope—the appearing of the glory of our great God and Savior, Jesus Christ, who gave himself for us to redeem us from all wickedness and to purify for himself a people that are his very own, eager to do what is good.

Verses 11–13 tell us to deny ungodliness and pursue godliness in light of God's grace. Paul tells believers to conduct themselves in this manner while waiting for the coming of our Lord Jesus Christ. Verse 14 is a description of Jesus's work and the purpose for that work: Jesus gave himself, which refers to his sacrificial death, to redeem us from all wickedness. To redeem "implies purchase from a state of bondage or condemnation."[46] The redemption is from all wickedness. The term for wickedness (*anomia*) presents the idea of utter lawlessness, a situation in which a person is enslaved to sin.[47] The second purpose for redemption was that Christ would "purify for himself a people that are his very own, eager to do what is good." Jesus's death resulted in the cleansing of believers, a people that God claimed for his own.[48] The result is also a transformation of the believers. They

---

[46] Robert W. Yarbrough, *The Letters to Timothy and Titus*, PNTC (Grand Rapids: Eerdmans, 2018), 531.

[47] Philip H. Towner, *The Letters to Timothy and Titus*, NICNT (Grand Rapids: Eerdmans, 2006), 761.

[48] Yarbrough, *The Letters to Timothy and Titus*, 532.

are no longer enslaved to sin, but now are eager/zealous for good works. These people are motivated and energized to do good works. Biblically-theologically, the good works would be in keeping with God's revealed will in his law. Towner notes that Paul uses the framework in the Old Testament for the new covenant that relates redemption, purification, and the zeal to do good works.[49] These works result from Christ's death and are the fulfillment of the new covenant promise that the law is written on believers' hearts. Towner explains:

> Consequently, with this closing phrase ("zealous for good deeds") Paul lifts the entire web of OT reflections into the contemporary situation, rounding off the theological rationale of Christian existence by returning to the ethical vocabulary most familiar to his readers. From the perspective of cause and effect, authentic Christian identity involves a creative act of "becoming" (redemption, purification) that makes a unique quality of "being" possible. Having already established a distinct OT covenant and New Covenant framework for understanding, "zeal for good deeds" can be seen within this frame. The appropriate response to grace was to be devoted to Torah (Exod 19:5; Deut 26:18). From Paul's eschatological Spirit-perspective, the faith response to covenant grace is the Spirit-generated fulfillment of Torah (suggesting the internalization of the law; cf. Jer 31:31–34 [MT], the reshaping of the heart/will to obey; [Titus] 3:5; Rom 8:1–9, Gal 5:17–18).[50]

In Titus 3:5–6, Paul refers to the Spirit as the agent of regeneration. If the intent of the law is accomplished in the desire and ability to do good works, the acts of justice and the defense of the marginalized are a component of the good works which are intended by God's redemptive work in Jesus Christ.

---

[49] Towner, *The Letters to Timothy and Titus*, 764.

[50] Towner, 764.

Theological Formation

This section will discuss some theological issues regarding redemption and social justice. The biblical evidence above suggests that redemption is used in three senses. The first is the act of redemption, which is deliverance from slavery in the Old Testament and the work of ransom and release through the death of Jesus. This aspect is addressed by reflecting upon atonement theology. The second sense is the status of redemption, which refers to those who have placed their faith in Jesus Christ. The theology of salvation (soteriology) will be the focus of this second aspect. The third sense is the consummation of redemption. Eschatological themes will be explored for this third aspect of redemption.

Atonement and Social Justice

Mark 10:45 uses the language of ransom to describe Jesus's death, while Gal 3:13 describes Christ's redeeming work by referring to his death. Mark 10:45 shows that this act of ransom is most likely a substitutionary act, while Gal 3:13 shows that Jesus redeemed us by becoming a curse for us, the substitutionary and sin-bearing aspect. The language of ransom and the act of redeeming in these passages suggests the penal substitution atonement metaphor. Penal substitution is the view that God the Father sent forth his Son (and the Son came voluntarily) as an act of love to die as our substitute, bearing our sin, and that that death satisfies the justice and wrath of the Father by his death. Steve Jeffrey, Michael Ovey, and Andrew Sach provide a beautiful definition of penal substitution:

> This understanding of the cross of Christ stands at the very heart of the gospel. There is a captivating beauty in the sacrificial love of a God who gave *himself* for his people. It is this that first draws many believers to the Lord Jesus Christ, and this that will draw us to him when he returns on the last day to vindicate his name and welcome his people into his eternal kingdom. That the Lord Jesus

> Christ died for us—a shameful death, bearing our curse, enduring our pain, suffering the wrath of his own Father in our place—has been the wellspring of the hope of countless Christians throughout the ages.[51]

Upon the first appearance, it is difficult to see how this explanation of the atonement is applicable to social justice. The working definition of social justice is that people would be treated equitably, working for systems and structures that are fair, and advocating for weak, vulnerable, and oppressed people. Sin, either as a personal transgression or as manifested as the curse on creation (Gen 3:17–19), is the reason for injustice. There must be a remedy for sin so that injustice will be removed. Penal substitution is the response to sin that rages in the human heart for unredeemed humanity. Jesus's death on the cross deals with our condemnation before God and reconciles us to him. Penal substitution also addresses the curse on creation, as humanity's redemption is linked to the redemption of the created order (Rom 8:18–25).[52] However, the death of Christ is also connected with the coming of the Spirit, who empowers and transforms believers so that they may live in accordance with God's heart and standards.[53] As believers are transformed individually, there are social consequences to the transformed life. As sin has social effects, so godliness has social effects. If sinful lives result in sinful people creating organizations and structures that reflect sinful hearts, then godly lives will transform systems that breed injustice. Our

---

[51] Steve Jeffery, Michael Ovey, and Andrew Sach, *Pierced for Our Transgressions: Rediscovering the Glory of Penal Substitution* (Wheaton, IL: Crossway, 2007), 21.

[52] For arguments that penal substitution grounds cosmic restoration, see Jeffrey, Ovey, and Sach, *Pierced for Our Transgressions*, 211; Michael Ovey, "The Cross, Creation and the Human Predicament," in *Where Wrath and Mercy Meet: Proclaiming the Atonement Today* (Milton Keynes: Paternoster, 2001), 100–35.

[53] I argue that penal substitutionary atonement is the grounding for the transforming work of the Holy Spirit. See Kenneth Reid, "Penal Substitutionary Atonement as the Basis for New Covenant and New Creation" (PhD diss., The Southern Baptist Theological Seminary, 2015), 178–209.

lives will reflect God's intent in our social behavior. Our transformation as individuals is grounded in the sacrifice of Christ on the cross.

Christus Victor, another view that provides much ground for social justice, is the theory that Jesus's death and resurrection bring victory over the powers and death. Since ransom and redemption are the language of liberation, then *Christus Victor* directly appeals to the liberation theme.[54] Kelly Kapic describes the theory:

> Christ comes as the conqueror who delivers the world from the oppressive forces of sin, death, and the devil. He achieves this by entering the world, freeing people from demonic influence through exorcism and healing, absorbing a fatal blow by swallowing up these powers of darkness, taking on human sin in death, and destroying claims on humanity by rising triumphantly. The victorious Christ brings new life, ushering God's people into a new kingdom that reigns over and against the devil's kingdom.[55]

This victory leads to new creation. The story of the fall points to God's redemptive work that will defeat the powers. God pointed to Jesus as having victory over Satan and the demonic realm (Gen 3:15). The defeat of the powers is one factor that may be behind the injustices of the world. Paul notes that we struggle against principalities and powers (Eph 6:12). While this is true individually, Millard Erickson states that this struggle occurs on the spiritual plane: "Behind the visible structures and institutions of society and culture, evil forces are at work using these invisible powers to enslave and blind believers, to attack them and to do them harm."[56] They influence

---

[54] The ancient ransom theory of the atonement proposes that Jesus died as a ransom to Satan. However, the Scriptures do not present Satan as a recipient of the ransom. Christus Victor provides more nuance and is more biblically grounded.

[55] Kelly M. Kapic, "Atonement," in *Evangelical Dictionary of Theology*, 3rd ed. (Grand Rapids: Baker Academic, 2017), 97.

[56] Millard J. Erickson, *Christian Theology*, 3rd ed. (Grand Rapids: Baker Academic, 2013), 592. On p. 593, he continues: "Paul does not tell us much about

systems and individuals—individuals who are not redeemed walk according to the prince and the power of the air (Eph 2:2). Though human sin is massive, demonic influence would explain the pervasiveness of injustice in such cases as glorifying lynching in the nineteenth and twentieth centuries, or in child sexual exploitation. Through *Christus Victor*, victory over the powers leads to the removal of evil eschatologically and their diminished power today. Victory at the resurrection also provides hope so that our labor is not in vain. The labor toward justice is encouraged by the resurrection because God's way, in the end, will win.

Moral influence or exemplar theories of the atonement point to Jesus's life and death as an example for humanity. The moral influence theory points to the cross as a demonstration of divine love. Michael Bird explains:

> "Some theologians, medieval and modern, have argued that the primary effect of Christ's death is not to change the *objective* state of humanity's relationship with God. Rather, the chief effect is to change the *subjective* state of a person's being. The cross demonstrates divine love and kindles a corresponding love in ourselves."[57]

The exemplar theory states that "Christ died in order that we would follow his example and imitate him."[58] Both theories explain the value of the

---

the specific forms in which the powers appear. What is clear, however, is that any of the patterns of a society can be used by the forces of evil to influence the thoughts and actions of the members of that society. John Yoder has suggested that these patterns include both intellectual structures (ologies or isms) and moral structures (the tyrant, the market, the school, the courts, race, and nation). To the extent that they control or at least influence humans, they are powers. The term 'structures' is appropriate, for the patterns utilized by the forces of evil form and constitute the very framework within which a person functions. They make their impact before or at a level below conscious influence and choice. Characteristically, the individual is not really conscious of their influence, or that other viable options exist."

[57] Michael F. Bird, *Evangelical Theology: A Biblical and Systematic Introduction*, 2nd ed. (Grand Rapids: Zondervan Academic, 2020), 453.

[58] Bird, 454. Cf. Erickson, *Christian Theology*, 716.

cross as influencing human action. Jesus's acts of love should encourage us to love as he loved. Jesus associated with and ministered to people who were on the margins of Jewish society, such as the Samaritan woman (John 4:7–26) and those suffering from leprosy (Matt 8:1–4). Jesus rebuked the Jewish leaders who neglected justice for their people (Matt 23:23–24) or exploited the vulnerable in the community (Mark 12:38–40). Jesus stated that the two greatest commandments are to love God and love people, which sums up the law (Matt 22:37–40). If social justice is an expression of love, and if Jesus modeled acts of justice and taught about justice, then we should do likewise. Moral influence and exemplar theories coincide with social justice by demonstrating the value of the cross with our actions. These atonement models do not carry a broad biblical foundation to consider these as the central or prominent meaning of Jesus's death. However, they have a biblical foundation and can be helpful with other theories in constructing a theology of atonement in relation to social justice.

There is a connection between these theories that present the plan of God. Penal substitution provides the basis for *Christus Victor*.[59] The power of the enemy to accuse is removed because of penal substitution. Furthermore, the curse on creation is removed. The enemy not only loses or has his power

[59] Jeremy Treat states, "First, in terms of theology, penal substitution has priority because of its explanatory power. Since systematic theology engages explicitly with doctrine and theory, the fact that penal substitution explains the 'how' of *Christus Victor* gives it priority in the doctrine of the atonement. Penal substitution does not do everything, but it provides insight into many of the other aspects of the atonement, especially *Christus Victor*. Second, penal substitution has priority in the sense that it is more directly related to the God-human relationship, which is the special focus of creation, fall, and redemption. In other words, penal substitution *directly* addresses the root problem between God and humanity (wrath/guilt), whereas *Christus Victor* addresses the *derivative* problem of human bondage to Satan. However, I must once again be clear that maintaining this type of priority for penal substitution does not imply that it does everything. Penal substitution is necessary but not sufficient for understanding the doctrine of the atonement in its entirety." Jeremy R. Treat, *The Crucified King: Atonement and Kingdom in Biblical and Systematic Theology* (Grand Rapids: Zondervan, 2014), 223–24.

diminished, but the conditions in creation that occasion injustice will be reversed. Because of the victory of Christ through penal substitution, we should act in a way that is consistent with Jesus's example and display his love.

Thus, key elements of each of the atonement theories address fundamental problems behind social injustice. Penal substitution and exemplar theories deal with the individual sin that causes injustice. *Christus Victor* addresses the demonic realm, which is one factor in influencing systemic injustice. Penal substitution provides the grounding for transforming behavior, while the moral influence and exemplar theories provide inspiration grounded in Jesus's life, conduct, and sacrifice.

Salvation and Social Justice

Ransom and redemption not only refer to the act of deliverance at the cross, they also emphasize the new condition of redeemed persons. In Eph 1:7, Paul refers to the present status of redemption. When the term redemption is applied to a person, it is also in reference to the broader idea that they are saved. This means that this person has a new relationship with God, whereby they are no longer alienated from God, counted guilty of their sins, and have a destiny apart from God, but that they have fellowship with God, are forgiven of their sins, and have a destiny with God in heaven and ultimately in the new heavens and the new earth. This section will discuss the salvific aspect of a person in light of social justice.

The first blessing of salvation to explore is adoption. Wayne Grudem notes, "Adoption is an act of God whereby he makes us members of his family."[60] Adoption is the blessing that those who are saved become children of God. Paul links redemption and adoption explicitly in Rom 8:23 and Gal 4:4–6. Romans 8:23 connects the consummation of the believer's adoption with the resurrection, while Gal 4:4–6 emphasizes the present reality of adoption: "But

---

[60] Wayne A. Grudem, *Systematic Theology: An Introduction to Biblical Doctrine*, 2nd ed. (Grand Rapids: Zondervan Academic, 2020), 913.

when the set time had fully come, God sent his Son, born of a woman, born under the law, to redeem those under the law, that we might receive adoption to sonship. Because you are his sons, God sent the Spirit of his Son into our hearts, the Spirit who calls out, '*Abba*, Father.'" Paul portrays the incarnation and the death of Christ as the acts that redeem those under the law. Those under the law are both Jews and Gentiles because both are under the dominion of sin.[61] The purpose of this redemption is to become children of God, and God has provided his Spirit and made us heirs. Paul's driving point is that believers are now the heirs of the promise.[62] Yet the Spirit is a critical gift from the Father to believers. Paul explained that the Spirit's reception shows that they are the people of God and no longer need to do the works of the law or be circumcised.[63] More will be explored about the Spirit below.

Those who are adopted should reflect the character of the Father. Trevor Burke discusses the moral imperative of God's children because of adoption and the work of the Spirit. He notes that God's children are commanded to put to death the misdeeds of the body (Rom 8:11).[64] They are led by the Spirit (Rom 8:14), which properly understood means to be led in a moral and ethical sense—it is not mere guidance but leading toward a life of holiness and rejecting sin.[65] Burke notes that our adoption should lead to holy living and that our conduct should reflect the conduct of God the Father.[66] He summarizes: "Paul's presentation of sonship by adoption is inextricably linked to the Spirit in that both are eschatological gifts and there is a clear moral responsibility to conduct oneself as a member of God's family."[67] Believers should

---

[61] Thomas R. Schreiner, *Galatians*, ZECNT (Grand Rapids: Zondervan Academic, 2010), 271.

[62] Schreiner, 263.

[63] Schreiner, 178.

[64] Trevor J. Burke, *Adopted into God's Family: Exploring a Pauline Metaphor*, NSBT (Downers Grove, IL: IVP Academic, 2006), 143–44.

[65] Burke, 145–46.

[66] Burke, 146.

[67] Burke, 147.

adopt the ethics and perspective of the Father. Since the Father is concerned with justice, and the Son has dealt with issues of justice, then the children of God should be concerned about social justice. If God's adopted children are truly reflecting his heart, they should orient their lives to defend the weak and marginalized people in the church and society and ensure that they and the systems and structures in their influence treat people fairly.

A second aspect of salvation is sanctification. Grudem states, "Sanctification is a progressive work of God and man that makes us more and more free from sin and like Christ in our actual lives."[68] Since sanctification is an ongoing blessing of salvation, it requires the work of both the Holy Spirit and the Christian.[69] Progressive sanctification fulfills the new covenant promise that God would write his law on the hearts of his people (Jer 31:33) and that the indwelling Spirit would cause people to obey the law (Ezek 36:27). If that is the case, then the whole law is the standard and expectation by which each Christian should live. It does not mean that they keep all the stipulations perfectly in this already/not-yet age. However, sanctification should produce people who love God and love their neighbor. The sanctification process should then result in believers committing acts of justice and loving the most vulnerable.

The Holy Spirit's sanctifying work transforms believers. The believer is indwelt by the Spirit (John 14:16–17; Rom 8:10; 1 Cor 6:12–20), and all believers receive the Spirit as a sign of their adoption (Rom 8:14–17; Gal 4:6). The Spirit is the agent of transformation as believers responsibly obey. Paul discusses this reality in Gal 5:16: "So I say, walk by the Spirit, and you will not gratify the desires of the flesh."[70] Verses 17–18 explain the conflict

---

[68] Grudem, *Systematic Theology*, 924.

[69] The view of sanctification expressed here is the traditional Reformed view in which sanctification is a progressive work of the Christian and the Holy Spirit and will not be completed in this life.

[70] Paul also discusses the work of the Spirit in the believer's transformation in Rom 8:1–17.

between the Spirit and flesh, while vv. 19–26 discuss the corresponding work of the flesh and the fruit of the Spirit. For our purposes, I will focus primarily on v. 16. The believer is commanded to walk by the Spirit, but the consequence is that the believer will not fulfill the desires of the flesh. This promise fulfills the prophetic expectation of the new covenant in which God will write the law on the hearts of his covenant people (Jer 31:33) and will give his Spirit so that his people will obey his law (Ezek 36:26–27) Ronald Fung explains:

> That the guidance of the Spirit can be experienced as a reality in the life of the believer is a sign that Jeremiah's prophetic word about the new covenant has been fulfilled. In OT times the Israelites knew of God's law as an external code, but in the NT dispensation the law of God is set in his people's understanding and written on their hearts (Jer. 31:31–34; Heb. 8:8–12); God's will is now an inward principle, the result of the leading of the Spirit within the believer.[71]

The Spirit's work in writing the law on the believer's heart is an essential aspect of the Christian experience. If the law is written on the heart, the disposition of people will follow God's desires as expressed in the law. This includes the motivation to treat one another fairly, to ensure that believers and unbelievers operate in systems that are fair, and that Christians

---

[71] Ronald Y. K. Fung, *The Epistle to the Galatians*, NICNT (Grand Rapids: Eerdmans, 1988), 248–49. Craig Keener comments, "In 5:16–25, Paul emphasizes here that the solution to the passions of the flesh is not more laws, but the Spirit who transforms from within. Paul has biblical grounds for affirming that, to the extent that we follow the eschatological Spirit, we follow God's commands (Ezek 36:26–27), Paul alludes to this text as part of the new covenant reality in 2 Cor 3:3, and probably alludes to it here as well: the Hebrew text of Ezek 36:27 speaks of the Spirit enabling God's eschatological people to 'walk' in his commands and do them." Craig S. Keener, *Galatians: A Commentary* (Cambridge: Cambridge University Press, 2019), 249.

will have a heart toward the weak and vulnerable. While this reality is lived in an already/not-yet fashion, God's people are empowered by the Spirit toward acts of justice and they advocate for justice in their spheres of influence.

To be a redeemed person, to be saved, naturally means that our agenda must change to God's agenda. Redeemed people are adopted into God's family. As such, they would act in ways that resemble the character of God. Redeemed people are being sanctified, becoming more conformed to the character of Christ in their conduct. Schreiner notes:

> The Galatians did not receive the Spirit in general; they received "the Spirit of his Son" (Gal 4:6). Further, Gal. 4:4–5 indicates that the Spirit was given on the basis of Christ's redeeming work, so that believers truly become God's children. The exhortations to walk in, be led by, march in step with, and sow to the Spirit (Gal. 5:16, 18, 25; 6:8) are rooted in the redemption that Christ achieved in the cross.[72]

The Spirit empowers believers to change, and his transforming work is the fulfillment of new covenant expectations of God's people. God empowers his people to follow his expectations, which include the expectations of justice.

Eschatological Redemption and Social Justice

The term redemption not only points to God's act of redemption at the cross or the status of the individual person who is redeemed, it also points to the plan of God for cosmic restoration. Paul discusses the eschatological aspects of redemption in Rom 8:18–25 and Eph 1:14; 4:30. In this sense, "redemption is the renewal and transformation of the creation."[73]

---

[72] Thomas R. Schreiner, *New Testament Theology: Magnifying God in Christ* (Grand Rapids: Baker Academic, 2008), 487.

[73] Letham, *Systematic Theology*, 58.

Eschatological redemption includes the final defeat of evil and the establishment of God's kingdom under the Messiah's rule, and the restoration of all things.

First is the defeat of evil. The defeat of evil includes the removal of sin as well as the defeat of demonic powers. The removal of evil occurs through the judgment of evildoers and banishment (Rev 20:10; 21:8). Recall that the demonic powers influence evil in this world. They take advantage of sinful humanity to multiply the destruction against God's intended plan. This is especially true if the systemic injustices of this world are influenced by the powers. God's plan of redemption brings forth justice by banishing the demonic powers, removing sin, and bringing judgment. Sin, Satan, and the demonic realm will be removed, and nothing will spoil God's new heavens and new earth.

Finally, all things will be restored. Redemptive history points to God's plan of restoration. A helpful concept is shalom, which "means *universal flourishing, wholeness, and delight*—a rich state of affairs in which natural needs are satisfied and natural gifts fruitfully employed, a state of affairs that inspires joyful wonder as its Creator and Savior opens doors and welcomes the creatures in whom he delights."[74] God's original design was for universal flourishing. Sin spoiled that reality. The renewal of the created order and the removal of evil will result in shalom in the eternal state. That those things must be restored means that they were once broken. Yet this world will have no more crying, pain, or grief because the old order of things will pass away (Rev 21:3–5). There will be no more curses or death, and God will dwell with his people. This state of affairs rules out injustice and brings forth perfect justice.

Another aspect of redemption is future-oriented. The completion of redemption is the resurrection of the body and the renewal of the created

---

[74] Cornelius Plantinga Jr., *Not the Way It's Supposed to Be: A Breviary of Sin* (Grand Rapids: Eerdmans, 1996), 10. Italics original.

order. This renewal speaks of the permanent elimination of sin and injustice. The powers will no longer be present. Unredeemed humanity is not a part of this new creation. Personal acts of injustice will be removed or transformed. The systemic dimension of injustice is removed because Jesus rules in this new heavens and new earth that has the absence of pain, crying, grief, and death.

Summary—Holistic Redemption and Social Justice

The Scripture and the theological categories above indicate that redemption is holistic. It begins with God's act of deliverance, first at the exodus and ultimately at the cross. God's people are redeemed because he has purchased them through the blood of Christ. Thus, believers as redeemed people are saved and have fellowship with God. Redemption also applies to the created order, so that one day the entire earth will be redeemed. God's work of redemption is the remedy to the injustices of this world, and social justice is grounded in the redemptive work of Jesus. Donald McLeod provides a helpful summary:

> God did more, however, than deliver his people from Egypt. He brought them to Canaan, the Promised Land. This was not, as modern Liberation Theology suggests, a merely earthly utopia from which political oppression, exploitation of the poor, and structural injustice had all been banished. These things mattered, of course; indeed, they matter enormously, not least because God himself loves justice and laid down stringent regulations with regard to the rights of the alien, the widow, the orphan and the needy (Exod 22:21–27). But the real hope, which Canaan merely prefigured, was of a heavenly country; and the wealth of that county consisted not of milk and honey, but of 'every spiritual blessing in the heavenly places' (Eph 1:3 ESV). The biblical concept of redemption never held out the promise of rest or freedom in this world. The

> exodus and the Promised Land, impressive and suggestive though they are, were but a pale shadow of a world-embracing redemption which would be consummated only when the first heaven and the first earth had passed away (Rev 21:1).[75]

Implications

One of the implications of redemption and social justice is that there are layers to God's redeeming work. God certainly has redeemed individuals, but he also redeems creation. One problem is when people emphasize one over the other. Some emphasize personal salvation and evangelism and neglect God's work of cosmic reconciliation. Others so emphasize cosmic reconciliation and de-emphasize God's evangelistic purposes for personal salvation. A false dichotomy can emerge that is not healthy. Our goal in theology and ministry is to be faithful to God's word.

Another debate concerns the meaning or content of the gospel. The gospel is the good news of Jesus Christ and his work for our salvation (1 Cor 15:3–4). But some argue that Scripture also speaks about the gospel of the kingdom, which is a wider referent than the evangelistic message of Jesus's death and resurrection. The gospel is certainly not less than God's saving work for each person, and any discussion about the gospel that minimizes or neglects this aspect of God's saving work misrepresents a fundamental aspect of the gospel. However, the gospel is also the good news about God's global concerns. To neglect this aspect also neglects God's concern for all humanity and creation itself.[76] DeYoung and Gilbert propose a narrow and wide lens for the gospel without compromising the message of salvation. The narrow referent is for personal salvation, while the wider referent is the gospel of the kingdom and cosmic renewal; it is interesting that

---

[75] Donald Macleod, *Christ Crucified: Understanding the Atonement* (Downers Grove, IL: IVP Academic, 2014), 222.

[76] DeYoung and Gilbert, *What Is the Mission of the Church?*, 91–113.

justice is important for both personal salvation and cosmic restoration.[77] Thus, justice and the gospel, if social justice is grounded in Scripture, are never in conflict.

Redemption is always first and foremost about God's work. Any approach to social justice must first be grounded in the death and resurrection of Jesus and the gift of the Holy Spirit. Any neglect of God's trinitarian redemptive work and any minimizing of personal faith in the work of Christ undercuts the very heart of God's approach to justice. However, the neglect of God's heart for justice ignores an important dimension of God's renewal of all things. God's plan is holistic.[78]

If redemption and justice include a personal and corporate/systemic dimension, ministry must follow suit. Our practices should reflect the priority and the heart of God. Personal evangelism and the proclamation of the message of salvation is the essential and nonnegotiable first priority. Yet any neglect of the real-life social situation that believers and unbelievers suffer may discourage others from hearing the gospel; it is a neglect of God's intended purpose and runs counter to Jesus's example of ministering to people's experiential needs.

Questions for Further Reflection

1. How would the idea of the wide-angle lens of the gospel and the zoom angle be helpful?
2. Do you and your congregation see a conflict between God's redemptive work and social justice?
3. Where is justice in your priority for your context? Is it a primary focus, a secondary focus, or not a focus at all?
4. How may justice intersect with the purpose of salvation?

---

[77] DeYoung and Gilbert, 100.

[78] Scot McKnight, *Kingdom Conspiracy: Returning to the Radical Mission of the Local Church* (Grand Rapids: Brazos, 2014), 152–53.

5. In your context, how do you envision redemption, for individuals and in light of justice?

Suggested Reading

DeYoung, Kevin and Greg Gilbert. *What is the Mission of the Church? Making Sense of Social Justice, Shalom, and the Great Commission.* Wheaton, IL: Crossway, 2011.

Keller, Timothy. *Generous Justice: How God's Grace Makes Us Just.* New York: Dutton, 2010.

Murray, John. *Redemption Accomplished and Applied.* Repr. ed. Grand Rapids: Eerdmans, 2015.

Offutt, Stephen, F. David Brokema, Krisanne Vaillancourt Murphy, Robb Davis, and Gregg Okesson. *Advocating for Justice: An Evangelical Vision for Transforming Systems and Structures.* Grand Rapids: Baker Academic, 2016.

Teevan, John Addison. *Integrated Justice and Equality: Biblical Wisdom for Those Who Do Good Works.* Grand Rapids: Christian's Library, 2014.

9

Justice and the Mission of the Church

— John Wind —

All who embrace Scripture as the uniquely authoritative written revelation of the only God agree that God is just and requires humanity to "do justice" in keeping with God's own character (Mic 6:8). Less agreed upon is what exactly God in his justice demands of the individual Christian, of the local institutional church, and of the broader civil state in order for that justice to be done.[1] An expanded term also up for debate today is "social justice." How does the biblical mandate to "do justice" compare with the contemporary call to pursue "social justice"? This chapter proposes a biblical framework for understanding the responsibility to do justice and then identifies some key facets of biblical justice with implications for the mission of the church. In doing so, it is important to distinguish this biblical sketch from any conceptions of justice that move clearly beyond or are opposed to the biblical portrait, lest we unwittingly invest the command to "do justice" with

[1] The US Constitution proclaims itself as designed "in order to . . . establish Justice" and one of its principal framers, James Madison, later reaffirmed that "Justice is the end of government. It is the end of civil society." James Madison, "Federalist 51," in *The Federalist*, ed. George W. Carey and James McClellan (Indianapolis: Liberty Fund, 2001), 271.

a meaning foreign to Scripture.[2] As Duncan Forrester remarks, "Christian notions about justice have interacted historically with other accounts of justice, often challenging, sometimes accommodating, frequently legitimating alternative views of justice."[3] In that spirit, the last part of this chapter will focus on recent understandings of "social justice," seeking to delineate the claims embedded in this idea and to identify any ways in which it corresponds or conflicts with biblical justice and the mission of the church.

The concept of covenant is a crucial component of any biblical framework for considering the question of justice and the broader question of the mission of the church. Peter Gentry and Stephen Wellum argue that "every loci of theology is affected by one's understanding of the relationship between the biblical covenants, given the fact that the covenants form the backbone of Scripture's story line."[4] The proposed framework below reflects one interpretation of the overall covenantal macrostructure of Scripture, with particular implications for the mission of the church and the question of justice. I present the same framework in much greater detail in the book, *Do Good to All People as You Have the Opportunity: A Biblical Theology of the Good Deeds Mission of the New*

---

[2] Stephen Charles Mott, for instance, in his book, *A Christian Perspective on Political Thought* (New York: Oxford University Press, 1993), argues that there is a "high degree of correspondence to biblical justice in the socialist commitment to justice, which in its highest form is distributed according to needs" (204). Mott defines "socialism" as "the conviction that the best society and the best environment for individual self-fulfillment is the one where the means of production are both owned and controlled by the community" (198) (i.e., owned and controlled by the government). While one might attempt to marshal evidence in favor of this economic model as the best one (though the empirical evidence of the last 100 years does not offer much obvious support for this contention), using the Bible as any evidence of divine sanction for this economic model seems questionable.

[3] Duncan B. Forrester, *Christian Justice and Public Policy* (Cambridge: Cambridge University Press, 1997), 227.

[4] Peter J. Gentry and Stephen J. Wellum, *Kingdom through Covenant: A Biblical-Theological Understanding of the Covenants* (Wheaton, IL: Crossway, 2012), 653.

Covenant Community.[5] The following will be only a brief selection of some aspects of that proposed covenantal framework, particularly those most relevant to the focus of the present chapter. Unlike the book-length treatment, which provides extensive argumentation in support of the framework, this chapter will mainly be limited to describing key aspects of the framework, aspects which will then function as the presuppositions for subsequently considering the ideas of "justice" and "social justice."

Biblical Texts and Exegesis: Covenantal Framework

The first presupposition of this proposed biblical framework is that God always relates to his creation by means of covenant. Some covenants God makes with all humanity and creation comprehensively (Adamic creation covenant and Noahic fallen creation covenant). Other covenants God only establishes with a subset of humanity, such as with Abraham and his descendants (Abrahamic and Mosaic covenants) or with followers of Jesus of Nazareth (new covenant, in both its inaugurated and consummated phases, with the consummated phase expanding to cosmic transformation). All these covenants, by their very nature, include binding privileges and responsibilities for the members of the covenant.

Second, humanity is presently in the age of the Noahic fallen creation covenant established in Genesis 9 (a covenant sharing both continuity and discontinuity with the Adamic creation covenant of Genesis 1–2) *and also in* the age of the inaugurated new covenant established by the complex of events stretching from the Last Supper to Pentecost (a covenant sharing both continuity and discontinuity with the Abraham and Mosaic covenants of the past and the consummated new covenant of the future). Believers are

[5] John A. Wind, *Do Good to All People as You Have the Opportunity: A Biblical Theology of the Good Deeds Mission of the New Covenant Community* (Phillipsburg, NJ: P&R, 2019).

members of the Noahic covenant by virtue of their humanity and members of the new covenant by virtue of their union with Christ.

Third, as given by God, all general human responsibilities and all uniquely Christian responsibilities (those premised on union with Christ and his church) are covenant responsibilities. All general *human* responsibilities (such as, justice in society) are governed by the Noahic fallen creation covenant. All uniquely *Christian* responsibilities (the mission of the church, which includes the responsibility to be faithful witnesses to those *outside* the new covenant and the responsibility to disciple those *inside* the new covenant) are governed by the inaugurated new covenant. Important to note: while these two covenants must be distinguished (since only Christians are members of both and since the covenants include differences in responsibilities, arenas of service, and promises), Christians' membership in the new covenant is nevertheless designed to impact *all* aspects of their membership in the Noahic covenant. While necessarily distinguished, these two covenants must not be separated.

Fourth, the covenant responsibilities of the individual Christian and of the local institutional church toward those *inside* the inaugurated new covenant community are different from their responsibilities toward those *outside*. One illustration of this distinction is found in Gal 6:10 where Paul commands Christians to "do good to everyone" but with a greater responsibility: "especially to those who are of the household of faith."

Fifth, the responsibilities of the individual Christian and of the local institutional church toward those *outside* the inaugurated new covenant community are twofold: first, to proclaim the good news of what Christ has done in inaugurating the new covenant, inviting all to enter this covenant. Second, to do good to all people as we have the opportunity (Gal 6:10). This "good deeds responsibility" is shared with all humanity under the Noahic fallen creation covenant of Genesis 9, including a general human responsibility to "do justice" in society, with the *lex talionis* of Gen 9:5–6 revealing mankind's "royal duty to champion justice"[6] and to pursue "proportionate

[6] W. Randall Garr, *In His Own Image and Likeness: Humanity, Divinity, and Monotheism* (Leiden: Brill, 2003), 158.

retributive justice with forbearance."[7] The good deeds responsibility of all humanity is a responsibility to pursue human flourishing for individuals and communities, the experience of daily provision, care, health, peace, and blessing in this life. This limited yet real human flourishing is possible under the Noahic covenant because God graciously restrains sin and maintains the natural world. As members of the Noahic covenant sharing this general responsibility, Christians also embody a greater reality in that their good deeds are governed by the clearer moral standards of Scripture, empowered by the indwelling Holy Spirit, and consciously directed toward the glory of God. Christian good deeds also always serve the "greatest good deed" of evangelism, in that, by their good deeds, Christians "adorn" and beautify the gospel message proclaimed verbally (Titus 2:10).[8]

Sixth, the verbal proclamation mission must maintain operational priority for the institutional local church even while many individual Christians give vocational priority to the good deeds mission in their personal lives. Some disagree that the mission of verbal proclamation should be given operational priority by the local church over the mission of good deeds. In response, some reasons why the local church *must* maintain this priority include the following. Verbal proclamation is a uniquely Christian vocation which will largely not occur if the local church neglects or downplays it. Verbal proclamation is the only means of bringing individuals into the eternal blessings of the new covenant, while doing good deeds at best provides temporal blessings. As Jesus says, "For what will it profit a man if he gains the whole world and forfeits his soul?" (Matt 16:26). Since the local church has limited resources of time, money, and personnel, verbal proclamation should likewise be given priority—questions of priority cannot be bypassed in a world of scarce resources. Additionally, any consideration by a local church of doing

---

[7] David VanDrunen, *Divine Covenants and Moral Order: A Biblical Theology of Natural Law* (Grand Rapids: Eerdmans, 2014), 128.

[8] This is not to imply that all Christian good deeds in society must be explicitly or directly connected to verbal proclamation of the gospel message. Obedience to humanity's God-given good deeds responsibility is valid in its own right.

good in matters of public policy and politics is complex and moves quickly into many issues not directly addressed by Scripture, meaning that when the local church gives priority to such matters, they typically speak beyond the authority of Scripture and beyond the competency and expertise of the institutional church. Important to repeat is that this operational priority is only for the local institutional church. Many individual Christians or groups of Christians outside those institutional structures will rightly give vocational and volunteer priority in their lives to doing all kinds of good deeds and to promoting general human flourishing across society. But the institutional local church must nonetheless maintain operational priority for the mission of verbal proclamation in its ministry to those still outside of Christ.

These six presuppositions provide the basic framework for examining the question, "What exactly does the biblical command to 'do justice' include?" The premise of the following examination is that proper biblical categories within which to understand the human (and Christian) responsibility to "do justice" in society are twofold: the good deeds responsibility of the Noahic fallen creation covenant and the good deeds mission of the inaugurated new covenant. As well, based upon the covenantal boundaries outlined above, when considering the question of justice, careful distinctions must be made: distinctions between God's own perfect justice in the age to come and humanity's limited and imperfect justice in this age and distinctions between the justice possible in the local church and that possible in broader human society.

Theological Formulation

Justice in Scripture

Debated questions are often matters of debated definitions. Some Christians rightly affirm that "justice is a core message of the Bible"[9] but then fail to pro-

[9] Eric Mason, *Woke Church: An Urgent Call for Christians in America to Confront Racism and Injustice* (Chicago: Moody, 2018), 51.

vide a clear and warranted definition of what biblical justice actually entails and instead appear to assume a consensus on the meaning of "justice" that is, in fact, lacking. This same lack of clear definition also plagues many secular discussions of justice, including that of John Rawls, the Harvard philosopher who established the trajectory of the larger discussion during the last fifty years with his publication of *A Theory of Justice* in 1971. As fellow philosopher Antony Flew observes, "Most remarkably . . . Rawls himself offers no definition of the word 'justice.' He must surely be the first author of a substantial treatise pretending to be about justice not to have done so."[10] Flew goes on to note that two advantages of leaving "justice" ill-defined are the greater ease of claiming one's favorite public policies as those that produce "justice" and the ability to position oneself "in unchallengeable occupation of the moral high ground."[11] Who, after all, wants to be seen opposing justice?

In seeking to define justice, Christians who look to Scripture for authoritative answers encounter an additional difficulty in that "the concept of justice is not explicitly defined in Scripture," at least not in the sense of a detailed and comprehensive model.[12] Instead, since the writers of Scripture "do not articulate a conception of justice," Nicholas Wolterstorff asserts that readers must attempt "to extract the underlying pattern of [the biblical writers'] thought from their testimony."[13] But among theologians and philosophers, "there is no consensus interpretation" of what the complete pattern of justice extracted from Scripture looks like.[14] What can be discerned from the biblical portrait is of a more fragmentary nature and must be supplemented and brought into conversation with insights found in

[10] Antony Flew, *Equality in Liberty and Justice*, 2nd ed. (New Brunswick, NJ: Transaction, 2001), xiii.

[11] Flew, *Equality in Liberty and Justice*, xiii.

[12] Steven B. Cowan and James S. Spiegel, *The Love of Wisdom: A Christian Introduction to Philosophy* (Nashville: B&H Academic, 2009), 378.

[13] Nicholas Wolterstorff, *Justice: Rights and Wrongs* (Princeton: Princeton University Press, 2008), 67.

[14] Wolterstorff, *Justice*, 66.

"conventional and commonly accepted accounts of justice" that occur outside of Scripture.[15] Furthermore, sensitivity to the macro-covenantal structure of Scripture means, for example, that seemingly straightforward civil laws given to old covenant Israel cannot be simplistically applied to either the new covenant church or to Noahic covenant societies. The social laws of old covenant Israel, Tim Keller notes, "were principles for relationships primarily between believers. Israel was a nation-state in which every citizen was bound to obey the whole law of God and also was required to give God wholehearted worship. This is not the situation in our society today."[16] Instead, suggests Keller, the abiding validity of such laws for members of the new covenant is unavoidably "inferential," requiring that "application must be done with care and . . . always be subject to debate."[17]

These difficulties notwithstanding, some important parameters of justice in the Bible arise from within the covenantal structure presupposed in this chapter. As outlined above, all humanity presently lives under the Noahic fallen creation covenant, a covenant which includes the general human responsibility to uphold "a proportionate retributive justice [as] the basic standard for human law."[18] The Noahic covenant standard, "Whoever sheds the blood of man, by man shall his blood be shed, for God made man in his own image" (Gen 9:6), is a standard of "proportionate retributive justice." This standard corresponds with the later Mosaic covenant standard, "But if there is harm, then you shall pay life for life, eye for eye, tooth for tooth, hand for hand, foot for foot, burn for burn, wound for wound, stripe for stripe" (Exod 21:23–25), a standard many

---

[15] Forrester, *Christian Justice*, 3.

[16] Timothy Keller, *Generous Justice: How God's Grace Makes Us Just* (New York: Dutton, 2010), 23.

[17] Keller, 31.

[18] Randy Beck and David VanDrunen, "The Biblical Foundations of Law: Creation, Fall and the Patriarchs," in *Law and the Bible: Justice, Mercy and Legal Institutions*, ed. Robert F. Cochran Jr. and David VanDrunen (Downers Grove, IL: IVP Academic, 2013), 41.

today condemn as barbaric. But in fact, this standard of "proportionate retributive justice" not only embodies a clear sense of proportionality between crime and punishment but also exhibits comparative restraint in contrast to the typically harsh penalties of the broader ancient Near Eastern context.[19] In addition to justice in Scripture requiring retribution for or remediation of wrongs, Steven Cowan and James Spiegel identify three further elements in the biblical portrait of justice: "procedural fairness . . . help for the needy . . . mercy for the oppressed."[20] Mercy for the oppressed is another expression of justice as remediation of wrong, in this case, the wrong of some form of oppression. Those in a general state of needing help may or may not themselves also be victims of injustice, but regardless of the cause(s) of their needy state, the one who is just inclines toward compassionate aid. The just one in Scripture also pursues restoration, or what John Teevan labels "relational justice," which "focuses on healing broken relationships."[21] Finally, justice in Scripture includes the fair application of the rule of law, following just procedures that impartially treat individuals according to shared and established standards (in Scripture, these standards are often divinely revealed moral absolutes). When those standards are transgressed, then retributive or remedial justice is required.

In seeking to understand "justice," Christians have also long sought supplementary insight from outside Scripture, including from Aristotle (384–322 BC), who pondered the meaning of "justice" not long after the completion of the Old Testament canon. In his survey of Aristotle on justice, Ronald Nash begins by noting that Aristotle identifies two different senses in which "a person can be said to be just": universal justice and

---

[19] Paul Copan, "Is Yahweh a Moral Monster?: The New Atheists and Old Testament Ethics," *Philosophia Christi* 10, no. 1 (2008): 7–27.

[20] Cowan and Spiegel, *The Love of Wisdom*, 379.

[21] John Addison Teevan, *Integrated Justice and Equality: Biblical Wisdom for Those Who Do Good Works* (Grand Rapids: Christian's Library, 2014), 14–15.

particular justice.[22] Universal justice is "coextensive with the whole of righteousness, with the whole of virtue. A person is just in the universal sense if he possesses all the proper virtues, if he is moral, if he keeps the laws, which Aristotle thought should accord with virtuous behavior. . . . act[ing] virtuously toward others."[23] Universal justice describes individuals of a just and virtuous character (whose words and actions necessarily reflect that character). When considering the Noahic fallen creation covenant, Noah, predating the Abrahamic covenant, seems to meet just this standard of universal justice, "a righteous man, blameless in his generation" (Gen 6:9). Another Old Testament figure who also appears to be living outside the Abrahamic and Mosaic covenants is Job, likewise described as one who was "blameless and upright, one who feared God and turned away from evil" (Job 1:1). These biblical examples seem to accord with Aristotle's understanding of universal justice, or what could be labeled, "justice as virtue."[24] As well, the aforementioned biblical facets of justice—mercy for the oppressed, help for the needy, restoration of relationships—also appear to fit well within the category of universal justice, that is, as actions that characterize the virtuous person. Nash goes so far as to suggest that "the vast majority of biblical allusions to justice appear to be examples of justice in this universal sense."[25] This conception of justice resonates with the demands made of all humanity in the Noahic covenant since the label "universal" designates this as the justice that "can be practiced by all . . . [that which] we normally hope to find . . . present in every human being."[26]

In contrast to universal justice, which ought to be practiced by all people, "particular justice" describes the justice which should be demonstrated by those occupying a particular role or functioning within a defined arena.

---

[22] Ronald H. Nash, *Social Justice and the Christian Church* (Milford, MI: Mott Media, 1983), 29.

[23] Nash, 30.

[24] Nash, 74.

[25] Nash, 30.

[26] Nash, 75.

This notion moves beyond the idea of justice as virtuous character to some of the actions that accord with that virtue, particularly as appropriate to certain roles and arenas. Particular justice, in contrast to universal justice, is also concerned with standards of behavior that are enforceable through government power, while much of the virtuous life of universal justice is beyond the power of the state to legislate, coerce, or correct. In general, Michael Sandel defines this justice for Aristotle as "giving people what they deserve."[27] Nash labels this, "justice as fairness," as it concerns "the question of fair treatment" within particular contexts.[28] Aristotle identifies three variants of particular justice: commercial justice, remedial justice, and distributive justice. Commercial justice concerns fair standards and practices among those involved in the exchange of goods and services within the economic sphere.[29] Commercial justice appears to be one expression of the above-identified biblical concern for "procedural justice." For example, Scripture consistently maintains the standards of giving others what is fair and deserved as employees (condemning those who "oppress the hired worker in his wages" [Mal 3:5]) and as customers (in the marketplace, "a false balance is an abomination to the Lord, but a just weight is his delight" [Prov 11:1]). When established standards of fairness in the marketplace or the rule of law in society are violated, then justice demands remediation, correction, and retribution—Aristotle's category of "remedial justice." The arena of this corrective justice is the civil or criminal court of law within which the recognized agent of the governing power (such as a king, a judge, or a jury) is responsible to seek justice in remedying the wrong. Again, this facet of justice appears to resonate with the already-stated biblical concern for "proportionate retributive justice," in which the state assigns punishments and penalties for crimes in proportion to the harm inflicted, including as

---

[27] Michael J. Sandel, *Justice: What's the Right Thing to Do?* (New York: Farrar, Straus and Giroux, 2009), 9.

[28] Nash, *Social Justice*, 75.

[29] Nash, 31.

exhibited archetypically in the law of the Noahic covenant, "Whoever sheds the blood of man, by man shall his blood be shed" (Gen 9:6).

Aristotle identifies one other area of particular justice: distributive justice. This conception of justice is less a matter of equal treatment under the law and more a matter of treatment corresponding to individual merit. Distributive justice concerns the communal "goods" of a society, with Aristotle's focus mainly on the "good" of political office, but also broadened to include social honors and privileges in general, along with the shared resources and wealth of the community (in contrast to individual possessions). Distributive justice is then a matter of how these communal "goods" ought rightly to be distributed among the members of that society, with government typically understood to be the agent of distribution. Cowan and Spiegel observe that "rather than pursuing an *equal* distribution of these "goods," Aristotle envisions a decidedly *unequal* result in which "each person's share should match what they actually deserve"—though Aristotle is uncertain which criteria(s) of merit should be employed in making these distributions.[30]

Identifying Aristotle's concept of distributive justice with justice as portrayed in Scripture is harder to do, though the scriptural principle requiring Christians to render "honor to whom honor is owed" (Rom 13:7) fits with Aristotle's general sentiment. It is noteworthy that many who advocate for "social justice" today likewise embrace an idea of justice requiring "distribution," but by this they typically mean a forced redistribution of individual wealth by means of government power in pursuit of equalized economic outcomes—a meaning radically different than Aristotle's distributive justice. As Flew notes, Aristotle and the Western tradition of justice were never a project to "equalize the conditions of all its subjects."[31] Thomas Sowell calls into question the legitimacy of such an equalizing goal since "neither logic nor empirical evidence

[30] Cowan and Spiegel, *The Love of Wisdom*, 378.

[31] Flew, *Equality*, 142.

provides a compelling reason for expecting either equal or random outcomes among individuals, groups, institutions or nations."[32] While Sowell freely acknowledges that discrimination and injustice are at times significant factors in unequal outcomes among humans (situations in which a just remedy ought to be sought), the Western tradition of justice, beginning with the Old Testament and with Aristotle, has never recognized *all* unequal outcomes among humans as evidence of injustice. Instead, the Western tradition understood that "equal rights and equal treatment of all does not mean equal performances."[33]

Emerging out of our survey of justice is the recognition of the inherent limitations of the human justice which is possible under the Noahic fallen creation covenant. While both the Old Testament and Aristotle have a fuller conception of justice (as virtue, as mercy for the oppressed, as help for the needy, and as restoration of relationships), one that moves beyond mere procedural and remedial justice, Beck and VonDrunen contend that such comprehensive justice "lies beyond the capacity of human government," and "since civil government cannot fully achieve justice in the biblical sense, it must stake out a more manageable set of objectives within the scope of its limited resources."[34] Reinhold Niebuhr, for example, makes

> a sharp distinction between absolute justice, which human beings find impossible to achieve, and the relative and temporary approximations to justice which result from the effective balancing of conflicting interests and give for a time an acceptable degree of justice in the social and economic orders. Policy can never hope to achieve more than such relative justice; the direct pursuit of absolute justice . . . leads to tyranny and disaster.[35]

---

[32] Thomas Sowell, *Discrimination and Disparities*, 2nd ed. (New York: Basic Books, 2019), 87.

[33] Sowell, 24.

[34] Beck and VanDrunen, "The Biblical Foundations," 48.

[35] Forrester, *Christian Justice*, 218.

According to Niebuhr, one reason why the "relative justice" possible through human agents in a fallen world must be distinguished from "absolute justice" (promised through God in the *eschaton*) is that potentially well-intended human attempts at "absolute justice," in pushing beyond human limitations (as creatures both finite and fallen), end not in justice but in "tyranny and disaster." When the limitations of human justice under the Noahic fallen creation covenant are ignored, Niebuhr describes "how easily and subtly justice degenerates into injustice, and how powerful groups assert the right to define what justice is and use notions of justice to disguise their own oppressions."[36]

But is the biblical portrait of justice limited to the justice possible under the Noahic covenant? Christians, after all, are also members of the inaugurated new covenant, groaning in anticipation of the perfect justice of the consummated new covenant kingdom to come. Forrester answers by describing the local church community as "called to be a kind of anticipation of the life and the justice of the City of God, a colony of heaven, a preliminary and partial demonstration as it were of the justice of God."[37] The full picture of the future justice of the city of God which Christians are called to anticipate and partially demonstrate includes both mercy and retribution. This retribution, as Paul describes it, is "the wrath to come" (1 Thess 1:10), Christ "inflicting vengeance on those who do not know God and on those who do not obey the gospel of our Lord Jesus," such that they "suffer the punishment of eternal destruction, away from the presence of the Lord" (2 Thess 1:8–9). Apart from the work of mercy accomplished by Christ in the new covenant, *only* retribution would be justly due to all humanity on the day of final judgment, "for all have sinned and fall short of the glory of God" (Rom 3:23). The mercy to be granted on that day will be granted only to those within the new covenant, mercy which is

[36] Forrester, 187.

[37] Forrester, 244.

therefore also a proper expression of God's justice since Christ has *already* borne the full retribution for sin otherwise due to believers.[38] But how then is God's perfect future judgment to be rightly reflected in the inaugurated new covenant community of today? How is it to be reflected in the Noahic fallen creation covenant community (broader human society) of today? In both communities, God's perfect justice is prefigured in a mixture of mercy and punishment, with the mercy pointing to the ultimate mercy found only in Christ and the punishment pointing to both the just retribution of a holy God toward unrepentant rebels and the restorative discipline of a loving Father toward his adopted children. This "new creation moral dynamic," as VanDrunen labels it, must not only be evident within the community of the local church but also "expressed in various ways by individual Christians' conduct in broader society."[39] This moral dynamic means that Christians must continue to "support the administration of justice in civil life" under the Noahic covenant, even while the eschatological ethic of the new covenant community also "penultimizes their support of the pursuit of retributive justice" and causes believers to be known as those who consistently "exercise a merciful, reconciling, and restorative love that transcends the claims of retributive justice."[40] But the ongoing realization of life lived within this tension is a constant challenge which involves, in some measure, upholding the ethic of the new creation (embodied in the eschatological institution of the church) within the boundaries of the still-existing old creation (and its Noahic covenant institutions). As VanDrunen states, "Determining how to witness to the new moral order while honoring the present moral order is perhaps *the* central issue of Christians ethics."[41]

---

[38] Any additional retribution would put the believer in an unjust position of double jeopardy.

[39] VanDrunen, *Divine Covenants*, 449.

[40] VanDrunen, 469.

[41] VanDrunen, 478.

Social Justice?

How does this portrait of justice in the Bible relate to contemporary calls for "social justice?" Sowell notes again the problem of definition since "so many advocate what they call 'social justice'—often with great passion, but with no definition."[42] Sowell also believes that the adjective "social" is redundant since "all justice is inherently social," necessarily expressed in relationships between persons.[43] Why then has a redundant and ill-defined term become popular? Like Flew's earlier recognition of the advantages of ambiguity when using the term "justice," Antonio Martino also identifies "social justice" as popular because it acts as a cipher upon which people can project their own ideas and can position themselves in the moral high ground. Social justice

> "can be used by different people, holding quite different views, to designate a wide variety of different things. Its obvious appeal stems from its persuasive strength, from its positive connotation, which allows the user to praise his own ideas and simultaneously express contempt for the ideas of those who don't agree with them."[44]

Michael Novak and Paul Adams seek to move beyond this less-than-helpful ambiguity by identifying "six different connotations or meanings" of "social justice" as commonly used today.[45] First, the haziest usage of the term is one which employs it interchangeably with "compassion." While "compassion" is certainly a biblical attitude which should characterize the one who is just, this usage—assuming that those who are compassionate must support whatever is said to promote social justice, with a lack of support

---

[42] Thomas Sowell, *The Quest for Cosmic Justice* (New York: Free Press, 1999), 3.

[43] Sowell, *The Quest*, 3.

[44] Antonio Anselmo Martino, "The Myth of Social Justice," in *Three Myths*, by Arnold Beichman, Antonio Anselmo Martino, and Kenneth R. Minogue (Washington, DC: Heritage Foundation, 1982), 23.

[45] Michael Novak and Paul Adams, *Social Justice Isn't What You Think It Is* (New York: Encounter Books, 2015) 29.

for such proposals indicating one's lack of compassion—is unhelpful and brings little clarity to the discussion.[46] Second, Novak and Adams identify the oldest usage of "social justice" as found within Roman Catholic social thought, with the first author to use the term being the Italian Jesuit Luigi Taparelli d'Azeglio in 1840 and with the phrase first appearing in a papal encyclical in 1932 (*Quadragesimo Anno*).[47] Within this tradition, "social justice" is "typically associated with some notion of the 'common good' . . . [defined as] 'the sum of those conditions of social life which allow social groups and their individual members relatively thorough and ready access to their own fulfillment,'" an idea which "avoids speaking of 'equality of condition' or 'collective equality,' in favor of emphasizing the opportunity for each unique individual to develop his or her talents to their full potential."[48] This usage of "social justice" appears broadly compatible with the Noahic covenant concern for general human flourishing in this age. Novak and Adams argue that, understood this way, "social justice" is "an attribute of citizens not of states," with social justice being "a virtue that can be exercised solely by individuals rather than a government institution," making it another expression of Aristotle's "universal justice" or "justice as virtue."[49] As demonstrated below, this distinctly Roman Catholic usage of "social justice" differs significantly from the common usage today within the secular realms of education, media, and politics.

Novak and Adams identify a third definition for "social justice," one that *is* common within the secular realms: social justice as "distribution." Broader than Aristotle's meaning of "distribution," this idea concerns "the fair distribution of advantages and disadvantages in society," in particular through the government power to tax and selectively redistribute wealth.[50]

---

[46] Novak and Adams, 35.

[47] Novak and Adams, 90, 106–20.

[48] Novak and Adams, 31.

[49] Novak and Adams, 51.

[50] Novak and Adams, 30.

This definition spills over into a fourth definition of social justice as "equality." In this case, government redistributes wealth and opportunity in pursuit of a (however ill-defined) goal of "equality of condition" among its citizens (in contrast to the more modest goal of "equality of opportunity").[51] This leads to a fifth definition, "social justice" as the larger "progressive agenda" of expanding government in order to increase redistribution in pursuit of equal outcomes.[52] Finally, in recent years, the equality agenda has extended beyond economic, racial, and female equality to include the "new civil rights" of equity for sexual identities (the LGBTQ+ movement), as well as framing the legal right for a woman to have an abortion as a matter of "social justice" for women.[53]

These last four uses of "social justice" emerged from the philosophical currents of recent decades, including the significant influence of the previously mentioned John Rawls. Teevan goes so far as to state, "'Social Justice,' for all practical purposes . . . is now recognized as justice as Rawls defined it."[54] What then are Rawls' crucial claims that undergird the concept of "social justice" common in secular society today? First, Rawls defines "all human outcomes as arbitrary."[55] Rawls asserts that individual human talent or effort

---

[51] Novak and Adams, 30. Nash describes the difference between these two as the difference between "an approach that insists that the attainment of justice is impossible apart from the realization of certain just results and a competing view that maintains that a just society is one that adopts just procedures. A theory that places its emphasis upon just procedures will recognize that there is no way of specifying or knowing in advance what a just result would be. All one can do is try to make the procedures as just as possible. Then, whatever results from those just procedures must be recognized as just." Nash, *Social Justice*, 53. In contrast, the issue in the first approach, according to Sowell is "not process principles but social results," a vision within which "moral rights . . . are rights to results." Thomas Sowell, *A Conflict of Visions: Ideological Origins of Political Struggles*, 2nd ed. (New York: Basic, 2007), 205, 215.

[52] Novak and Adams, 33.

[53] Novak and Adams, 34.

[54] Teevan, *Integrated Justice*, 58.

[55] Teevan, 49.

cannot be used (even in part) to explain unequal human outcomes. In spite of the "tendency for common sense to suppose that income and wealth, and the good things in life generally, should be distributed according to moral desert" (what is merited or deserved), Rawls "rejects this conception."[56] For Rawls, even "inequalities of birth and natural endowment are undeserved."[57] Instead, if all wealth and ability "can properly be treated as a collective windfall gain,"[58] that is, if one's possession of more wealth or ability than another is truly arbitrary without any reference to merit or right, then government transgresses no moral boundaries when it redistributes wealth and opportunities. Second, though arbitrary, according to Rawls, this unequal distribution of human outcomes is, nonetheless, unjust. Roger Scruton restates this claim as "inequality in whatever sphere—property, leisure, legal privilege, social rank, educational opportunities, or whatever else we might wish for ourselves and our children—is unjust until proven otherwise."[59] "Social justice" therefore requires "an equalization of outcomes to eliminate that unjust arbitrariness."[60] In contrast to "equality of opportunity," understood as a "fair and open competition for scarce opportunities," social justice must ensure that "every competitor is as likely to succeed as every other competitor."[61] Third, if this is so, the righteous instrument of social justice is the power of the state since justice is expressed in "the force society uses to assure equalization."[62] Because of Rawls' claim that the natural distribution of human benefits is fundamentally arbitrary, extensive government redistribution not only avoids charges of unjust confiscation of personal possessions but actually embodies

[56] John Rawls, *A Theory of Justice* (Cambridge: Belknap, 1971), 310; quoted in Sandel, *Justice*, 160.

[57] Flew, *Equality*, 150.

[58] Flew, 140.

[59] Roger Scruton, *Fools, Frauds, and Firebrands: Thinkers of the New Left* (London: Bloomsbury, 2015), 4.

[60] Teevan, *Integrated Justice*, 49.

[61] Flew, *Equality*, 175–76.

[62] Teevan, *Integrated Justice*, 49.

what is *demanded* by justice.[63] As Teevan notes, "the assumption is that unless we are working for equality of outcomes through institutions, we are not working for true justice. Any system that does not focus on the redistribution of income is fundamentally unjust."[64] David Schaefer agrees with this analysis, observing that Rawls "teaches that no government is just if it allows people to earn rewards from the honest use of their own skills and talents, unless they somehow compensate the 'least advantaged' members of society for their gains."[65] Some follow Rawls only in part, disagreeing that merit, effort, and natural endowment play *no* role in human outcomes while nonetheless believing that "if individual economic benefits are not due *solely* [emphasis added] to individual merit, there is justification for having politicians redistribute those benefits."[66] Even while recognizing the role of merit, effort, and natural endowment, this partial Rawlsian view is still convinced that "group outcomes in human endeavors would tend to be equal, or at least comparable or random, if there were no biased interventions"[67] in favor of those identified as advantaged. This assumption therefore warrants government redistribution based upon the belief that "politicians, bureaucrats and judges will produce either efficiently better or morally superior outcomes by intervening" in favor of those identified as disadvantaged.[68]

While Rawls' fundamental claims about "social justice" (complete arbitrariness of all human outcomes, with merit or natural endowment playing no role; all unequal outcomes as fundamentally unjust; government power required to equalize all outcomes) are not readily compatible with the biblical

---

[63] Sowell observes that this view "sees transfers of material benefits to the less fortunate not simply as a matter of humanity but as a matter of justice." Sowell, *A Conflict of Visions*, 215.

[64] Teevan, *Integrated Justice*, 50.

[65] David Lewis Schaefer, *Illiberal Justice: John Rawls vs. the American Political Tradition* (Colombia, MO: University of Missouri Press, 2007), 11.

[66] Sowell, *Discrimination and Disparities*, vii.

[67] Sowell, 152.

[68] Sowell, 215.

portrait under the Noahic and new covenants, Forrester is right to identify some strengths of Rawls' approach. First, Forrester commends Rawls' general desire to give priority to justice. Second, in agreement with scriptural revelation, Rawls "affirms and assumes human equality." Third, like the Bible, Rawls expresses a concern for the poor. Lastly, while all justice cannot be reduced, as Rawls does, to a matter of "fairness" (as he defines it), the notion of fairness, as addressed earlier in this chapter, is nonetheless "a central component of any adequate account of justice."[69] While joining Forrester in affirming Rawls in these ways, on balance, Rawls' conception of social justice exhibits more weaknesses than strengths. One of those weaknesses is the validation of class warfare that his view implies, since all inequalities are inherently unjust and wealthier classes are necessarily oppressing poorer classes. In contrast, Sowell warns that "history shows how dangerous it can be, to a whole society, to automatically and incessantly attribute statistical differences in outcomes to malevolent actions against the less successful."[70] Rawls' approach appears to unavoidably pit members of society against one another, since "socioeconomic disparities are automatically somebody's fault."[71] Another weakness is Rawls' assumption of human competency through the power of government to achieve equality of outcome, even while appearing unconcerned about the danger of government using its ever-expanding power to do evil instead of good. Sowell describes this as a situation where "an inequality of economic outcomes is replaced by a far more dangerous increased inequality of power."[72] Rawls' high view of the competency of human governments appears out of step with the more restrained vision of the Noahic fallen creation covenant concerning the limitations of the state in this age.

While understanding Rawls' fundamental claims concerning justice is crucial to understanding "social justice" as commonly employed today,

---

[69] Forrester, *Christian Justice*, 133–34.

[70] Sowell, *Discrimination and Disparities*, 121.

[71] Sowell, 117.

[72] Sowell, 147.

another key influence shaping "social justice" is what's known as "critical theory." Critical theory was "conceived in the intellectual crucible of Marxism."[73] Like Marxism, the variants of critical theory share the conviction that "the world has to be changed, transformed, revolutionized if justice is to be recognized and realized."[74] But unlike Marxism in its traditional form, which emphasizes only the need to overthrow structures of *economic* oppression, critical theory seeks to uncover and eliminate *any* structures of oppression in society.[75] This is why some label critical theory "cultural Marxism" (in contrast to a narrower "economic Marxism"). Critical theory "divides the world into oppressed groups and their oppressors" and pursues the liberation of the oppressed (as well as often the punishment or marginalization of the oppressors).[76]

Apologist Neil Shenvi describes the practice of critical theory today as founded upon seven premises.[77] Premise one gives priority to an individual's group identity, in particular whether one is "part of a dominant, oppressor group or a subordinate, oppressed group with respect to a given identity marker like race, class, gender, physical ability, age, and so forth."[78] Premise two asserts that "oppressor groups subjugate oppressed groups through the exercise of hegemonic power. . . . [which is] the ability

---

[73] Stephen Eric Bronner, *Critical Theory: A Very Short Introduction*, 2nd ed. (Oxford: Oxford University Press, 2017), 2.

[74] Forrester, *Christian Justice*, 167.

[75] Bronner, *Critical Theory*, 2.

[76] Neil Shenvi, "The Language of Social Justice: A Friendly Rejoinder to Joe Carter," *Neil Shenvi—Apologetics* (blog), https://shenviapologetics.com/the-language-of-social-justice-a-friendly-rejoinder-to-joe-carter/.

[77] For a full engagement with critical theory, see Neil Shenvi and Pat Sawyer, *Critical Dilemma: The Rise of Critical Theories and Social Justice Ideology—Implications for the Church and Society* (Eugene, OR: Harvest House, 2023).

[78] Neil Shenvi, "Social Justice, Critical Theory, and Christianity: Are They Compatible?—Part 1," *Neil Shenvi*—Apologetics (blog), https://shenviapologetics.com/social-justice-critical-theory-and-christianity-are-they-compatible-part-1/. The remaining quotes in this paragraph are all from this blog post.

to impose your group's values, expectations, and norms on the rest of society." Among other means of subjugation, oppressor groups institutionalize their power to oppress the powerless through the systems and structures of society. When people benefit from these oppressive structures ("privilege"), those people are guilty of oppression, regardless of their personal awareness or intentions. According to premise three, all oppressed groups share a common experience of oppression and thus find solidarity with one another, regardless of how diverse their group identities. Narrower group identities (race, class, etc.) may vary, but the broader group identity ("the oppressed") unites them. The subjugation experienced by all oppressed groups is recognized as the primary source of unequal outcomes for those groups, inequities which Rawls likewise sees as the fundamental indication of injustice. Premise four is therefore a demand for justice, with all efforts at "freeing groups from oppression" seen as a righteous expression of humanity's "fundamental moral duty." The pursuit of justice *is* the pursuit of the liberation of the oppressed. Premise five gives priority to the "lived experience" of oppressed groups over any supposed objective counter evidence or rationale offered by oppressor groups. Instead, oppressors must defer to the opinion of the oppressed group. This approach appears to overthrow any final appeal to shared objective standards, such as the rule of law, reason, or historical fact. Indeed, premise six declares that "oppressor groups hide their oppression under the guise of objectivity," giving further reason to distrust and dismiss the perspective of those labeled as oppressors. Finally, premise seven recognizes that those who are members of two or more oppressed groups "experience oppression in a unique way" that gives increased weight to their perspective (the concept of "intersectionality").

Premises five, six, and seven combine to describe a whole new theory of how we gain knowledge, known as "standpoint epistemology." According to Helen Pluckrose and James Lindsay, in this theory of knowledge, all human knowing is "'situated,' which means that it comes from one's 'standpoint' in society, by which [this theory's proponents] mean one's membership in intersecting identity groups."[79] Because knowledge is tied to one's standpoint, "objective truth [is] unobtainable."[80] Instead, "knowledge comes from the lived experience of different identity groups, who are differently positioned in society and thus see different aspects of it."[81] Furthermore, "belonging to a marginalized group provides special access to truth, by allowing members insight into both dominance and their own oppression."[82] Note that this theory assumes that all people sharing the same marginalized identity "will have the same experience" and will "interpret [their experience] in the same ways."[83] Because of this shared experience and interpretation, "having oppressed identities allows extra dimensions of sight," which provide the marginalized "a richer, more accurate view of reality—hence we should listen to and believe their accounts of [reality]."[84] Those with multiple oppressed identities ("intersectionality") should be listened to even more closely and believed, giving priority and deference to the lived experience of the oppressed over any supposed claims of science or reason. In fact, some deny that "science and reason belong to all humans and are the same for all humans" but instead are merely the means of maintaining hegemony by "white Western men," with the result that "legitimate disagreement" with the viewpoint of those in marginalized groups is "not an option."[85]

An illustration of how "social justice" as understood today that incorporates both the concepts of critical theory and of Rawls is found in the book *Promoting Diversity and Social Justice: Educating People from*

---

[79] Helen Pluckrose and James Lindsay, *Cynical Theories: How Activist Scholarship Made Everything about Race, Gender, and Identity—and Why This Harms Everybody* (Durham, NC: Pitchstone, 2020), 139.

[80] Pluckrose and Lindsay, 139.

[81] Pluckrose and Lindsay, 78.

[82] Pluckrose and Lindsay, 150–51.

[83] Pluckrose and Lindsay, 194.

[84] Pluckrose and Lindsay, 195.

[85] Pluckrose and Lindsay, 196.

Privileged Groups by Diane Goodman. Goodman asserts that social justice "involves addressing issues of equity, power relations, and institutionalized oppression. It seeks to establish a more equitable distribution of power and resources . . . changing unjust institutional structures, policies, and practices, and challenging the dominant ideology."[86] Note the additional emphasis on institutional, structural, and ideological oppression. According to Goodman, these "systems of oppression are characterized by dominant-subordinate relations" which "allow one group to benefit at the expense of another."[87] Goodman even provides an "oppression chart" that lays out different areas of oppression (racism, sexism, heterosexism, transgender oppression, classism, ableism, ageism, religious oppression, and xenophobia) along with an identification of the corresponding oppressors and oppressed.[88] Social justice defined this way not only addresses more explicit evidence of oppression but also "grievances that span the generations, overlapping networks of oppression" and "the intangible privileges enjoyed by the majority."[89] As should be clear by now, social justice understood this way moves well beyond the more traditional Christian and Western conceptions of justice examined earlier. Rather than a vision of justice appropriate to human limitations under the Noahic fallen creation covenant, social justice aims for "a comprehensive rearrangement of society."[90] Noah Rothman, in fact, argues that social justice is "less a theory of justice than a new way of thinking about how society should be ordered," a way of thinking that "requires a social reversal."[91] Sowell labels this as a "quest for

---

[86] Diane J. Goodman, *Promoting Diversity and Social Justice: Educating People from Privileged Groups*, 2nd ed. (New York: Routledge, 2011), 4.

[87] Goodman, 5.

[88] Goodman, 7.

[89] Noah Rothman, *Unjust: Social Justice and the Unmaking of America* (Washington, DC: Regnery Gateway, 2019), 167.

[90] Scruton, *Fools, Frauds, and Firebrands*, 4.

[91] Rothman, *Unjust*, 4, 101.

cosmic justice" because it pursues a vision of equality that is ultimately beyond human power and wisdom.[92]

Implications

Limitations mark human experience. As creatures, Adam and Eve were tempted to disregard those limitations when the serpent declared, "You will be like God" (Gen 3:5). As fallen creatures, humanity knows the limits of time, resources, and human moral goodness, even as Christians long for the promised full removal of sin's corruption and for complete freedom in Christ. This age of the Noahic fallen creation covenant is an age of limitations, an age which does not finally satisfy but which only increases the believer's anticipation for the age to come. Human (and Christian) efforts to "do justice" share these limitations. Recognizing the constraints of human justice under the Noahic covenant should also help Christians discern the difference between biblical and nonbiblical ideas of justice. Christians must reject the idea of "social justice" if it includes any of the following seven elements: one, the denial or marginalization of the moral significance of human merit, effort, and natural endowment; two, the demand that governments forcibly equalize all outcomes; three, the false division of humanity into oppressors and oppressed based on group identity; four, the stress on sin resulting unconsciously from group membership rather than on sin resulting consciously from individual choice; five, the suggestion that only some groups are enmeshed in systems of sin rather than all humans unavoidably enmeshed as a result of the fall; six, the claim that only members of certain groups have access to truth ("standpoint epistemology") rather than all humans having the same fundamental access through God's special revelation in Scripture or general revelation in nature; or, seven, the assertion that humans can comprehensively reorder society in order to achieve some form of utopian, cosmic

---

[92] Sowell, *The Quest for Cosmic Justice*, 13.

justice. Such attempts to remedy injustice usually only create more injustice. But even while rejecting such mistaken notions of justice, Christians should be exemplars of the human responsibility to do good, fostering human flourishing and justice in the courts, in politics, in the marketplace, and in all spheres of society. For Christians, such just living must be rooted in virtuous character and must surpass mere observance of the rule of law and procedural fairness to mercy for the oppressed, help for the needy, and restoration of relationships. The local church, through the work of discipleship, should cultivate members as abundant doers of good and justice in society, and yet the institutional church itself must give operational priority to its unique vocation of proclaiming the verbal message of the gospel to a broken world, the greatest good that can be offered. This priority also recognizes the limitations of our good deeds and of our justice in this age. The combined efforts of all humanity are still impotent to transform the world into a place of perfect justice, while the gospel message of Christ's new covenant work is the only gateway to a "new heavens and a new earth in which righteousness dwells" (2 Peter 3:13). Cosmic justice will be achieved, but only Christ himself can achieve it.

Questions for Further Reflection

1. To what ideas of "justice" have you been previously exposed? How do those ideas compare to this chapter?
2. How is your understanding of the covenants of Scripture similar to or different from the views proposed in this chapter?
3. After reading this chapter, what role do you believe the pursuit of justice should play in the mission of the church?
4. After reading this chapter, how should our understanding of the covenants and of justice impact how we think about and participate in the political realm?
5. As described in this chapter, where have you personally encountered the promotion of the ideas of "social justice"?

Suggested Reading

Christian Authors

Baucham Jr., Voddie T. *Fault Lines: The Social Justice Movement and Evangelicalism's Looming Catastrophe*. Washington, DC: Salem, 2021.

Novak, Michael and Paul Adams. *Social Justice Isn't What You Think It Is*. New York: Encounter, 2015.

Shenvi, Neil and Pat Sawyer. *Critical Dilemma: The Rise of Critical Theories and Social Justice Ideology—Implications for the Church and Society*. Eugene, OR: Harvest House, 2023.

Teevan, John Addison. *Integrated Justice and Equality: Biblical Wisdom for Those Who Do Good Works*. Grand Rapids: Christian's Library, 2014.

Wind, John Anthony. *Do Good to All People as You Have the Opportunity*. Phillipsburg, NJ: P&R, 2019.

Non-Christian Authors

Bronner, Stephen Eric. *Critical Theory: A Very Short Introduction*, 2nd ed. Oxford: Oxford University Press, 2017.

Lindsay, James. *Race Marxism: The Truth about Critical Race Theory and Praxis*. Orlando: New Discourses, 2022.

Murray, Douglas. *The Madness of Crowds: Gender, Race, and Identity*. London: Bloomsbury Continuum, 2019.

Pluckrose, Helen and James Lindsay. *Cynical Theories: How Activist Scholarship Made Everything about Race, Gender, and Identity—and Why This Harms Everybody*. Durham, NC: Pitchstone, 2020.

Sowell, Thomas. *Discriminations and Disparities*. Rev. ed. New York: Basic Books, 2019.

10

The Pastoral Team and Mercy Ministries as Tangible Expressions of Justice

— D. A. Horton —

Introduction

The local church has the privileged duty of verbally and visibly manifesting glimpses of God's kingdom within its community.[1] When local churches prioritize this task, they function as instruments guided by the Holy Spirit,

[1] The terms *verbally* and *visually* derive from the discourse on global missions, which originated from the Edinburgh gathering in Scotland in 1910. This conversation eventually led to the development of two distinct approaches, ecumenical and evangelical, in the 1960s. This chapter is framed within the context of the evangelical approach, complemented by the nuanced method known as Misión Integral. For a comprehensive understanding of the historical discourse on missions, readers are encouraged to read Kenneth Nehrbass, *Advanced Missiology: How to Study Missions in Credible and Useful Ways* (Eugene, OR: Cascade, 2021), esp. 82–84. Additionally, see Charles Van Engen, "'Mission' Defined and Described," in *Missionshift: Global Mission Issues in the Third Millennium*, ed. David J. Hesselgrave and Ed Stetzer (Nashville: B&H Academic, 2010), 7–29. Regarding the method of Misión Integral, see C. René Padilla, *Discipulado y Misión: Compromiso con el reino de Dios* (Buenos

who orchestrates a continuous symphony of praise to the one true and living God worldwide. How each local church utilizes this privilege to proclaim and demonstrate the gospel is a decision they must make based on the unique circumstances of their context. The establishment of biblical guidelines, pastoral supervision, regular prayer practices, and the activation of each member's unique gifts is necessary.

Evangelicalism encompasses a range of perspectives, interpretations, and reactions towards justice. The perspective of this chapter views justice as a fundamental attribute of God that humans can imperfectly embody in our decision-making processes regarding interpersonal, legal, and social matters. This includes the allocation of resources and the protection of human rights, guided by principles of fairness and moral integrity.[2]

Aires: Ediciones Kairós, 1997). Cf. C. René Padilla and Juan José Toscano, *What is Integral Mission?* trans. Claudia Lorena Juárez (Oxford: Regnum, 2021).

[2] Harris Rall bases his definition of justice, as depicted in the Scripture, on his interpretation of the Hebrew and Greek terms employed. The author asserts that the original Hebrew and Greek words are synonymous with the terms "righteousness." This translation is commonly used, and in approximately half of the instances where the terms "just" and "justice" appear in the Authorized Version (AV), the American Revised Version (ARV) has replaced them with "righteous" and "righteousness." It is important to consistently remember that these two concepts are fundamentally identical. Harris Franklin Rall, "Justice," in *International Standard Bible Encyclopedia*, ed. James Orr, John L. Nuelsen, and Edgar Y. Mullins (Chicago: Howard-Severance, 1915), 3:1781–82. Rall also identifies the two scriptural expressions of justice as human justice and the justice of God. He frames human justice as the conduct between humans regarding their rights, and the justice of God as an essential characteristic of his perfect nature. He supports his definition of human justice as a theme in the Scripture in the following categories. He concludes that it is a New Testament understanding of righteousness that reflects God's character. He then provides Scripture support for the justice of God. He says it is applied to business regarding honest measures and weights (Lev 19:35, 36; Deut 25:13–16; Amos 8:5; Prov 11:1; 16:11; Ezek 45:10). He says justice is demanded in the courts regarding the rights of the rich, poor, Israelite, sojourner—all should be equally regarded (Deut 16:18–20; Exod 23:1–3, 6–9). Justice is also the establishment of the rights of others, and justice administered this way is seen as mercy as it relieves the oppressed, protects the fatherless, and gives representation to the widow (Isa 1:17; cf 11:4; Jer 22:15, 16; Ps 82:2–4). He says the same idea appears in Deut 24:12, 13; Ps 37:21, 26; 112:4–6, where

To focus this discussion on practical application within the local church in the context of North America's globalization and under the guidance of respected pastors, the term "mercy ministries" will encompass justice-related issues previously discussed to inspire readers to act rather than just talk.[3]

---

the term used is "righteous" instead of "just." The New Testament associates justice with righteousness, as justice or righteousness is typically described as a reflection of a person's character, with God's character serving as the standard (1 John 3:7; Matt 5:48). God's justice is his kingly power engaged on behalf of humanity. God is a just savior (Pss 51:14; 71:15; 103:17; Isa 45:21; 46:31; 51:5), who performs acts of deliverance (Judg 5:11). In the New Testament, God's justice is proclaimed to be administered through Jesus's judging humanity rightly (Matt 16:27; cf 25:14–46; Luke 12:45–48; Rom 2:2–16; 6:23; 2 Cor 5:10; Col 3:24, 25; 2 Thess 1:8, 9; Heb 2:2, 3; 10:26–31). Michelle Tooley defines justice as a philosophical concept that leads to fairness, proper treatment, and a fair allocation of resources. She then frames the scriptural theme of justice as "more than a mathematical distribution of goods. The Bible speaks of justice as a chief attribute of God, with biblical justice inextricably tied to God's mercy and grounded in the relationship between God and humankind." Michelle Tooley, "Just, Justice," in *Eerdmans Dictionary of the Bible*, ed. David Noel Freedman (Grand Rapids: Eerdmans, 2000), 757. She also interprets righteousness and justice as legal terms that encompass ethical and moral principles, ensuring equal treatment for all individuals under the law. She further explains, "Both *ṣĕḏāqâ* and *mišpāṭ*, Hebrew words for 'righteousness' and 'justice,' can be understood in legalistic terms. Heb[rew] *ṣĕḏāqâ* can refer to ethical and moral standards or equality of all people before the law. Likewise, *mišpāṭ* can refer to law, the process of deciding a case in civil or religious government, execution of a judgment, or rights of an individual under civil or religious law." Hebrew *ṣĕḏāqâ* and *mišpāṭ*, as also Greek *dikē* and *dikaiosýnē*, often are translated as "judgment" and "righteousness," words that are not commonly associated with justice in modern times. However, when considering situations of oppression or injustice, it becomes evident that they are crucial to the concept of justice in both the Old Testament and the New Testament. Tooley also connects justice to God's character (Deut 32:4; Isa 5:16). It is measured within a community by their treatment of the poor and oppressed (Isa 1:16–17; 3:15), which provides reasoning for the prophets' calling God's covenant community to repent of their injustice (Mic 6:8).

[3] See "Canada in 2041: A Larger, More Diverse Population with Greater Differences between Regions," *The Daily*, September 8, 2022, https://www150.statcan.gc.ca/n1/daily-quotidien/220908/dq220908a-eng.htm; Vimal Sivakumar, "Looking Ahead to Canada's Demographics in 2041," *CIC News*, September 9, 2022, https://www.cicnews.com/2022/09/looking-ahead-to-canadas-demographics-in-2041-0930535.html#gs.a3417w; William H. Frey, "The Nation is Diversifying Even Faster than Predicted,

The rationale for adopting this methodology will become clearer as we accurately define fundamental principles such as mercy and ministry, conduct a thorough examination of biblical texts that relate to the responsibilities of a Pastoral Leadership Team (PLT), identify theological frameworks, and consider the practical implications that arise from these. The analysis and reflection in this chapter will explore the multicultural demographics of North America in relation to Alan Hirsch's *5Q: Reactivating the Original Intelligence and Capacity of the Body of Christ*, incorporating both scholarly and practical aspects. The ongoing administration of pastoral service beyond mercy ministry to the local body should be managed by a team of qualified leaders.[4]

Biblical Texts and Exegesis

Mercy in Scripture

The Bible presents mercy as a fundamental characteristic of God, which he expects individuals in a covenant relationship with him to imitate consistently, albeit imperfectly. John Frederick provides a summary of the Hebrew roots, namely *rḥm*, *ḥnn*, *ḥml*, *ḥsd*, and *nḥm*, which collectively convey the

---

According to New Census Data," *The Brookings Institute*, July 1, 2020, https://www.brookings.edu/articles/new-census-data-shows-the-nation-is-diversifying-even-faster-than-predicted; Katharina Buchholz, "Demographic Change Accelerates in the U.S. [Infographic]," *Forbes*, May 30, 2023, https://www.forbes.com/sites/katharinabuchholz/2023/05/30/demographic-change-accelerates-in-the-us-infographic/. In this chapter, we discuss mercy ministry as a distinct category of specialized ministry, separate from other types offered during corporate midweek and weekend services. These other types include children and youth ministries, greeters/ushers, small groups, men and women ministries, and worship ministries. This chapter discusses mercy ministry, which addresses urgent interpersonal, legal, and social needs that may or may not require ongoing support.

[4] Pastoral service includes the administration of church ordinances, counseling, leadership, preaching, teaching, and visitations. This chapter envisions the distribution of these aspects to a pastoral team, rather than relying solely on one individual.

concept of mercy through themes of compassion, grace, love, and pity.[5] Complementing this, Edward Meyers asserts,

> Mercy (Heb. *rāḥam, ḥānan*) is an essential quality of God (Exod. 34:6; Deut. 4:31; Ps. 103:8). This is the quality (*ḥesed*, "covenant love"), demonstrated throughout their history (cf. Deut. 30:1–6; Isa. 14:1; Ezek. 39:25–29), by which God faithfully keeps his promises and maintains his covenant relationship with his chosen people despite their unfaithfulness (Gk. *éleos;* Rom. 9:15–16, 23; Eph. 2:4). Israel was often reminded of the relationship between God's *ḥesed* and their covenant with God (Deut. 7:9; 1 Kgs. 8:23; Neh. 1:5; Isa. 55:3; Dan. 9:4).[6]

J. W. L. Hoad suggests that the Hebrew terms *ḥesed* and *hen* in the New Testament can be equated with the Greek *charis* which is commonly translated as "grace." In the New Testament, the concept of mercy is interpreted by Hoad as extending "compassion to one in need or helpless distress, or in debt and without claim to favourable treatment."[7] E. E. Carpenter and P. W. Comfort also connect the Greek *eleos* to *charis,* closely related to the Hebrew *ḥesed*, as a foundational understanding of mercy it is "the single most prominent attribute revealed" about God in Scripture.[8]

Consider mercy as a flowing stream or pure water. The continuous and abundant source of this phenomenon can be attributed to God. He

---

[5] John Frederick, "Mercy and Compassion," in *Lexham Theological Wordbook*, ed. Douglas Mangum, Derek R. Brown, Rachel Klippenstein, and Rebekah Hurst, Lexham Bible Reference Series (Bellingham, WA: Lexham, 2014).

[6] See Edward P. Myers, "Mercy," in *Eerdmans Dictionary of the Bible* (Grand Rapids: Eerdmans, 2000), 885.

[7] J. W. L. Hoad, "Mercy, Merciful," in *New Bible Dictionary*, 3rd ed., ed. I. Howard Marshall, A. R. Millard, J. I. Packer, and Donald J. Wiseman (Downers Grove, IL: IVP, 1996), 751.

[8] Eugene E. Carpenter and Philip W. Comfort, *Holman Treasury of Key Bible Words: 200 Greek and 200 Hebrew words Defined and Explained* (Nashville: B&H, 2000), 125.

satisfies the deep longing in the hearts of those who sincerely seek him, fulfilling their eternal needs (Eccl 3:11). God has entrusted his people with the responsibility of serving others, both within and outside the covenant community. This has been true in both the Mosaic covenantal era with Israel and in the age of the new covenant with Jesus's global church.

This service involves offering acts of mercy and providing spiritual guidance, ultimately leading individuals to God, the divine source. The tangible expressions of God's merciful divine plan are easily comprehensible. It involves God showing mercy to those who actively seek him, filling their hearts like cups. These individuals are then responsible for sharing the mercy they have received with others, using both verbal and visual methods. Furthermore, this act of sharing serves the purpose of guiding others toward a deeper connection with God.

Ministry in Scripture

Scripture portrays ministry as an act of obedience to God, where individuals engage in providing beneficial service to both creation and humanity. The two ministries related to humanity will be classified as both *wholly* and *holy*. The ministry encompasses the universal commands that God has bestowed upon all of humanity. In Gen 1:28, God blessed both men and women, giving them the responsibility to exercise global authority, nurture relationships, and establish societal structures. Additionally, they were given the responsibility of nurturing and preserving the natural world (Gen 1:28–30). According to Bruce Waltke, using language to bless God carries "a sense of loyalty to future generations."[9]

In the context of Genesis 1, this perpetual blessing grants humans dominion over all creatures in the sea, on land, and in the sky (see Gen 1:26).

---

[9] Bruce K. Waltke, "The Kingdom of God in the Old Testament: Definitions and Story," in *The Kingdom of God*, ed. Christopher W. Morgan and Robert A. Peterson (Wheaton, IL: Crossway, 2012), 70.

Only humanity has been given this divine blessing and entrusted with the corresponding responsibility. Therefore, it is crucial that this form of ministry remains relevant and indispensable in the present day.

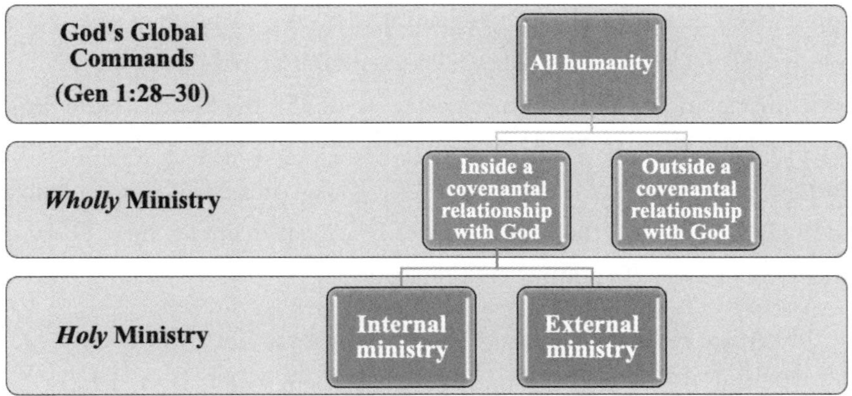

Figure 1: *Wholly* and *Holy* ministry

It is imperative to acknowledge a crucial caveat that establishes a clear differentiation between a ministry that is entirely dedicated to a specific purpose and a ministry that is considered sacred or divine in nature. In Genesis 3, Adam's disobedience toward God has distorted the paradigm of *wholly* ministry. This distortion has been transmitted equally to all human beings as a consequence of Adam's actions (cf. Rom 5:12–14). In the realms of society where *wholly* ministry has the potential to manifest, sin exists, intricately intertwined within the essence of humanity (cf. Ps 51:5), misdirecting the behaviors, intentions, and systems on both personal and organizational scales, influenced by malevolent and wicked forces (Eph 2:1–3).

Paul elucidates in Rom 1:18–25 the reasons behind the limited acceptance of a comprehensive ministry, attributing it to the human tendency to worship created items and demonstrate their allegiance through acts of disobedience toward the only true and living God. Only individuals who are in a covenant relationship with God can engage in *holy* ministry through both verbal and visual methods.

Peter Toon identifies the roles of *holy* ministry unto God in the Old Testament as confined to Israel's prophets, priests, kings, and collective people.[10] After God's election of Abraham (Genesis 12) and the establishment of national Israel through the exodus from Egypt (Exodus 1–18), God entered a covenant with Israel, designating them as a kingdom of priests and a holy nation (Exod 19:6). The different roles of sacred service in the history of Israel included the high priest (Exod 28:35), the Levites (Num 3:6), the prophets (Deut 18:15–22; 1 Sam 3:20; 7:15), the king (1 Sam 8:5–20), and the entire nation of Israel (Lev 19:2). Goheen presents a comprehensive command from God that outlines how Israel can maintain their holiness and ability to serve in a ministerial capacity:

> They are to be holy because they belong to a God who is holy: "Be holy because I, the Lord your God, am Holy" (Lev. 19:2). This exhortation is followed by comprehensive demands on Israel's life that will mark it as a distinctive people. Every area of life is to be holy to the Lord: respect in family relationships (v. 2); freedom from idolatry (v. 3); concern for the poor (vv. 9–10), the vulnerable (v. 14), the elderly (v. 32), and the foreigner (v. 33); fairness in economic dealings (v. 13); interpersonal integrity (v. 11); justice in courts (v. 15) and in speech (v. 16); concern for the safety and well-being of neighbors (v. 16), even love of neighbor (v. 18); sexual faithfulness (vv. 20–22); care of the nonhuman creation (vv. 23–25); distance from pagan religion (vv. 26–28); commercial honesty (vv. 35–36); and more. Thus, Israel would live as a holy nation in the midst of nations as one whose life has been transformed.[11]

---

[10] Peter Toon, "Ministry, Minister," in *Evangelical Dictionary of Biblical Theology*, ed. Walter A. Elwell, Baker Reference Library (Grand Rapids: Baker, 1996), 530.

[11] Michael W. Goheen, *A Light to the Nations: The Missional Church and the Biblical Story* (Grand Rapids: Baker Academic, 2011), 39.

The biblical account in Jer 2:21 highlights Israel's continuous disobedience, leading God to express disappointment by saying, "Yet I planted you a choice vine, wholly of pure seed. How then have you turned degenerate and become a wild vine?" Adam and Israel have consequently established a somber context for Jesus's righteous ministry as God incarnate. Christ's ministry during his initial coming was marked by service. He lived a life that fully aligned with God's law and ultimately sacrificed himself on behalf of humanity, who had failed to fulfill it (Matt 20:28; Mark 10:45). The life and work of Jesus established a harmonious equilibrium between verbal and visible ministry, setting a precedent for his disciples to follow (Luke 4:18–19).

The resurrection of Jesus serves as a confirmation that the payment for sin has been accepted by God. Individuals from diverse backgrounds who learn about Jesus can be considered righteous and forgiven by God (Rom 4:24–25). Those who repent and put their faith in Jesus become part of the universal body of believers, known as the church (1 Cor 12:13; 2 Cor 5:17–21). As a result, they are granted the opportunity to engage in *holy* ministry.

In the New Testament, the Greek term *diakonos* is associated with the *holy* ministry and can be translated as "minister" or "servant". According to Thomas Lindsay, the sacred vocation of ministry within the ecclesiastical context includes discipleship (John 12:26). Additionally, it involves the utilization of spiritual gifts (Rom 12:7; 1 Cor 12:5). Furthermore, ministers are called to attend to the material needs of others (Acts 6:2; 11:29; 12:25). Teaching Scripture is also a crucial component of the ministry, initially carried out by primarily the apostles (Acts 1:17; 20:24; Rom 11:13; Eph 4:11–12). Lastly, financial benevolence likewise finds appropriate emphasis (Rom 15:25; 2 Cor 8:4, 19).[12]

Alan Cairns complements Lindsay, offering a distinction of the sacred vocation, highlighting the significance of leadership positions bestowed by Christ upon his church. He adds,

---

[12] T. M. Lindsay, "Ministry," in *International Standard Bible Encyclopedia*, 3:2057.

> Yet there is a more restricted sense in which *minister* is used. In 1 Tim. 4:6 a good minister is evidently one, like Timothy, set apart to a particular work and place of leadership in the church. To perform this ministry, the apostles ordained elders in every church (Acts 14:23). Paul spoke to Timothy (1 Tim. 5:17) of elders who rule and elders who labour in the Word and doctrine. In Acts 20:28 he told the Ephesian elders that they were God-appointed bishops. Peter (1 Pet. 5:1–3) speaks to the elders as those who have the bishopric (oversight) over the flock of God and who have the task of feeding the flock.[13]

The establishment of an additional diaconate office in Jerusalem was a collaborative effort between the congregation and the apostles, even though the entire global church is called to actively serve in *holy* ministry. Brian Tabb asserts, "Congregational selection and the apostles' laying on of hands suggest the establishment of a formal ministry role in the Jerusalem church (Acts 6:5–6)."[14] The diaconate was established to meet the needs within the local church through acts of benevolence and physical care (Acts 6:1–7).

The qualifications for this office are presented by Paul in 1 Tim 3:8–13, wherein v. 11 specifically emphasizes the inclusion of women in this role.[15] The list of qualifications closely aligns with the criteria set for elders.[16] A. F. Walls says,

---

[13] Alan Cairns, *Dictionary of Theological Terms* (Greenville, SC: Ambassador Emerald International, 1998), 281.

[14] Brian J. Tabb, "Deacon," in *The Lexham Bible Dictionary*, ed. John D. Barry, David Bomar, Derek R. Brown, Rachel Klippenstein, et al. (Bellingham, WA: Lexham, 2016).

[15] Some translations render γυναῖκας as "wives" (CSB), "their wives" (KJV, ESV), and "women" (NASB). G.W. Knight discusses interpretations of Paul's audience and the inclusion of women in *The Pastoral Epistles: A Commentary on the Greek Text* (Grand Rapids: Eerdmans, 1992), 170–73. Some churches permit women to serve as deaconesses, while others interpret this passage as referring to a wife supporting her deacon husband in local church needs.

[16] Since churches differ when using terms such as elder and pastor, the term *pastor* in this chapter should be understood as addressing the same office Paul shared

> "These would be particularly appropriate for those with responsibilities in finance and administration, and the prominence of social service in the early church would make *diakonos* an especially suitable word for such people—the more so since the love feast, involving literal table-service, was a regular agency of charity."[17]

In the divine plan for *holy* ministry within the global church, the apostles played a crucial role as prominent leaders who finalized the establishment of the foundation. They built upon the ministry of Jesus, who is regarded as the cornerstone (Eph 2:20). Jesus provided a flawless definition of mercy ministry. The global church should have a comprehensive understanding of mercy ministry, encompassing both verbal and visual acts of compassion that address the needs of individuals within and beyond its own community. Pastors are the individuals whom Jesus entrusted with the responsibility of nurturing and equipping the members of the local church to engage in acts of mercy ministry. The biblical exegesis in this chapter serves as the scriptural scaffolding for this argument.

A Pastoral Path for Mercy Ministry

An understanding of Eph 4:1–10 establishes the contextual framework. Paul, identifying himself as an apostle, presents a compelling exhortation to the readers, urging them to live in accordance with a sound theological comprehension of their salvation, their unity with fellow believers in the body of Christ, and the mystery of the gospel. Paul's initial six verses exhort the saints to embody the unity that Christ has placed them in, considering their

---

qualifications for in 1 Tim 3:1–7; Titus 1:6–16 (cf. 1 Pet 5:1–11). The term *leader* used in this chapter speaks to auxiliary staff roles with leadership responsibilities in local churches. Examples of such an auxiliary are associate pastor, youth pastor, worship director, etc. *Lay leaders* are members of the congregation who have been given voluntary leadership roles.

[17] A. F. Walls, "Deacon," in *New Bible Dictionary*, 262.

diverse backgrounds in terms of social class, culture, ethnicity, and gender. In Eph 4:7–10, the apostle elucidates the magnanimity of Jesus in sharing gifts upon every individual local church. These gifts establish a structure of collaboration within both the leadership and membership of the local church.

Alan Hirsch identifies Eph 4:1–6 as Paul establishing the fundamental principles for achieving unity within the church. This is demonstrated by the removal of barriers such as race, identity, gender, and slavery, which were previously used to separate God's people.[18] Thomas L. Constable agrees and adds in this section, "Seven elements of unity follow that unite believers in the church. Believers should remember them when tempted to break unity. Again, all three members of the Trinity are in view and play a part in this process."[19] John Peter Lange says that the love and unity of the body of Christ described in vv. 1–3 is an expression of the outflow from the triune Godhead.[20] Despite their diverse differences, a local church that operates in love and walks in unity serves as a finite yet tangible example to other local churches and the rest of humanity of the God who redeemed them.

Building on this, Peter O'Brien says vv. 7–10 highlight a focus on "the issue of diversity in relation to Christ's distribution of grace."[21] Paul speaks of each believer in the "one body" as a recipient of Christ's gift of grace (v. 7), and earlier in Eph 2:8–10, salvation was said to be a gracious gift of God. Hence, in 4:7 the gift of grace that Christ gives is salvation. In v. 8, Paul loosely quotes Ps 68:18 to demonstrate the fulfillment of Christ's actions and, secondly, to provide a vivid description of a conquering king

---

[18] Alan Hirsch, *5Q: Reactivating the Original Intelligence and Capacity of the Body of Christ* (Los Angeles: 100 Movements, 2017), 5–7.

[19] Thomas L. Constable, *Notes on Ephesians*, *StudyLight*, 2018, accessed May 12, 2018, https://www.studylight.org/commentaries/eng/dcc/ephesians-4.html).

[20] Johann Peter Lange, Karl Braune, M. B. Riddle, and Philip Schaff, *A Commentary on the Holy Scriptures: Ephesians* (Bellingham, WA: Logos Bible Software, 2008), 134–43.

[21] Peter O'Brien, *The Letter to the Ephesians*, PNTC (Grand Rapids: Eerdmans, 1999), 286–87.

distributing the spoils of victory. O'Brien says, "Paul cites the Psalm using the verb 'gave' in an explanatory way and places the emphasis on the persons given back ('gifts,' vv. 8, 11) and the ministries they are to fulfill (vv. 11–16)."[22]

Allen P. Ross adds that Paul followed the Jewish exegetical interpretation (the Targum) of his day. He explained that "the conqueror distributed the gifts to His loyal subjects" because "the apostle applied the idea to Christ's victory over the forces of evil and His granting spiritual gifts (cf. Eph 4:11) to those on His side."[23] G. V. Smith contends that Jesus gives those he saves to the local church as a gift. Since it is understood that both men and women are included in the body of Christ (cf. Gal 3:27–29), the gift of grace given by Christ is for every believer. Since the word "men" placed at the end of the Ps 68:18 quotation is a general reference to humanity rather than the male gender, it is safe to conclude that Jesus gives both men and women as gifts in membership to all local churches.[24]

This backdrop clarifies Paul's direction for leadership praxis in the local church in Eph 4:11: "And he gave the apostles, the prophets, the evangelists, the shepherds and teachers." Hirsch interprets the aorist indicative *edōken* ("he gave") as Paul highlighting the past action of Christ's giving, a "once-and-for-all-time event."[25] Alternatively, Constantine R. Campbell examines the aorist indicative from a perspective of remoteness, likening it to observing a parade from a helicopter as opposed to ground level.[26] In each of these distinct approaches to the aorist indicative, they allow for the past gift to

[22] O'Brien, *Ephesians*, 287.

[23] Allen P. Ross, "Psalms," in *The Bible Knowledge Commentary: Old Testament*, ed. John F. Walvoord and Roy B. Zuck (Wheaton, IL: Victor, 1985), 843.

[24] Paul uses the plural *anthrōpois* in the quote of Ps 68:18, which leans towards a more general reference to humanity than his use of *anthrōpos* in Eph 5:31 when he is specifically addressing the male gender.

[25] Hirsch, *5Q*, 6–7.

[26] Constantine R. Campbell, *Basics of Verbal Aspect in Biblical Greek* (Grand Rapids: Zondervan, 2008), 37–38.

have present use. The leadership gifts that Jesus imparts to his church will continue to be present within the church until his return.

An immediate question arises regarding the number of gifts Jesus has given. Hirsch advocates for five roles of Eph 4:11, represented by the acronym APEST, and supports his reasoning with the syntax of the governing verb *edōken*.[27] He explains that APEST roles "come as an inseparable unit" because they "all come together under the sway of the ruling verb, *edothe* (verses 7, 11)" as Christ gave, individually, all five gifts of APEST as a complete "unit or not at all."[28]

At first glance, the exegetical zero sum requiring APEST to remain a whole unit of five gifts contradicts Granville Sharp's First Rule.[29] James Parks defines Granville Sharp's First Rule as

> "a grammatical construction consisting of an article with a substantive, the conjunction *kai*, and an anarthrous substantive agreeing in case and number with the previous. Sharp surmised that the lack of an article in the second substantive indicated both substantives were concerning the same entity instead of separate entities."[30]

Daniel Wallace's analysis of the article-noun-*kai*-noun plural construction argues that because both nouns—*poimenas* and *didaskalous*—are plural, the Granville Sharp rule does not apply to the construction.[31] Instead, the grammatical syntax indicates pastors are a subgroup of teachers, such that "all pastors are to be teachers, though not all teachers are to be pastors."[32]

---

[27] The acronym APEST corresponds to apostles, prophets, evangelists, shepherds, and teachers.

[28] Hirsch, *5Q*, 6–7.

[29] Cairns, *Dictionary of Theological Terms*, 199.

[30] James Parks, *Greek Grammatical Constructions Documentation* (Bellingham, WA: Faithlife, 2015).

[31] Daniel B. Wallace, "The Semantic Range of the Article-Noun-kai-Noun Plural Construction in the New Testament," *Grace Theological Journal* 4, no. 1 (1983): 59–84.

[32] Wallace, "Semantic Range," 83.

Building on Wallace's conclusion, this chapter identifies pastors as a subgroup of teachers within the APEST framework. Recognizing all gifts while treating *poimenas* as a subgroup of *didaskalous* renders APES-T.

Paul's original audience had the privilege of engaging directly with him as an apostle. Prophets who fearlessly proclaimed God's word and predicted the revelations that God had given (cf. Acts 11:27–30) were also present during the writing of this letter. In Eph 2:20, Paul refers to apostles and prophets as part of the foundation of the church, with Jesus as the cornerstone. In Eph 3:4–5, Paul explains that the mystery of Christ was not revealed to previous generations, but rather to the holy apostles and prophets. This allows the reader to understand Paul's argument about the unity of the global body of Christ, which includes both Jews and Gentiles (cf. Eph 3:6). Constable asserts that the main duty of Jesus's apostles was to the church and its congregations as their teachings and role served as the foundation for the faith.[33]

Evangelists like Philip (cf. Acts 8:6–40; 21:8) were also present in the first century, as were shepherd-teachers who met the qualifications outlined by Paul (see 1 Tim 3:1–7; Titus 1:6–16; cf. 1 Pet 5:1–11). These diverse and gifted leaders in the body of Christ have been appointed to "equip the saints for the work of ministry, for building up the body of Christ" (Eph 4:12). O'Brien identifies those mentioned in v. 11 as individuals tasked with

> "helping and directing other members of the church so that all may carry out their several ministries for the good of the whole. An emphasis on 'word' ministries corresponds with Romans 12:6–8 and the ranking of 1 Corinthians 12:28, while the connection between the 'special' ministers and others enhances our understanding of the relationship between gifted members and gifted leaders."[34]

---

[33] Constable, *Notes on Ephesians.*

[34] O'Brien, *Ephesians,* 303.

Gifted leaders were commissioned to utilize their giftedness to equip church members for ministry work. T. David Gordon warns against assuming that only the leaders of the church are responsible for equipping others. Instead, he emphasizes that each member has a role to play in helping to equip others.[35] The church leadership is responsible for raising and developing leaders from the church's laity to assist in their mutual preparation. The analogy of a team suggests that the process described has the potential to create a deep bench for each church. This is because there are amazingly gifted members who are always ready to serve whenever they are called upon.

Verse 12 is connected to v. 11 through the word *pros*, which links the equipping of the church back to the reason why Jesus gave gifts.[36] The APES-T PLT is collectively responsible to "equip the saints for the work of ministry, for building up the body of Christ." Paul uses the term *katartismos* to describe this process. His idea involves assisting someone who is "fully qualified" for an assignment, mission, or task.[37] The leaders are responsible for helping everyone under their leadership to become qualified, prepared, resourced, and ready to engage in the work of the ministry in the local church.

Consider a sports team manager responsible for ensuring that each player is equipped with the correct uniform and playbook to suit up and compete. All Christians in the global church have been given the same uniform and playbook. The prophet Isaiah predicts the uniform will be provided by the Messiah.[38] In Isa 59:17, the depiction of the figure includes the imagery of wearing righteousness as a breastplate and salvation as a helmet, along with

---

[35] T. David Gordon, "'Equipping' Ministry in Ephesians 4?" *JETS* 37, no. 1 (1994): 69–78.

[36] Robert G. Bratcher and Eugene A. Nida, *A Handbook on Paul's Letter to the Ephesians*, UBS Handbook Series (New York: United Bible Societies, 1993), 102.

[37] Johannes P. Louw and Eugene Albert Nida, *Greek-English Lexicon of the New Testament: Based on Semantic Domains* (New York: United Bible Societies, 1996), 678.

[38] James Smith identifies the Redeemer who will come to Zion as Christ Jesus (Rom 11:26). *The Major Prophets* (Joplin, MO: College Press, 1992), 161.

garments symbolizing vengeance and zeal. The anthropomorphic language portrays God as a warrior adorned in righteousness and vengeance. The distinctiveness of the Messiah guarantees that the attributes with which he is adorned will not be bestowed upon anyone else. Nevertheless, this does not prevent him from providing those he saves with attire symbolizing salvation.

The ESV rendering of Isa 61:10–11 speaks of this messianic clothing:

> I will greatly rejoice in the Lord; my soul shall exult in my God, for he has clothed me with the garments of salvation; he has covered me with the robe of righteousness, as a bridegroom decks himself like a priest with a beautiful headdress, as a bride adorns herself with her jewels. For as the earth brings forth its sprouts, and as a garden causes what is sown in it to sprout up, so the Lord God will cause righteousness and praise to sprout up before all the nations.

In this text Isaiah says God is the one who "has clothed" him with the garments of salvation and "covered" him with the robe of righteousness. The verb meaning "to clothe" (*labesh*) occurs elsewhere in Isaiah with God as the subject. In Isa 22:21 God clothes Eliakim with Shebna's robe, and in Isa 50:3, God says of himself, "I clothe the heavens with blackness." Similarly, the garments in Isa 61:10 (*beged*) also occur in Isa 36:22 and 37:1 when describing the torn clothes of Eliakim, Shebna, Joah, and King Hezekiah. This term occurs elsewhere in the Old Testament to denote a variety of clothing items, including Esau's finest attire (Gen 27:15), everyday garments (Gen 37:29; Prov 6:27), priestly vestments (Exod 28:2–4; Lev 16:4, 23–24), regal attire (Gen 41:42; 2 Kgs 5:5), ceremonial dress (Eccl 9:8; Ezek 23:26), and—of particular import for our purposes—soiled garments that God would replace with dignified clothing (Zech 3:3–5). In Isaiah 61, God is the one who supplies garments of salvation to those he saves, and he clothes them with the garments.

In the New Testament, particularly in Rom 13:14, Paul provides guidance to his readers to "put on the Lord Jesus Christ," employing the verb *endysasthe*. In Gal 3:27, Paul utilizes the term *endysasthe* to convey to his audience, "For as many of you as were baptized into Christ have put on Christ." Regarding the former, Leon Morris says,

> "*Clothe yourselves* translates the verb rendered 'put on' in verse 12; it signifies not that which is merely external but habitual association and identification with Christ. 'Putting on Christ' is a strong and vivid metaphor. It means more than 'put on the character of the Lord Jesus Christ,' signifying rather 'Let Christ Jesus himself be the armor that you wear'" (NEB).[39]

Kenneth Boa and William Kruidenier add, "The church—those faithful, spiritual descendants of Abraham—are clothing themselves with the Lord Jesus Christ, and displaying the glory of God to the world."[40]

Related to Gal 3:27, F. F. Bruce says, "To be 'baptized into Christ' is to be incorporated into him by baptism, and hence to be 'in Christ.'"[41] Timothy George adds,

> "In the present context, however, the likening of baptism to a 'putting on' of Christ most nearly approximates the ancient practice of stripping off old clothes and putting on fresh ones as a part of the baptismal rite itself. Baptism by immersion, the normal pattern in apostolic times, required of necessity a changing of garments.[42]

When an individual accepts Christ as their savior, they are baptized into the body of Christ (1 Cor 12:13) and Christ bestows upon them the garments of salvation. The analogy of a uniform offers a tangible representation of the global church receiving new garments. Similar to professional sports

---

[39] Leon Morris, *The Epistle to the Romans*, PNTC (Grand Rapids: Eerdmans, 1988), 473.

[40] Kenneth Boa and William Kruidenier, *Romans*, Holman New Testament Commentary, vol. 6 (Nashville: B&H, 2000), 402.

[41] F. F. Bruce, *The Epistle to the Galatians: A Commentary on the Greek Text*, NIGTC (Grand Rapids: Eerdmans, 1982), 185.

[42] Timothy George, *Galatians*, NAC (Nashville: B&H, 1994), 280.

teams, the individuality of each team member is evident through the distinct name, number on their uniform, and the position they hold. This highlights the uniformity in Christ without dissolving the individuality of each follower of Christ.

The playbook should be regarded as Scripture. The PLT is expected to offer meticulous and faithful exegetical instruction aimed at facilitating a comprehensive comprehension of how to apply Scripture in everyday life (implementing the teachings). Engaging with Scripture on a daily basis enables individuals to effectively communicate their faith and actively participate in acts of mercy ministry within their local community. It would be beneficial for the PLT to provide training for each member of the local community on how to study Scripture. This training will enable them to subsequently instruct others on the application of Scripture (cf. Rom 12:6–7; Gal 6:6; Col 3:16; Titus 2:1–6).

A process that enables leaders to equip the members of their congregation is necessary. This process, which Paul calls "building up of the body of Christ," needs implementation. Paul uses the term *oikodomē*, which conveys a figurative understanding of spiritual strengthening likened to a building being constructed.[43] Paul normally utilizes *oikodomē* throughout his writings to depict building up other Christians by using spiritual gifts (1 Cor 14:12; 2 Cor 12:19; Rom 14:19) and edifying others (Rom 15:2; Eph 4:29).

Ephesians 4:13 continues Paul's sentence by establishing a timeline for the duration of the PLT responsibility to equip the saints: "until we all attain to the unity of the faith and of the knowledge of the Son of God, to mature manhood, to the measure of the stature of the fullness of Christ." This timeline extends until every member of the local church reaches full maturity in their walk with the Lord. If the Lord continues to add baptized members to the local church through evangelism, the need to equip will persist until

---

[43] Frederick W. Danker, W. F. Ardnt, and F. W. Gingrich, *A Greek-English Lexicon of the New Testament and Other Early Christian Literature*, (Chicago: University of Chicago Press, 2000), 696–97.

Jesus's glorious return. The picture that Jesus is trying to paint of his bride is admirably shared by Richard Strauss, who writes,

> God is not trying to produce successful Christian business people who can impress the world with their money and affluence. He is not trying to fashion successful church leaders who can influence people with their organizational and administrative skills. Nor is He trying to fashion great orators who can move people with persuasive words. He wants to reproduce in His followers the character of His son—His Love, His kindness, His compassion, His holiness, His humility, His unselfishness, His servant attitude, His willingness to suffer wrongly, His ability to forgive, and so much more that characterized His life on earth.[44]

Every local church that remains faithful to Christ's command can demonstrate to its community what a mature local church looks like when its members have successfully endured through trials (cf. Jas 1:2–5). Ephesians 4:14 speaks of mature saints whose level of maturity is clear, for they are no longer "children tossed to and fro by the waves and carried about by every wind of doctrine, by human cunning, by craftiness in deceitful schemes." The phrasing of "human cunning, by craftiness in deceitful schemes" speaks of a methodized system of deceit. Bengel connects this phrase to Satan, who is the "parent of error" (cf. Eph 6:11) and is known to operate through schemes against the body of Christ.[45]

Paul's writings emphasize the importance of church leaders safeguarding the congregation from internal threats, often referred to as "wolves." In Acts 20:28–30, Paul addresses the Ephesian elders and instructs them,

---

[44] Richard L. Strauss, "Like Christ: An Exposition of Ephesians 4:13," *BibSac* 143, no. 571 (1986): 264.

[45] David Brown, Andrew Robert Fausset, and Robert Jamieson, *Commentary Critical and Explanatory on the Whole Bible* (Oak Harbor, WA: Faithlife, 1997), 350.

> "Pay close attention to yourselves and to all the flock, in which the Holy Spirit has made you overseers, to care for the church of God, which he obtained with his own blood. I know that after my departure fierce wolves will come in among you, not sparing the flock; and from among your own selves will arise men speaking twisted things, to draw away the disciples after them."

The PLT provides sound doctrine to the congregation, refuting false teachers and their teachings, and guiding people from a basic understanding to a deeper level of knowledge. This ensures their spiritual growth and maturity. In essence, their role is to exemplify Eph 4:15–16, demonstrating how to live out these principles: "speaking the truth in love, we are to grow up in every way into him who is the head, into Christ, from whom the whole body, joined and held together by every joint with which it is equipped, when each part is working properly, makes the body grow so that it builds itself up in love." This requires the PLT to combine effective teaching with a commitment to living a holy life in all areas, while also fostering a sense of community among its members. The objective is to create a system of mutual accountability where individuals can motivate each other to not only listen to sound doctrine but also apply it in their lives (Jas 1:22–25).

Scripture also provides guidance on how to address and help brothers and sisters who have erred and become involved in sin, as well as the steps needed for their restoration (Matt 18:15–18; 2 Cor 7:9–11; Gal 6:1–2). Titus 3:10–11 offers guidance to pastors and teams on handling individuals who seek to disrupt the unity that Christ is striving to establish through division. Paul also educates the congregation on holding leaders accountable, ensuring they provide sound teaching and set an example of holy living. The process of addressing any infraction is discussed in 1 Tim 5:19–22. Within this system of accountability, obedience to Christ will occur, and Jesus, who is joined to the body, will grow as each member engages in ministry work.

In summary, Jesus provides his church with a variety of gifts (people) to promote its growth and maturity. Jesus has equipped leaders with diverse skills to work together as a team. Jesus provides the local church with four types of leaders (APES-T) who have diverse gifts and work together to equip each member to live fully on mission for Jesus. Following this approach systematically will strengthen the body while safeguarding it from the deceptions of Satan. The PLT speaks truthfully and lovingly, living transparently before the congregation. This inspires them to engage in mercy ministry and perform good deeds.

Theological Formation

The church in the twenty-first century is significantly different from the establishment of Christ's church two millennia ago. Therefore, it is important to evaluate the fourfold ministries in the modern era. Should all four continue operating in the same way as they did during the early stages of the church? In this section, we will evaluate each of the roles in APES-T and discuss their implications in the following section.

Apostle

Constable interprets Paul's use of *apostolos* in Eph 4:11 as a servant who has been sent out by their master, in contrast with the office of apostle, which was reserved for those who had seen the risen Christ and had received personal appointment from him (Acts 1:21–22; 1 Cor 15:8–9; Gal 1:1; 2:6–9).[46] J. Armitage Robinson suggests that "missionary is a modern equivalent term."[47] Foulkes interprets Paul as using the term *apostolos* to refer to the "spiritual gifts of certain individual leaders, rather than their offices."[48]

---

[46] Constable, *Notes on Ephesians*, 93–96.

[47] J. Armitage Robinson, *St. Paul's Epistle to the Ephesians* (London: Macmillan, 1903), 98.

[48] Francis Foulkes, *The Epistle of Paul to the Ephesians*, TNTC (Grand Rapids: Eerdmans, 1963), 117.

Gregg Allison suggests that the office of apostle was "given uniquely to the twelve apostles of Jesus Christ and a few others (e.g., Paul)," and that "this gift empowered these divinely appointed eyewitnesses of Jesus' resurrection to proclaim the gospel and be the foundation of the church, to perform signs and wonders, to exercise peculiar authority in the first churches, and (in the case of some) to write what we now call the New Testament."[49] Louis Berkhof stated that this classification only applies to those twelve men and Paul whom Jesus chose and who received their commission directly from God or Jesus himself. They were witnesses of Jesus's life, specifically his resurrection, and were conscious of the Holy Spirit's inspiration in their work, teaching, and in having the power to perform miracles which ratified their message.[50]

The office of the apostle ceased with the glorification of the last member. The church fathers understood apostolic succession not to mean the office of apostle remained but that the doctrine of the church and its function come directly from the content revealed to those twelve men and Paul whom Jesus selected.[51] It is not in harmony with the biblical qualifications of an apostle or the testimony of church fathers to claim that the office of apostle should be practiced today.

---

[49] Gregg R. Allison, *Sojourners and Strangers: The Doctrine of the Church*, Foundations of Evangelical Theology (Wheaton, IL: Crossway, 2012), 414.

[50] Louis Berkhof, *Systematic Theology* (Edinburgh: Banner of Truth, 1998), 585.

[51] Historical theologian Justo González cites Clement of Rome, Ignatius of Antioch, and Tertullian as affirming that leadership in the church came not from apostles but from bishops (pastors) and deacons. See *A History of Christian Thought: From the Beginnings to the Council of Chalcedon*, vol. 1 (Nashville: Abingdon, 1970). Apostolic succession, then, was understood as the teachings of the bishops of the church being in line with those of the apostles. Similarly, according to J. N. D. Kelly, Cyprian affirmed that "the bishops stand in the place of the apostles, not only in the sense that they are their lineal successors, but that like them they have been chosen and established in their offices by the Lord's special decree." Although Cyprian interpreted the office of a bishop as more of an overseer of a parish of churches, it is important to note that he also believed that the office of apostle had ceased. *Early Christian Doctrines*, 2nd ed. (New York: Harper and Row, 1960), 204.

This consensus suggests that individuals referred to as *apostolos* within the local church context could be viewed as having a similar role to that of a missionary or church planter. This proposed interpretation of *apostolos* enables the integration of apostolic ministry in APES-T within a modern local church context. Hirsch concurs with the notion that individuals characterized as apostolic typically exhibit a holistic viewpoint, place importance on the innovative elements of the church, take the lead in establishing new initiatives, and endeavor towards the continuous rejuvenation of the church/organization.[52] Hirsch defines the apostolic mark as "the people-movement that participates in the redemptive and transformative mission of God in the world."[53] The complete manifestation of the apostolic mark occurs when the church is consistent in its theology, engaged in all areas of life, culturally dynamic, adaptable in its organization, scalable, and part of a church planting movement. The apostolic mark aims to bring about social transformation, achieve widespread acceptance of the gospel, and unite the church in its purpose and mission.[54]

The pastor, who is in possession of the apostolic mark, should prioritize mobilizing people for various forms of mercy ministry. This can encompass activism, evangelism, spiritual practices, and volunteer work. It is crucial for the pastor to exemplify these qualities to the congregation and encourage the laity to engage in missional activities. By doing this, they can inspire laypeople to start their own mercy ministries and mobilize others. This can be accomplished through a leadership pipeline under their guidance.

Prophet

In 1 Cor 14:3, Paul identified prophets as individuals who edified, exhorted, and comforted the church. John E. Johnson states that most prophets in the

---

[52] Hirsch, *5Q*, 101–2.

[53] Hirsch, 134.

[54] Hirsch, 136.

early days of the church "spoke the truth that God has previously revealed (cf. Acts 13:1; 1 Cor 11:5; 14:26–33)."[55] Malcolm Yarnell explains that within the Reformation tradition, the gift of prophecy is defined as "forth-telling" or proclaiming the gospel, differentiating it from the role of the prophet, who engaged in both proclaiming and "foretelling." Normative modern prophecy can be heard from pulpits. It contains edification, exhortation, and consolation (1 Cor 14:3), and it never contradicts Scripture.[56]

The offices of apostle and prophet played a foundational role in establishing the church, making the gift of prophecy, specifically in terms of forthtelling, still relevant in present times. Hirsch views this gifting as those who vertically cultivate a culture that is centered on God and horizontally emphasize the importance of God's people obeying, repenting, speaking truth with authority, advocating for justice, striving for holiness, communicating a sense of urgency, and promoting learning through questioning.[57] In local churches, individuals who have been given a prophetic voice by Jesus would practice these qualities to complement the second gifting in the APES-T model.

Hirsch identifies the prophetic mark as "the holy people that stand for God in the world, calling all to faithfulness, to true worship, to receptive obedience to God and his word, and the prayerful participation in the prophethood of all believers."[58] The mature expression of the prophetic mark is seen when the church becomes an alternative society (a prefigurative community) with a strong and solid commitment to worship, prayer, spiritual warfare, holiness, justice, and incarnational witness. The prophetic leader's ability to mobilize prophetic voices among the laity will lead to the formation

---

[55] John E. Johnson, "The Old Testament Offices as Paradigm for Pastoral Identity," *Bibliotheca Sacra* 152, no. 606 (1995): 182–200.

[56] Malcolm B. Yarnell III, "The Person and the Work of God the Holy Spirit," in *A Theology for the Church* (Nashville: B&H Academic, 2014), 546.

[57] Hirsch, *5Q*, 103–6.

[58] Hirsch, 134.

of a revitalized community. This community will be characterized by a covenant relationship with God and a deep reverence for his presence.[59]

The pastor with the prophetic mark should be known as a truthteller of God's design for both the internal life of the body and society at large. An example of one such prophetic voice in the modern American landscape is Pastor Chris Brooks, who stated that evangelicals would benefit from enhancing their approach to mercy ministry (or justice) in various areas such as economic fairness, educational equality, immigration reform, the sanctity of life, women's rights, and religious liberty.[60]

Evangelist

The role of the evangelist is not listed as a foundational role in Eph 2:20 or 3:5. Therefore, the question arises: should it be interpreted as an office confined to the early stages of the church or as a spiritual gift? Berkhof identifies Philip, Mark, Timothy, and Titus as evangelists in the early church but acknowledges that "little is known about these evangelists."[61] Constable states that evangelists preached the gospel both locally and abroad and that their ministry was crucial in equipping individuals to lead others to faith in Christ.[62]

Allison argues that evangelists are "the Holy Spirit's endowment and empowerment of persons who communicate—and of personal acts of communicating—the gospel of Jesus Christ, and who equip others to do the same," while referencing this as a gift of evangelism, not a role or office.[63] The leader with the gift of evangelism must effectively address challenges, objections, and questions that arise during verbal and visual mercy ministry. Having experienced leaders and members who excel in evangelism

---

[59] Hirsch, 136.

[60] Christopher Brooks, *Urban Apologetics: Why the Gospel is Good News for the City* (Grand Rapids: Kregel, 2014), 18–20.

[61] Berkhof, *Systematic Theology*, 585.

[62] Constable, *Notes on Ephesians.*

[63] Allison, *Sojourners and Strangers*, 416.

will provide valuable on-the-field training. According to Hirsch, evangelists effectively communicate the church's story in a compelling, accessible, and understandable manner. They serve as social connectors and essentially act as recruiters.[64]

There is no need to establish the office of an evangelist based solely on an argument from silence, as there is no list of biblical qualifications for an evangelist, unlike for apostles, prophets, and shepherd-teachers. The primary role of the evangelist is to preach the gospel, and the evangelist's God-given communication ability is essential for effectively conveying the gospel to the listener. Paul instructed Timothy to carry out the duties of an evangelist (cf. 2 Tim 4:1–5) by faithfully preaching the Word of God. Hence, an evangelist is an individual who can effectively communicate God's Word to listeners and equip members to do the same.

Hirsch defines the evangelistic mark as "The Body of saved people that joyfully proclaim the good news and call all to experience freedom and salvation in and through Jesus."[65] The mature expression of this mark enables the church to truly embrace the good news, as it becomes a redemptive, contagious, culturally relevant, and consistently supportive movement of people. The mature, evangelistic church possesses these attributes: a redeemed community that is growing in their faith, a thriving society that is built on a restored relationship with God, and a grace economy that is built on sharing.[66]

The pastor with the evangelistic mark should focus his energy on helping members in the congregation learn ways to communicate the gospel using clear language and concepts. These can be used as illustrations that help nonbelievers understand biblical truth. The evangelistic pastor should lead others in the practice of evangelism, while also training them to effectively equip others to share the gospel.

---

[64] Hirsch, *5Q*, 106–8.

[65] Hirsch, 134.

[66] Hirsch, 136.

Shepherd-Teacher

Though Paul's use of *poimēn* is exclusive to Eph 4:11, it is connected to the shepherd who looks after and cares for a flock (*poimnion*). Paul intersects *poimnion* with the role of the overseers in Acts 20:28 which conveys the concept of a shepherd who acts as a protector.[67] John Eadie explains that Paul describes "overseers of local churches who both pastor and teach (cf. 1 Tim 3:2; Titus 1:9; 1 Pet 5:1–3)."[68] Bruce Ashford identifies pastors as those who specifically are called "to equip the saints for the work of ministry."[69] Likewise, Michael Green highlights the bishops as God's gift to the church, tasked with building up the saints, while the saints themselves regularly engaged in the ministry of evangelism.[70] Allison argues that Paul's use of shepherd-teacher is "not so much about a church office as it is about graciously gifted people given by Christ to the church for its edification (vv. 7–16)."[71]

Hirsch distinguishes between the two roles of shepherding and teaching. The shepherd cultivates a loving community, protects the body, supports healing, and encourages shalom and wholeness.[72] The teacher contributes wisdom and understanding to foster development of a worldview, facilitate theological discussions, and nurture a love for the Scriptures.[73] Exegetically, these descriptions align with Jesus's act of giving gifts allowing the shepherd-teacher to be seen as an individual providing pastoral care for the flock.[74]

---

[67] BDAG, s.v. "*poimnion*."

[68] John Eadie, *Commentary on the Epistle to the Ephesians*, 2nd ed. (Edinburgh: T&T Clark, 1977), 304.

[69] Bruce Riley Ashford, ed., *Theology and Practice of Mission: God, the Church, and the Nations* (Nashville: B&H, 2011), 311.

[70] Michael Green, *Evangelism in the Early Church* (Grand Rapids: Eerdmans, 2004), 239.

[71] Allison, *Sojourners and Strangers*, 291.

[72] Hirsch, *5Q*, 109.

[73] Hirsch, 110–11.

[74] Even though Hirsch separates the shepherd-teacher gift, a comprehensive summary of Hirsch's perspectives on both shepherd and teacher will emphasize his ideas on measuring these qualities, maturity, and societal impact.

According to Hirsch, the shepherding mark is defined as "the family of God's redeemed people that nurtures a faithful, reconciled community that witnesses to the Resurrection through its common life." The teaching mark refers to "the wise and intelligent people that passionately seek truth and share all the treasures of the wisdom, insight, and knowledge of God hidden in Christ Jesus, faithfully nurturing understanding and communicating truth in the world."[75]

The mature expressions of these marks are when the church is seen as a reconciled, healed, and forgiven human community. A well-practiced community of learners forms living relationships, with increasing self-awareness and the ability to offer wisdom for living well. The impact of a shepherding-teaching church on society can be seen through their living as a united and wise community that loves all people, regardless of their characteristics, because they share a common bond in Christ. They proclaim God's truth while expressing their love for him through their minds, souls, and strength.[76] The shepherd, as a skilled leader and teacher, should blend passion for God's word with consistent acts of love toward both believers and nonbelievers. Additionally, they should involve community members in providing care and educating others.

The PLT model, which maintains an accountable relationship with the congregation, is a biblically acceptable model of local church polity. Since Jesus gives gifts to his church to equip the saints for ministry, which leads to maturity and growth, it is biblically permissible to see support for apostolic (e.g., missionaries and church planters), prophetic (forthtellers), evangelistic (effective communicators of the gospel), and shepherding-teaching gifts demonstrated by church leaders. Therefore, it is reasonable to conclude that the APES-T fourfold ministry model is applicable in contemporary church leadership. Lastly, this chapter discusses the implications of equipping the laity to engage in mercy ministry with the APES-T PLT.

---

[75] Hirsch, 134–35.

[76] Hirsch, 136.

Implications

In their book *Designed to Lead*, Eric Geiger and Kevin Peck emphasize the importance of local church leaders creating a pipeline or system for lay members to receive the training they need for ministry. In discussing the importance of a system, they propose,

> Without a system, all you have is wishful thinking. If developing leaders is a conviction, then that conviction will drive you to construct. The presence of a construct to help your church develop leaders, not just sign up volunteers, reveals development is important. The absence of a system reveals the conviction has not overwhelmed you to action.[77]

North American church planters commissioned by a church, network, or denomination often undergo an assessment process. The process should provide candidates with insight into their calling, experience, strengths and weaknesses, theological convictions, philosophy of ministry, and leadership abilities.[78] If the candidate passes the assessment and receives approval from the network or denomination, it is advisable for them to identify their primary APES-T gift and then focus on assembling a team of leaders whose gifts fill the leadership gaps.

If the planter does not have a network to rely on, or for those who are pastoring existing churches or who have started the church revitalization process, it would be beneficial to connect with experienced local pastors who can provide guidance through a recommended assessment. The assessment

---

[77] Eric Geiger and Kevin Peck, *Designed to Lead: The Church and Leadership Development* (Nashville: B&H, 2016), 185.

[78] The list of attributes provided are a collection of assessment goals from the following church planting networks: Anglican Church of North America (https://www.always-forward.com/), Assemblies of God (https://churchmultiplication.net/), Converge (www.converge.org/church-planting/assessment), Presbyterian Church in America (https://pcamna.org/church-planting/), Send Network (https://www.namb.net/send-network/church-planting/), and The Summit Collaborative (https://summitcollaborative.org/plant/).

should analyze their lifestyle based on the standards outlined in 1 Tim 3:1–7; Titus 1:6–16; and 1 Pet 5:1–11. It should also consider their theological convictions,[79] natural leadership qualities,[80] and emotional, family, and mental health.[81] Finally, the assessment should identify their gifting using the APES-T framework, which can be evaluated through the 5Q Vocational Assessment.

Once the pastor has been assessed and is ready to build their team, Jeff Christopherson says four elements should be present to successfully lead the potential leaders who are demonstrating qualities of leadership: keep and maintain consistent team meetings, develop a culture of authenticity, allocate time in your schedules for one-on-ones with key leaders, and develop your team by discussing books you read, videos you watch, and interviews with other leaders you engage with.[82]

Although the APES-T PLT consists of individuals with diverse talents, each member should strive for unity with the other pastors in terms of identity, calling, and purpose. Each pastor should be a man who has experienced spiritual rebirth and not a recent convert (1 Tim 3:6). Ken Blanchard emphasizes the importance of a leader's identity being rooted in God:

> But if you need a lot of external recognition, stop and take a look at your own self-esteem. I've heard it said that the devil's definition of self-worth is that *who you are is a function of your performance plus the opinion of others*. If the devil can hook you on that, he's got you, because now your focus is on fearing people, not fearing

---

[79] It would be most prudent for the church to use the statement of faith in their bylaws, or one provided to them by their denomination.

[80] J. Oswald Sanders provides readers with twenty-six introspective and thought-provoking questions to assess if they and others affirm their leadership qualities in *Spiritual Leadership: Principles of Excellence for Every Believer* (Chicago: Moody, 2007).

[81] Peter Scazzero provides a thorough self-examination of one's emotional state and provides prescriptive guidance for a pathway towards health. See *The Emotionally Healthy Leader: How Transforming Your Inner Life Will Deeply Transform Your Church, Team, and the World* (Grand Rapids: Zondervan, 2015).

[82] Jeff Christopherson, *Kingdom First: Starting Churches That Shape Movements* (Nashville: B&H, 2015), 156–58.

> God. . . . Make sure your self-worth is grounded in the knowledge of God's unconditional love for you, and remember that God doesn't make junk.[83]

Each pastor must collaborate through corporate prayer and study of Scripture to remind one another of the blessings of knowing Christ, being covered by his righteousness, and how to remain fully equipped with the armor of God to resist the attacks of the enemy (cf. Eph 6:10–18).

The pastoral APES-T PLT must exemplify what it means for "each part working properly" (cf. Eph 4:16) before the rest of the congregation. They must strive for unity while embracing the diversity that exists within the congregation and, if possible, the broader community. This can be achieved when each leader operates in their area of strength and allows other leaders to guide them and the rest of the team in areas where they are weak. This is an act of humility as it requires each pastor to willingly give up power. Participative leadership, as supported by global scholarship,[84] promotes creativity, motivation, and active stakeholder contributions by sharing decision-making responsibilities across different levels of an organization.[85]

---

[83] Ken Blanchard, "Reflections on Encouraging the Heart," in *Christian Reflections on the Leadership Challenge*, ed. James M. Kouzes and Barry Z. Posner (San Francisco: Wiley, 2004), 108.

[84] Kurt Lewin's study on leadership identified three forms of leadership: authoritarian, participative, and delegative. He concluded that the participative (or democratic) style was the most effective and powerful. For further information, refer to the study conducted by Kurt Lewin, Ronald Lippitt, and Ralph K. White, "Patterns of Aggressive Behavior in Experimentally Created 'Social Climates,'" *The Journal of Social Psychology* 10 (1939): 271–99.

[85] See Kowo Solomon Akpoviroro, Bola Kadiri, Sabitu Olalkan Owotutu, "Effective Participative Leadership Style on Employee's Productivity," *International Journal of Economic Behavior* 8, no. 1 (2018): 47–60; Xu Huang, Joyce Iun, Aili Liu, and Yaping Gong, "Does Participative Leadership Enhance Work Performance by Inducing Empowerment or Trust? The Differential Effects on Managerial and Non-Managerial Subordinates," *Journal of Organizational Behavior* 30, no. 1 (2010): 122–43; Anit Somech, "Directive Versus Participative Leadership: Two

Kouzes and Posner value the necessary quality of sharing leadership. They state,

> "Leaders accept and act on the paradox of power; you become more powerful when you give away your power . . . [P]eople who are not confident about their power, regardless of their organizational position or place, tend to hoard whatever shreds of influence they have. Powerless managers tend to adopt petty and dictatorial styles."[86]

In contrast to the powerless, Christ is the perfect model, as he prioritized serving others rather than being served (Matt 20:28) and demonstrated his commitment to serving those he was raised to lead by dying on their behalf (Mark 10:45).

Each pastor on the PLT should be securely grounded in their identity in Christ and affirmed in their calling to have a deep relationship with him. In addition, each pastor should operate with a soft heart that acknowledges Jesus has sent each pastor and member as gifts to their local churches. In this scenario, the PLT will exemplify the Eph 4:1–16 model for the congregation. This will allow individuals to focus on the complexities of their specific talents and abilities and to prepare and empower others for ministry in their own areas of giftedness.

The following content proposes a framework, encapsulated by the acronym F.A.B.R.I.C., for effectively managing both internal and external mercy ministry initiatives.[87] The primary objective of this section is to envi-

---

Complementary Approaches to Managing School Effectiveness," *Educational Administration Quarterly* 41, no. 5 (2005): 777–800; Thembelani Elvis Jentile, "Pastoral Leadership in a Congregational Church Setting: The Case of the Baptist Convention of South Africa," *Verbum et Ecclesia* 42, no. 1 (2021): 1–10.

[86] James M. Kouzes and Barry Z. Posner, *The Leadership Challenge: How to Make Extraordinary Things Happen in Organizations*, 5th ed. (San Francisco: Wiley, 2012), 244.

[87] F.A.B.R.I.C. The text addresses six areas of ministry that the local church should prioritize both internally and externally. The domains encompass Family, Authority, Business, Religion, Institutions, and Culture. For a concise elucidation

sion shared pastoral oversight and the role of the lay leadership council in promoting mercy ministry as a strategy for evangelism and discipleship. Different churches have varying structures of polity, allowing for the contextualization of the existing local church leadership model to suit each congregation's specific needs. This applies to church plants, existing churches, and those undergoing a merger or revitalization process.

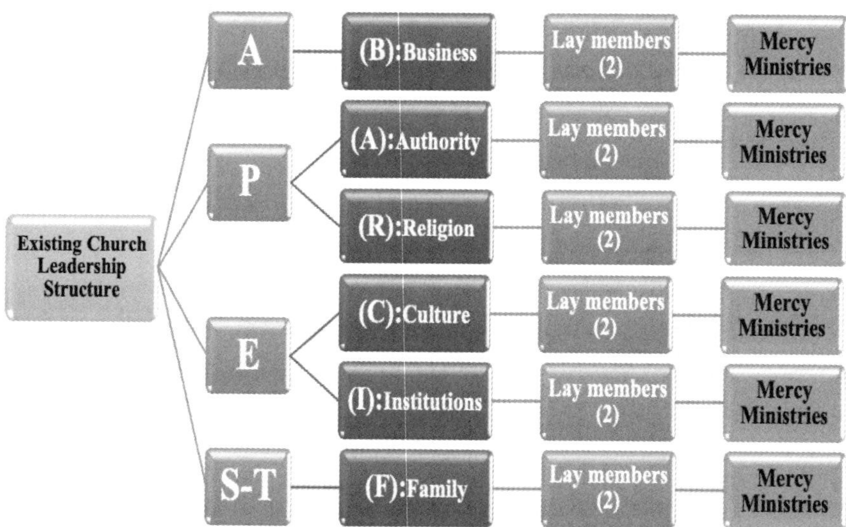

Figure 2: PLT, FABRIC, Lay Leadership Council, and Mobilization[88]

---

of each constituent, refer to D. A. Horton, *Intensional: Kingdom Ethnicity in a Divided World* (Colorado Springs: NavPress, 2019), 140–42.

[88] Figure 2 proposes a hypothetical scenario in which the pastor with a dominant apostolic gift has competency to oversee the Lay Leadership Council members and mercy ministry opportunities correlated to the Business category of F.A.B.R.I.C. The pastor with a dominant prophetic gift has oversight of the Lay Leadership Council members and mercy ministry opportunities under both Authority and Religion categories. The pastor with a dominant evangelistic gift for evangelism would manage relationships with members of the Lay Leader Council and oversee mercy ministry opportunities that fall under the Culture and Institutions of F.A.B.R.I.C. And the dominantly shepherd-teacher-gifted pastor would oversee the Lay Leader Council members and mercy ministry opportunities associated with Family.

The figure presented here is a visual representation of a PLT pipeline designed to streamline the execution of mercy ministry initiatives.

- **Step 1:** The responsibility for selecting qualified candidates to form the APES-T PLT lies with the current local church leadership with vetting by the congregation. If those who are currently serving in pastoral leadership are qualified and desire to remain in leadership, they should, like all other candidates, complete the 5Q assessment.[89] The existing church leadership alongside members of the congregation should conduct the analysis of the assessment results. The candidates are presented and classified based on their dominant APES-T gift and then presented to the congregation for a vote of affirmation. Once each of the four roles has been approved by a vote, the APES-T PLT is installed.
- **Step 2:** The PLT assesses the competency, experience, and willingness of each member to acquire additional education required to oversee one or at most two specific components of the F.A.B.R.I.C. The PLT provides the congregation with information about the specific member responsible for overseeing each aspect of F.A.B.R.I.C., before distributing the 5Q assessment to members to conduct a survey on the presence of gifts within the congregation.
- **Step 3:** The PLT and congregation actively engage in communal prayer and dialogue. The goal is to identify and categorize different forms of mercy ministry using the acronym F.A.B.R.I.C. The PLT will begin accepting nominations from the congregation for individuals who are considered highly qualified for two lay leadership positions within each letter of the F.A.B.R.I.C. framework.[90] This

---

[89] Detailed information about the process and tools for the 5Q assessment can be found on the official website: https://5qcentral.com/tests/.

[90] Examples of exceptional qualifications may include a strong commitment to Christ and active participation in the local church, along with extensive experience in a related professional field, relevant certifications or degrees, or significant life experiences that are relevant to the position.

group of leaders will be referred to as the Lay Leadership Council (LLC). The PLT will conduct individual interviews with each candidate and compile a final list. The list will include one male and one female candidate for each role in the LLC. The congregation will vote to confirm the members of the LLC, and the PLT will proceed with installing the LLC. The LLC will then create the Mercy Ministry Policy and Procedure (MMP&P) manual.

- **Step 4:** The LLC presents the MMP&P manual for approval through a congregational vote. The LLC consistently identifies potential internal and external opportunities for mercy ministry. These opportunities are regularly shared with the entire congregation. The execution of mercy ministry follows the guidelines outlined in the MMP&P manual to ensure that it effectively meets the practical needs of individuals requiring assistance.

The table below illustrates how different forms of internal and external mercy ministry can be organized and members can be mobilized to help meet felt needs.

FABRIC	Internal Mercy Ministry	External Mercy Ministry
(F): Family	*Benevolence (clothing, healthcare, financial assistance, and food)* *Adoption/foster, blended family support, marriage enrichment, single parent support* *Assistance for adults and children with special needs* *Grief and loss support* *Housing assistance for those facing homelessness and more*	*Benevolence (case by case)* *Adoption/foster and blended family outreach* *Community respite events* *Community vigils* *Housing assistance for those facing homelessness* *Marriage enrichment, divorcee and single parent support, and more*

(A): Authority	*Citizenship assistance* *Community service opportunities* *First responders care and support* *Incarceration care and support* *Legal counsel* *Asylum seeker/refugee resettlement assistance, and more*	*Citizenship assistance* *Community service opportunities* *First responders care and support events* *Asylum seeker/refugee resettlement cooperation, and more*
(B): Business	*Apprenticeship assistance* *Career counseling* *Financial planning* *Job attainment and more*	*Patronizing local businesses* *Career fair hosting, job attainment, résumé building classes, mock interviews, and more*
(R): Religion	*Apologetic training* *Religious/spiritual abuse recovery* *Soul care retreats* *Counseling/therapy assistance and more*	*Community prayer events* *Civic dialogue for communal flourishing* *Human rights events*
(I): Institutions	*Education: GED assistance, financial aid, tutoring* *Elderly: care packages and visitations* *Jail/Prison: approved visitations, care packages, educational support, halfway housing, and reentry support*	*Education: GED assistance, financial aid, tutoring, and volunteerism* *Elderly: care packages, visitations, volunteerism* *Jail/Prison: approved visitations, care packages, educational support, halfway housing, and reentry support*

(C): Culture	*Creation care (lawn and yard care)* *Emotional intelligence classes* *Multiethnic and cultural celebration support* *Sensory need assistance* *ESL classes, foreign language classes, and more*	*Creation care (lawn and yard care)* *Community gardening* *Community multiethnic and cultural celebrations* *Community art, music, and theater events* *ESL classes, foreign language classes, and more*

Table 1: Example of a Mercy Ministry Organizational Chart

The proposed process enables entire congregations to consistently participate in various forms of mercy ministry. In the concluding section of this chapter, we will explore strategies for implementing mercy ministry. Local churches, regardless of their growth or decline, offer guidance for implementation.

Conclusion

A team leadership approach in the local church is not only in line with biblical principles but is also a more effective way to provide holistic care for the congregation of believers. Ephesians 4:1–10 provides valuable insights into Jesus's bestowal of grace upon every believer and his distribution of gifts to the church, which consists of individuals he has redeemed. Ephesians 4:11–16 highlights the role of leaders in the church and highlights that Jesus has provided a fourfold framework (APES-T) of distinct leadership types as special gifts to enable members of the local body to engage in ministry work. These leaders would greatly benefit from integrating their work within the community to which God has called them. They should utilize a pipeline that connects the laity and leadership in alignment with the APES-T giftings. This approach will empower laypeople to receive discipleship and training for leadership roles. By implementing this approach, every member of the local church can receive competent and intentional care and discipleship.

Leaders empower lay members to sustain their ministry efforts and ensure that each member is aware of their spiritual gifts bestowed by Jesus. In this scenario, the church will grow in their capacity to love and make a significant impact on their local community, aligning with the teachings of the kingdom as described in Scripture. While Eph 4:11–16 is important in this chapter, it should not be the only text considered when discussing leadership development or identifying APES-T gifts. Each passage cited in this chapter contributes to a comprehensive understanding of the qualifications of pastors, the development of leadership skills, and their influence on the local community where the church is located. When analyzing Eph 4:11–16 and applying the leadership model, the body of Christ can achieve unity because Christ provides all the necessary resources for proclaiming his message. The local church can benefit from mature believers who integrate evangelism, discipleship, and involvement in mercy ministry. This will help address the leadership crisis currently faced by many churches in North America.

Questions for Further Reflection

1. In what ways should the normal use of "mercy" and "ministry" in the Bible shape a Christian's approach to mercy ministry?
2. What are some distinctions made between wholly ministry and holy ministry in this chapter?
3. What practical implications would arise from implementing a fivefold APEST leadership structure as opposed to a fourfold APES-T leadership structure?
4. Consider the opportunities for mercy ministry at your local church and the surrounding community in which it is situated. What are instances of perceived needs within and outside the ecclesiastical community, and how can they be categorized within the F.A.B.R.I.C. framework?

5. In what ways does it benefit a church pastoral team to have lay members providing them with on-the-field advice and leadership regarding the implementation of mercy ministry within and outside of the church?

Suggested Reading

Bradley, Anthony. *Ending Overcriminalization and Mass Incarceration: Hope from Civil Society*. Cambridge, UK: Cambridge University Press, 2018.

Corbett, Steve and Brian Fikkert. *When Helping Hurts: How to Alleviate Poverty without Hurting the Poor . . . and Yourself*. Chicago: Moody, 2021.

Hirsch, Alan. *5Q: Reactivating the Original Intelligence and Capacity of the Body of Christ*. Los Angeles: 100 Movements, 2017.

Keller, Timothy. *Center Church: Doing Balanced Gospel-Centered Ministry in Your City*. Grand Rapids: Zondervan, 2012.

Padilla, C. René and Juan José Toscano. *What is Integral Mission?* Translated by Claudia Lorena Juárez. Oxford: Regnum, 2021.

CONCLUSION

In addition to the "Questions for Further Reflection" at the end of each chapter, it is helpful to conclude this volume with a final set of questions perhaps not directly answered in the chapters but which may be a question our readers have. The following list of questions are not exhaustive but represent the kinds of questions readers may want to consider from here, whether those questions are more theoretical or more practical. Additionally, our answers are not meant to give a full treatment of the issue but are suggestive of the possible ways forward for individual Christians and pastors. From an organizational standpoint, the more theoretical questions are first, followed by the more practical questions.

Question 1: What should Christians think about Critical Theory, and is there any room for its use in the Christian worldview?

This question deserves its own book![1] Still, we can suggest a few ways forward in our current cultural moment. First, we should recognize that not every Christian agrees on the answer to this question. This is sometimes because of real and substantial disagreements between Christians, but sometimes such disagreements are only apparent because Christians can use the

---

[1] For the interested reader, the best recent explanation and critique of Critical Theory is by Neil Shenvi and Pat Sawyer, *Critical Dilemma: The Rise of Critical Theories and Social Justice Ideology—Implications for the Church and Society* (Eugene, OR: Harvest House, 2023).

label "Critical Theory" (CT) in different ways. For instance, if one Christian thinks that CT is more or less synonymous with Marxism, he is likely to reject it outright (as well he should!). However, if another Christian thinks that CT is not a worldview but is a more or less useful tool to detect social injustice, he is more likely to accept its use. The important thing for us is to determine what is behind the label.

With this said, it behooves us to grasp some of the core commitments of CT, especially in its contemporary expression. First, CT sees all relationships through the lens of oppression and power. In any given relationship, the individual is either an oppressor or the oppressed, based on the possession (or lack thereof) of power in that relationship. In turn, this identification determines whether the individual is just or unjust. Such an analysis can be worked out across the lines of one's ethnicity, economic status, gender, and so on. Second, CT disallows the "oppressor" from determining whether an action is just or unjust, for the oppressor does not accurately perceive injustice from their place of "privilege." Indeed, the oppressor cannot do so, for injustice is ultimately determined by the oppressed, the ultimate basis for which is that person's "lived experience." Third, CT defines justice as the removal of power from the oppressors that results in universal equal outcomes. Such justice is enacted not on the basis of one's merits but on the basis of one's identity as oppressor or oppressed. In this sense, discrimination can be just so long as it is a means to ending the oppressor's power.

To the degree to which this description of CT's core commitments is accurate, Christians should reject it, for such a view runs contrary to biblical teaching and the Christian worldview. While CT rightly recognizes justice as a proper goal for society as well as the continuing problem of oppression, its portrayal of oppression, truth, and justice is antithetical to core tenets of the Christian faith. For example, while the Bible often condemns oppression, it does not condemn someone as an oppressor on the basis of their ethnicity, economic status, or gender, but on the basis of their own sinful motives and actions (Ezek 18:1–20). Oppression, which can be enabled by one's possession of power, is sinful not because possessing power is inherently sinful but because it misuses that power to the detriment of others. Further, while CT rightly claims that we should listen to the oppressed, the Bible does not ground the truth about injustice in the subjective experience of the oppressed but in the character of God and whether individual motives and actions align with his standards of justice. Of course, sometimes our experiences can either blind us to the truth of injustice or help us sense it more keenly. Still, truth is not ultimately determined by a person's "lived experience," and even those who are genuinely oppressed can be blind to reality (Prov 18:17). Finally, as seen throughout this book, biblical justice is not defined as equal outcomes enacted through the removal of power. Rather, it involves treating one another according to what one deserves and in accord with God's own impartial standard (Deut 16:18–20).

For these reasons, while we understand that CT can point out commonsense observations that are not unique to CT, we do not think it is profitable for Christians to look to CT as the solution to the problem of injustice, for it is ultimately theologically bankrupt, atheistic in its foundation, and hopeless in its outlook.

Question 2: How does the gospel relate to justice? Is justice a part of the gospel?

This question rightly assumes a relationship between the gospel and justice, but like so many questions, the answer depends on our definitions—in this case, on what we mean by "the gospel." The good news of the gospel can be used in a broad or narrow sense. In the broad sense, the gospel can refer to the Christian hope of experiencing the beatific vision in the new heaven and new earth. In this sense, justice is a part of the gospel, for our hope includes no more sin and no more injustice. We will dwell with other believers in perfect justice and righteousness forever (2 Pet 3:13; Rev 21:27; 22:3).

In the narrow sense, the gospel refers to the basis on which this Christian hope is founded. It is the message that "Christ Jesus came into the world to save sinners" (1 Tim 1:15). On the basis of Jesus's perfect life, atoning death, and life-giving resurrection, all those who repent of their sins and trust in him alone as Savior and Lord are forgiven, justified, and cleansed of their guilt before God (Rom 1:17; 4:25; 1 Cor 15:1–4). In this sense, justice is not a part of the gospel but is a necessary ramification of it. In other words, our right treatment of others is not the basis of or the means by which God forgives us our sins and declares us righteous in his sight. Rather, inasmuch as our just actions are the product of God's transformative grace in our hearts, justice is the necessary ramification of the gospel. All our good works, including our just actions toward others, adorn the gospel but do not comprise it (Titus 2:10).[2] As D. A. Carson observes, "Failure to distinguish between the gospel and all the effects of the gospel tends, over the long haul, to replace the good news as to what God has done with a moralism that is finally without the power and the glory of Christ crucified, resurrected, ascended, and reigning."[3]

At the same time, since our good works are the necessary evidence of our justification, a failure to exhibit tangible and observable good works shows our faith is dead (Jas 2:14–26). Jesus teaches that "by your words you will be acquitted, and by your words you will be condemned" (Matt 12:37), and according to Hebrews, we must pursue holiness because "without it no one will see the Lord" (Heb 12:14). In this sense, though the gospel is good news precisely because it tells us what God has done for us, our good works, which include our justice and righteousness, comprise the necessary

---

[2] For a helpful distinction between the gospel and social justice, see the denial of Article VI of "The Statement on Social Justice and the Gospel" (https://statementonsocialjustice.com, accessed June 30, 2023): "We deny that anything else, whether works to be performed or opinions to be held, can be added to the gospel without perverting it into another gospel. This also means that implications and applications of the gospel, such as the obligation to live justly in the world, though legitimate and important in their own right, are not definitional components of the gospel." See also Neil Shenvi and Pat Sawyer, *Critical Dilemma*, 424–25.

[3] D. A. Carson, *The Gospel and the Modern World: A Theological Vision for the Church*, ed. Brian J. Tabb (Wheaton, IL: Crossway, 2023), 89; originally published as "Editorial," *Themelios* 34 (2009): 2.

evidence for our reception of the gospel and our genuine hope for the restoration of the cosmos when Jesus returns.

Question 3: How does the *imago Dei* affect social justice conversations?

Because social justice issues unavoidably speak to the nature and dignity of man, Christians should think carefully about how to engage these conversations to promote a biblical understanding of the *imago Dei*. Christians promote various emphases when discussing this topic. Some prefer to emphasize substantive aspects of being an image-bearer, focusing upon the human ability to have rational thought and moral reasoning. Others focus upon the relational aspects of being image-bearers, especially since the text immediately says, "He created him in the image of God; he created them male and female" (Gen 1:27). Thus, one can see why relational understandings are worth pursuing. Still others focus on functional realities about being an image-bearer, and these usually pertain to the language of image-bearers having dominion and responsibility over creation.

While not dismissing these approaches, theologian Anthony Hoekema insists we look to Jesus. He claims,

> "We must learn to know what the image of God is by looking at Jesus Christ. What must therefore be at the center of the image of God is not characteristics like the ability to reason or the ability to make decisions . . . but rather that which was central in the life of Christ: love for God and love for man."[4]

As we discuss humanity's inherent dignity, we can explain how this relates to Jesus's work on our behalf. Through his life, death, and resurrection, Jesus restores and redeems the image of God in humanity. Sin has marred and distorted the image of God in us, but through faith in Christ, we are reconciled to God and transformed into his likeness (2 Cor 3:18). As

[4] Anthony Hoekema, *Created in God's Image* (Grand Rapids: Eerdmans, 1994), 22.

we follow Jesus and grow in our relationship with him, we are conformed more and more to his image.

Question 4: How should we respond when someone takes the moral high ground by claiming that their view on a particular issue is a matter of justice?

Perhaps you have been in a conversation before in which you did not agree with the other person on a particular cultural issue, and the other person claims that they are right because the issue in view is "a matter of justice" or "a justice issue." Their claim may or may not be right, but the claim itself is a rhetorical move to take the moral high ground in the conversation. After all, who wants to be on the side of injustice? In such instances, how should we respond?

The place to start is to ask what the person means by "a justice issue." Does he mean that his view alone is what constitutes the only just response to the issue, or that his view is one among many appropriate responses? Does he mean that the issue necessarily impacts the just treatment of others? What kind of justice is the person talking about? One based on impartial treatment of others or one that seeks universal equal outcomes? Put negatively, what specifically would be unjust about the situation if the issue did not get resolved as the person wished? Asking precise follow-up questions like these is a constructive way forward in the conversation because it puts the onus on the other person to clarify what they mean and to defend their view.

Another constructive response is to maintain a sense of compassion throughout the conversation. You probably will not appreciate someone attempting to take the moral high ground, and you will have a righteous zeal welling up within you to clarify the truth of the matter. Such zeal is good! Still, in our zeal to uphold the truth, we will probably be unpersuasive in the end if we do not remember why we are in the conversation in the first place: to pursue the truth with others, not apart from them. After all, we want the truth to prevail by others around us believing it!

Alongside such compassion, boldly state the truth of the matter. Let's suppose the issue is, in fact, a matter that touches on justice, but not in the way that the other person thinks. Then say so! We live in an age in which Christians need to be biblically literate and unashamed to speak the truth in the world. Indeed, such is the burden of this book. Ultimately, we live our lives before God, and we are obligated to hold forth his glorious truth to the world, even if the world rejects it.

One final word: We strongly recommend having these kinds of conversations in person or at the very least over the phone. Debates on social media far too often end up with more heat than light precisely because the selected medium is not an appropriate space to have the kind of in-depth conversations that actually sway a person's opinion. So, pick the right time and the right medium, and then lean in to these conversations.

Question 5: How should we respond when a professing Christian refuses to think social justice matters at all in the Christian life?

First, it is important to remember that Christians approach social justice concerns from multiple angles. Some Christians have high expectations for their churches to engage in justice causes, while many others prefer such action to be pursued, if at all, from individual efforts. Due to the catholicity of the church and the cultural realities many Christians encounter around the world, we should seek unity rather than uniformity when discussing how we engage the cultural challenges of our time. Additionally, to those who refuse to think of social justice as applying to the Christian life we can respond by engaging in a thoughtful and respectful discussion about relevant biblical passages (see the first section of this volume for a guide), which show that Christianity is relevant for modern life.

One could also discuss the gospel and its implications for life. Carl F. H. Henry (1913–2003) sought to challenge the isolationist posture of Fundamentalists and the accommodationist practices of the social gospel movement. When addressing this topic, he claims, "Social justice is not, moreover, simply an appendage to the evangelical message; it is an intrinsic part of the whole, without which the preaching of the gospel itself is truncated. Theology devoid of social justice is a deforming weakness of much present-day evangelical witness."[5] Social justice is not the whole of the gospel, but Henry claims that it testifies to the whole, for, he adds,

> "The Gospel resounds with good news for the needy and oppressed. It conveys assurance that injustice, repression, exploitation, discrimination and poverty are dated and doomed, that no one is forced to accept the crush of evil powers as finally determinative for his or her existence. Into the morass of sinful human history and experience the gospel heralds a new order of life shaped by God's redemptive intervention."[6]

Henry's presentation foregrounds the heart of the gospel, that we are sinners in desperate need of the salvation Christ offers to those who repent and believe. But the gospel also produces sanctified works to be done against the tides of darkness, knowing our eschatological hope that Christ will return and justice will prevail. Thus, Christians must realize that this is our Father's world, and until he renews the cosmos, we should look upon fallen creation with an urgency to preserve and promote the gospel.

Question 6: How should Christians use conversations about social justice to compel secular audiences to think about apologetics questions?

Social justice issues often touch upon deeper worldview questions, such as the nature of human dignity, the source of moral values, or the existence of evil and suffering. Christians should use these opportunities in a manner consistent with Peter's instruction, whereby we are prepared to "give a defense to anyone who asks you for a reason for the hope that is in you" (1 Pet 3:15). Being prepared to make a defense does not mean

[5] Carl F. H. Henry, *God, Revelation and Authority* (Wheaton, IL: Crossway, 1999) 4:551.

[6] Henry, 4:542.

that Christians must become expert apologists with an in-depth understanding of every cultural issue. It is good and right to say, "I don't know," when confronted with an unfamiliar topic. While we give thanks for those Christian apologists who serve in professional capacities, Peter's emphasis speaks to every believer.

Perhaps the first step one could take is that of active listening, whereby one seeks to understand the concerns and proposed solutions from any given secular audience. From this, one could explain how the Christian faith motivates believers to care for the marginalized, promote human dignity, and seek justice. By demonstrating the connection between one's beliefs and one's actions, one can pique the curiosity of secular audiences and perhaps open the door for more dialogue about spiritual matters. If possible, find areas of common ground between one's secular audience and Christianity. Secular audiences often emphasize shared values like human rights, compassion, and fairness, and these topics offer Christians an opportunity to show how Christianity offers a robust foundation for these values and how it provides a more comprehensive and coherent explanation for the existence and pursuit of justice.

Finally, one should anticipate and address potential objections or skepticism that secular audiences may have towards Christianity. Be prepared to discuss topics like biblical interpretation, the problem of evil, or the role of the church in history. Present thoughtful and well-reasoned responses that demonstrate the intellectual coherence and relevance of the Christian faith. Finally, recall Peter's admonition that we are to give a defense "with gentleness and reverence, keeping a clear conscience, so that when you are accused, those who disparage your good conduct in Christ will be put to shame" (1 Pet 3:16).

Question 7: Should a pastor address "justice" issues from the pulpit?

Those who have been preaching pastors for any length of time know that congregants will occasionally express a desire for their pastors to address current events from the pulpit. How should a pastor respond to these requests, particularly when it comes to matters of justice? When facing such requests, a pastor would be wise to ask at least two questions: (1) "Do I need to preach on this?" and (2) "Do I need to preach on this right now?"

As for the first question—"Do I need to preach on this?"—a pastor should discern the Bible's clarity on the issue. Some issues the Bible does not address clearly or in a straightforward way. Some issues are quite complex because they require juxtaposing numerous biblical principles and then extrapolating from them application to the modern context. Take, for instance, the question of immigration policy in the United States. While the Bible clearly teaches that we should treat all people with dignity and respect, including immigrants, it does not directly speak to what kind of immigration policy would best serve the United States and those desiring US citizenship. Perhaps as an individual a pastor is already persuaded of what is the best policy, but as a pastor he must recognize that his responsibility in a sermon is to speak what God has revealed. If the issue is so complex that it requires hermeneutical gymnastics to arrive at a conclusion, then preaching on that issue will probably cause more confusion than understanding, and it may give the wrong sense to the congregation that the pastor is using the pulpit to promulgate his own concerns.

Additionally, a pastor should discern the importance of the issue for the church. Even if the Bible clearly and directly addresses an issue, this is not a mandate to preach on it. Some cultural issues may be trendy now but in a few months will be long-forgotten. Or perhaps the issue affects only a small minority of the congregation instead of the congregation at large. In such cases, a pastor would be wise to stay focused on preaching the whole counsel of God, lest he and the congregation be easily distracted by every cultural wind that blows. Of course, even if a pastor chooses not to preach on a topic, it does not mean he cannot address it elsewhere. For instance, if a few in the congregation are affected by a particular issue, it is appropriate for a pastor to shepherd those people so that they think more biblically about it.

The second question—"Do I need to preach on this right now?"—requires similar pastoral wisdom. Even if the Bible speaks directly to an issue of great importance to a church, it may be prudent for a pastor to wait for some time before addressing it from the pulpit. Sometimes congregants want their preaching pastors to address issues and events that are hot off the press. Certainly this can be appropriate, but sometimes a pastor may want to take time to consider the matter further to allow for a more robust treatment of the issue (e.g., in a three-part sermon series). Or perhaps immediately addressing the issue would involve a major modification to the preaching schedule, which may not be advantageous to the pastor or the congregation. In such cases, it is appropriate for a pastor to let the congregation know that he is aware of the issue and will address it in a forthcoming sermon.

The principle is this: If the Bible speaks clearly and directly to a particular issue, and the issue is of great importance to the church as a whole, then a pastor will want to seriously consider preaching on the issue at the appropriate time.

Question 8: Where are the best resources on topics like justice, Critical Theory, and the mission of the church?

Resources on justice abound, but not every resource makes the careful distinctions necessary for constructive Christian thought on justice. What follows are some exemplary resources on the topics of social justice, Critical Theory, and the mission of the church as it relates to justice.

For a good evangelical introduction to social justice, we recommend Thaddeus J. Williams's *Confronting Injustice Without Compromising Truth: 12 Questions Christians Should Ask About Social Justice* (Grand Rapids: Zondervan Academic, 2020). Williams carefully distinguishes between a social justice that is in keeping with the Christian worldview and the kind of social justice antithetical to it. Additionally, Michael Novak and Paul Adams's *Social Justice Isn't What You Think It Is* (New York: Encounter Books, 2015) provides careful nuance to origins and usage of the phrase "social justice."

For introductions to Critical Theory, we recommend Stephen Eric Bronner's *Critical Theory: A Very Short Introduction*, 2nd ed. (New York:

Oxford University Press, 2017) as well as Helen Pluckrose and James Lindsay's *Cynical Theories: How Activist Scholarship Made Everything about Race, Gender, and Identity—and Why This Harms Everybody* (Durham, NC: Pitchstone, 2020). The latter is particularly poignant in its articulation of contemporary Critical Theory and where it is headed. The best recent critique of Critical Theory from an evangelical Christian perspective is Neil Shenvi and Pat Sawyer's *Critical Dilemma: The Rise of Critical Theories and Social Justice Ideology—Implications for the Church and Society* (Eugene, OR: Harvest House, 2023).

For resources on the individual Christian's pursuit of justice and how that relates to the mission of the church, we recommend John Anthony Wind's *Do Good to All People as You Have the Opportunity* (Phillipsburg, NJ: P&R, 2019), a distillation of which appears in Wind's chapter in this book. Additionally, Kevin DeYoung and Greg Gilbert's *What Is the Mission of the Church? Making Sense of Social Justice, Shalom, and the Great Commission* (Wheaton, IL: Crossway, 2011) articulates that the mission of the church must be kept distinct from the individual Christian's pursuit of justice.

GENERAL INDEX

SCRIPTURE INDEX

John

Acts

Romans